# THOMAS MANN

THOMAS MANN

# TWENTIETH CENTURY VIEWS

The aim of this series is to present the best in
contemporary critical opinion on major authors,
providing a twentieth century perspective on
their changing status in an era of profound
revaluation.

Maynard Mack, *Series Editor*
Yale University

# THOMAS MANN

## A COLLECTION OF CRITICAL ESSAYS

Edited by
*Henry Hatfield*

**Prentice-Hall, Inc.,** *Englewood Cliffs, N.J.*

For my former students in Berlin

Second printing ...... October, 1965

© 1964 BY PRENTICE-HALL, INC.

ENGLEWOOD CLIFFS, N.J.

LIBRARY OF CONGRESS CATALOG CARD NO.: 64-12244

*Printed in the United States of America—C*

P 55189
C 55190

# Preface

It is my pleasant duty to thank various members of the staff of Widener Library, most especially Mr. Walter Grossmann, for valuable assistance; and Alfred A. Knopf, Inc. for permission to use my own translations of various sentences originally quoted in German in some of the essays included here. (The authorized translations by Mrs. H. T. Lowe-Porter are published by Alfred A. Knopf, Inc.) I am grateful to my wife and to Miss Ingeburg Zemmrich for typings and retypings. Finally, it should be acknowledged that the translations of the essays by Mann and Rilke and those by Messrs. Blume, Holthusen, and Weigand are my own, as are those of various German passages in other articles. In editing some of the contributions, notably those of Miss Wilkinson and Mr. Weigand, I have drastically reduced the amount of documentation. Quite possibly some reader may be interested, e.g., in exact page references to a text of Mann referred to in either of these essays; if so, he should consult the originals.

H.H.

# Table of Contents

# THOMAS MANN

# Introduction

## by Henry Hatfield

In this collection I have tried to provide a cross section of responsible critical opinions about Thomas Mann. The "views" presented here are literally "twentieth century," ranging from Rilke's essay of 1901 to articles published very recently. Generally speaking, the critics represented here do not pretend to say the last, absolute word on Thomas Mann, who himself makes no such claim in his very relaxed piece reprinted here. Rather, each writer aims to give his own aspect of the truth. As Wellek and Warren have pointed out, every sensible estimate of a work of literature adds to the richness of our perception of it, and this book is meant as a contribution to "perspectivism," in their sense. Beyond that, I hope that readers will find the various contributions stimulating—*fermenta cognitionis*.

In contrast to Charles Neider's procedure in his valuable anthology, *The Stature of Thomas Mann* (New Directions, 1947), I have included only entire essays or uncut sections of books, hoping that what my volume loses in variety it may gain in other respects. The contributors come from England, the United States, and the German-speaking countries; had there been slightly more space at my disposal, I would have included one of the several excellent French essays on Mann. A letter inviting a prominent East German literary historian to contribute went unanswered. Although I regret that the "German Democratic Republic" cannot be represented here, I feel that this omission is not a significant loss. (A highly intelligent Marxist view of Mann may be found in Georg Lukács's book of 1949 and in various of his essays; Mr. Neider's volume contains a brief excerpt from Lukács, in translation.)

One of my major concerns has been to avoid the monotony of unvaried praise. Alas, the intelligent English and American critics who dislike Mann's work—and there presumably are quite a few of them—do not seem to have written about it at any length. I am not referring to the familiar complaints of the middle-brow book reviewer: that Mann's novels tend to be long (how true!), that his books are unrelievedly serious and "heavy" (how false!). Fortunately, Herr Holthusen has provided an attack not devoid of *furor teutonicus*. Several others of Mann's more

1

formidable German opponents have their say in "Aspects of Contradiction"; Mr. Blume has lucidly summarized their views.

Turning to the various contributions, we find that Rilke's early review of *Buddenbrooks* attracts not merely because of its authorship; it is marked by enthusiasm and verve. If we can read his somewhat patronizing words—"we shall have to take note of this name"—only with a rather wry amusement today, they at least reveal an appraisal of *Buddenbrooks* far more just than Stefan George's brusque and total rejection of the novel. At the end of his brief discussion, the young poet reverts to his lyrical subjectivity. Whatever *Buddenbrooks* may be, it is not an "act of reverence toward life . . . which is good and just in its enactment"— words more applicable to the verses of Rilke's friend Lou Andreas-Salomé, say, than to Mann's story. Thus the decision to supplement Rilke's remarks with a more prosaic but "text-centered" essay on *Buddenbrooks* may be defended.

If any work of Mann's has been "explicated" almost to death, it is *Tonio Kröger.* Yet there is always something valuable still to be said about any major work in any field if the critic cares enough really to wrestle with the work. Miss Wilkinson did care enough, and her truly brilliant interpretation of *Tonio* abandons the clichés about artist *vs.* burgher, and other too-familiar themes, to concentrate on a deeply felt, authentically personal essay. The reader is grateful for her discussion of the structure of the *novella,* for her distinction between the "man . . . who acts and one who watches" in it, and above all for the grace and lucidity of Miss Wilkinson's style.

*Royal Highness* is the most underrated of Mann's novels, and Hermann Weigand's essay on it therefore has a place in the tradition founded by Lessing of "vindicating" neglected or harshly judged works. While *Royal Highness* may well be the "most graceful of German novels," as a French critic put it, it does after all support a considerable weight of symbolic autobiography.

In treating *Death in Venice,* a story which has been analyzed almost as often as *Tonio Kröger,* Mr. von Gronicka acknowledges his debt to the excellent interpretations by Franz Mautner[1] and Vernon Venable.[2] He is able to go beyond them in demonstrating the *novella's* incredible richness of mythological reference. It is almost too much that, as Mr. von Gronicka shows, Aschenbach is linked with Wotan as well as with the classical world.

To discuss *The Magic Mountain,* a novel long subjected to solemn pontifications, Erich Heller has adopted the dialogue form used by Friedrich Schlegel, one of his favorite critics. The choice was a happy

---

[1] In *Monatshefte,* XLIV (1952), 20-26.
[2] In *Virginia Quarterly Review,* XIV (1938), 61-76; reprinted in *The Stature of Thomas Mann.*

one, for the dialectic, shifting points of view enable Mr. Heller to do justice to the complications and contradictions of this dialectic novel. Like Schlegel, he is very witty and makes abundant use of epigram and paradox. If the reader is at times perhaps more dazzled than enlightened, that too is reminiscent of reading Schlegel, and was presumably part of the intention of this sparkling "conversation."

Mark Van Doren's consideration of *Joseph and His Brothers* as comedy is in effect another vindication. (It is one which would have particularly delighted Mann; see his remarks on humor in this anthology.) Of course Mr. Van Doren does not lose sight of the more serious elements in the tetralogy. His concept of the comic is both broad and profound. At times it reminds one of Schiller's surprising statement that comedy is "higher" than tragedy as a genre, since it possesses more serenity and aesthetic detachment. Mr. Van Doren's entire approach to *Joseph* is a fresh one; his view is never hampered by academic blinders. Reading his essay, one quickly becomes aware that it is the work of a man who is himself an artist.

No one, I think, has dealt more adequately with *Doctor Faustus* than has Erich Kahler. His essay stresses the theme and style of the various "terminal books" (*Endbücher*), in which novelists as different as Proust and Kafka, Gide and Musil, have reached what seems to be a *ne plus ultra*. In *Doctor Faustus*, he points out, the theme of the "end" is linked to that of deliberate rebarbarization, a note recalling Nietzsche, Spengler, Hamsun, and D. H. Lawrence. After succinctly reviewing Thomas Mann's work from the early *novellas* on, he makes one of the first clear descriptions of the extreme "structuralism" of the novel: "It is a structure in which each detail has an exact symbolic reference, a structure of utter complexity, . . ."

As Herr Holthusen wrote me recently, his later discussion of Mann[3] is much more favorable than is his brochure on *Doctor Faustus, The World Without Transcendence* (1949), the first sections of which appear in translation here. At that time, he was angered by the conviction that Mann was consigning the whole German tradition, from Luther to the present, to damnation. Some readers may feel, as I do, that Herr Holthusen was too harsh in this long essay, but no one can question his acuity and his polemical skill.

In "Variations on Picaresque," Robert B. Heilman successfully applies the methods of comparative literature to *Felix Krull*. Noting in passing that *felix* is synonymous with *faustus,* he argues a relation between the rogue novel and the *Faust* theme; and he has developed at some length the equation *"picaro* equals artist." One finishes reading his essay in a mood of cheerful agreement with his conclusion: Thomas

[3] See his essay "Kritik und Einbildungskraft" in *Kritik und Verstehen* (Munich, 1961).

Mann demonstrated originality and boldness in making fresh use of familiar themes.

By providing a cross section of hostile comment, Mr. Blume's contribution reminds us what an incredibly bad "press" Mann often received from German literary historians, not only Nazis but highly "respectable" *deutsch-national* scholars. One of the most learned of them described poor Hanno Buddenbrook as the most repulsive child in German literature. (One hopes he has read *The Tin Drum* in the meantime; the punishment would fit the crime.) Another, writing in the most prestigious professional journal in the field of Germanics, claimed that the key to *Buddenbrooks* was a "predisposition to uremia (*urinsaure Diathese*) lasting through four generations." This judgment shows originality, at least. To leave the sphere of the *Schimpflexikon:* Mr. Blume, in his cool rebuttals of Mann's foes, clearly draws the distinction between the aesthetic sphere and other realms of being. Despite Kant and Schiller, it is a distinction too often lost sight of by German critics, though since the emergence of Wolfgang Kayser and Emil Staiger a more sophisticated attitude has become evident. Doubtless Mr. Blume's most striking point is this: the literary work of a creative writer has a higher "truth content" than do his letters, diaries, etc. (In context it is clear that this thesis has nothing to do with any charge of insincerity.) Whether this may be applied to all writers is perhaps debatable, but as far as Thomas Mann is concerned, Mr. Blume has made his case.

Probably "Humor and Irony" is less important in itself, though it is very good, than in its revelation of Thomas Mann as a private individual. He appears here as he indeed did in life—genial, charming, modest, fond of making little jokes and telling stories. His oral style is very informal; he did not worry about casual repetitions or incomplete sentences which, in his "real" prose, he would have shunned like the plague.

If one turns from the writers represented in this book to Mann criticism in general, one encounters certain characteristic distortions. The most obvious ones are rooted in political prejudice. In Germany, Mann's championship of the Weimar Republic was harshly resented by nationalistic commentators, all the more so since he had maintained a conservative position during the First World War. Thus his most embittered foes were those of the Right. Again and again they tried to discredit his books as "unGerman" because they were ironic and "intellectual," the products of a mere writer, not a creative artist (*Dichter*). Not all of these critics were swayed by conscious political bias, but they generally adhered to the belief that an author should avoid rational thought and create spontaneously, unconsciously, and above all (to use one of their favorite clichés) "organically." ("Organically" is a nice word; but, as Peter Demetz has observed, it has never been clearly proved that works of art grow in quite the way that vegetables do.) As Mann became more the European, less the romantic German, objections of this sort increased. The Nazis, of course, were happy to draw upon the arguments of the conservative Right in the hope of destroying Mann's German reputation, once his opposition to fascism became clear. In fairness, it should be added that Mann was not only blamed but at times praised, especially in the United States, for irrelevant political reasons; but those who thought him a great novelist because he disliked Hitler and supported the New Deal were, if often silly, anything but vicious.

During the late Thirties and early Forties an extreme cult, the 200 per cent Mannites, emerged. Some of their effusions have been preserved in Mr. Neider's *The Stature of Thomas Mann,* like flies in an extremely large chunk of amber. One should distinguish sharply between Thomas Mann and his hangers-on and completely uncritical admirers. When Robert Musil wrote sarcastically of the "Mann circus," he was moved in part by envy, no doubt, but his designation is characteristically accurate. With devastating irony, uninhibited by any sense of gratitude, Mann portrayed two members of his own "circus" in *Doctor Faustus,* under the names of Kunigunde Rosenstiel and Meta Nackedey.

Less obvious and perhaps more serious distortions have been caused by two related opinions about Mann: that he was vastly erudite, and that he was a profound and original philosopher. Given the nature and scope of books like *The Magic Mountain, Joseph,* and *Doctor Faustus,* these notions are very natural ones, but I am convinced that they are based on misconceptions. A great artist, always avid for raw material to transmute into art, Mann immersed himself in volumes of Babylonian lore, classical mythology, theology, treatises on various diseases. "Reading with the pencil," as he called it, he took copious notes. Like a student before an examination or a lawyer getting up a case, he would assemble a mass of concentrated information which he then dismissed from his mind, once it had served its purpose. Convinced furthermore that the material was in itself indifferent until he had given it aesthetic form, he apparently cared nothing about the soundness of his "sources," as such. Thus a book on the "lost continent" Atlantis, or an elementary popular work on mythology, or even Frank Harris' very "far-out" discussion of Shakespeare's life, could be quite as useful to him as the most accurate scholarship, the most penetrating psychology. But these comments should not be construed as an attack on Mann. Profoundly the artist, he used at times the methods of the scholar, much as some of his contemporaries exploited the techniques of journalism. The role of "Professor Mann" was not after all entirely a mask, as his representation of one part of his personality in Serenus

Zeitblom shows. And in certain of his essays, particularly in those devoted to Goethe, he drew on a wealth of genuine knowledge, of personal cultural experiences, not on the results of hasty cramming. In any case, Mann will stand or fall as a master of prose fiction, not as a philosopher, political scientist, or essayist. Like most of the contributors of this volume, I am convinced that he will stand—and stand triumphantly.

# Thomas Mann's *Buddenbrooks*

## *by Rainer Maria Rilke*

Without any doubt we shall have to take note of this name. In a novel of 1100 pages Thomas Mann has given evidence of a capacity and an ability that cannot be ignored. It was his intention to write the history of a family that is going under—the "decline of a family." Only a few years ago a modern author would have been content to show the last stage of this decline, the last heir, dying of himself and of his fathers.[1] Thomas Mann felt that it would be unjust to concentrate in a last chapter on the catastrophe to which generations in fact contributed; and conscientious as he is, he begins at the point when the family's fortunes have reached their peak. He knows that beyond this peak the inevitable decline sets in: at first in a barely perceptible dissolution, becoming more and more marked, until at last nothing remains.

Thus he was faced with the necessity of narrating the life of four generations, and Thomas Mann's way of solving this unusual problem is so surprising and interesting that, though it takes days, one reads these two weighty volumes with attention and suspense, without tiring or skipping anything, without the least sign of impatience or haste. One has time, one must have time for narration of the calm and natural succession of these happenings, precisely because nothing else in the book seems to be there for the reader, because there is no point at which —over the head of events as it were—a writer superior [to his material] bends down to an [equally] superior reader,[2] in order to persuade him and carry him along. For that very reason one is wholly involved and almost personally engaged, quite as if one had found in some secret drawer old family papers and letters, in which one slowly read ahead, to the limit of one's own memories.

"Thomas Mann's *Buddenbrooks*," by Rainer Maria Rilke. From *Rainer Maria Rilke: Bücher Theater Kunst* (Vienna, 1934), ed. Richard von Mises, 14-18. (Originally in *Bremer Tageblatt*, No. 86, April 16, 1902.) Reprinted by permission of Frau Ruth Fritsche-Rilke of the Rilke Archive, and of the Insel Verlag. Translated by Henry Hatfield.

[1] (That is, dying of the innate weariness, the "decadence," of his family.)

[2] Rilke is making the point that in *Buddenbrooks* the author does not stand above the novel, preserving his aesthetic distance (hence "superior"), but presents it simply and directly.

Thomas Mann felt quite rightly that he had to become a chronicler, that is, a calm and unexcited reporter of events, to narrate the history of the Buddenbrooks; and that it would nevertheless be his task to be a poet, and to imbue many figures with convincing vitality, with warmth and substance. He has combined both aims most happily by interpreting his role as chronicler in a modern way and endeavoring, not simply to record salient data, but to include conscientiously everything apparently unimportant and slight, a thousand particulars and details; for after all, everything actual has its value, is a tiny bit of that life that it was his purpose to describe. And in this manner, by this deeply felt absorption in particular events, by a grand (*grosse*) justice vis-à-vis all happenings, he attains a liveliness of representation which is due less to the material itself than to the continuous materialization of all things. Here something of Segantini's[3] technique has been transformed to another milieu: the thorough and impartial management of every passage, the careful compilation of the material, causing everything to appear important and essential; the surface traversed by a hundred furrows, which seems unified, informed with life to the observer; and finally the objective element, the epic manner of narration, which gives even cruel and frightening matters a certain character of necessity and of being ordained by law.

The history of the old Lübeck patrician family of the Buddenbrooks (the name of their firm is Johann Buddenbrook), which begins with Johann Buddenbrook Senior about 1830, ends with little Hanno, his great-grandchild, in our own day. It includes feasts and family gatherings, baptisms and hours of death (particularly oppressive and terrible hours of death), weddings and divorces, great business successes and the unfeeling, incessant reverses of fortune, such as the life of a merchant entails. The story shows the calm, unself-conscious life of an older generation and the nervous, self-observing haste of its descendants; it shows small and ridiculous people violently thrashing about in the tangled nets of their destinies. It reveals also that even those who are somewhat more far-seeing are not in control of their good fortune or disaster, both of which arise from a hundred small movements and spread out and draw back, almost impersonal and anonymous in their origin, while life goes forward like a wave.[4] It is shown with particular subtlety how the decadence of the family manifests itself above all in the fact that the individual members have changed the direction of their lives, as it were: no longer is it natural for them to live [with their energies directed] toward the exterior world; rather, the tendency to-

[3] Giovanni Segantini (1858-1899), Italian painter, influenced by Millet. Much of his work is realistic in intention.

[4] The image (I believe) compares the individual to a particle of water, moving in a small, restricted circle, while the great wave of life, having briefly agitated his existence, sweeps on beyond him.

ward introversion becomes more and more apparent. Even Senator Thomas Buddenbrook must subject himself to strain, in order to satisfy his ambition. In the case of his brother Christian, this turning away from practical life has led to a dangerous and pathological self-scrutiny which extends to his internal physical condition and destroys him by its inexorable torture. The last of them too, little Hanno, walks about with his glance turned inward, listening attentively to the inner world of his soul, from which his music streams forth. In him there exists the potentiality of another ascent (of a different sort, to be sure, from the one the Buddenbrooks hope for)—the potentiality, infinitely endangered, of becoming a great artist; it is not realized. The sickly boy is ruined by the banality and ruthlessness of his school, and dies of typhus.

His life, a day of his life, takes up considerable space in the second volume. And however cruelly fate seems to be treating the boy, here too we hear only the excellent chronicler who supplies a thousand matters of fact without permitting himself to be swept away into anger, or into acquiescence.

And besides the colossal labor and the poet's gift of seeing, this noble objectivity deserves praise; it is a book in which there is no trace of arrogance on the author's part. An act of reverence toward life—life that is good and just in its enactment.

# Thomas Mann's *Buddenbrooks:*
# The World of the Father

*by Henry Hatfield*

T. S. Eliot once remarked on the "usefulness" of a type of poetry "which could cut across all the present stratifications of public taste," and cited the plays of Shakspere, with their "several layers of significance" as examples of works of the desired universality of appeal. Eliot was writing only of poetry, but his *aperçu* illuminates the enormous success of *Buddenbrooks*. Essentially a rather complicated and deeply pessimistic book, it has an abundance of sheer narration, of humor, of easily grasped character and local color, which make its vast popularity natural enough; and also a certain sympathetic warmth in dealing with character which is more agreeable to most readers than the cool temperature of the early *novellas*. One need know nothing of Wagner or Schopenhauer, of the theory of decadence or the metaphysical allure of death to find the novel absorbing, and this is all to the good. Nor need one have heard of the leitmotif to "get" the effect of Mann's repetitions; indeed it would be difficult to miss most of them. To say this is not, of course, to disparage the less obvious attractions of the book: its tendency and meaning, its overtones and associations. The comparison with Galsworthy's *Forsyte Saga,* sometimes facilely and misleadingly made, can be enlightening. *Buddenbrooks,* besides its "popular" elements, has precisely what the *Saga* does not: the broad range of "layers of significance," unexpected finesses, and a technique which, if at times obviously used, points ahead from the straightforward historical arrangement of nineteenth-century narration to the musical complexities of the novel of the twentieth century. Mann's own reference to Wagner's *Ring* furnishes a needed clue.

Despite his doubts about the bulk and nature of the book, Mann completed *Buddenbrooks* in about two and a half years; it was published early in 1901. The actual writing was begun in Italy, where he spent a year with his brother Heinrich. Yet there is no trace of the South in the novel. This was no "Italian journey" in Goethe's sense; it had nothing to do with the traditional attempt of the German writer to experience the Mediterranean and classic world; it was rather a period of deliberate self-isolation, which afforded no doubt perspective and concentration on his work. Mann tells us that his mood at the time was made up of "indolence, a bad conscience as a bourgeois, and the secure sense of latent talents." For the "bad conscience" there were presumably two reasons: his rejection of any sort of middle-class career, and his choice of the decay of his own family as a subject. At times, Mann must have felt that he was committing an indiscretion if not a downright betrayal. Thomas Buddenbrook is closely modeled after Mann's own father, and his exotic wife Gerda would seem, to a lesser extent, reminiscent of Mann's mother, Julia Da Silva-Bruhns. Psychologically, the novel may be said to represent a sort of reckoning with the father image by a young man who has broken with family tradition and gone off to carry on a "questionable" existence in Munich and Italy. He has rejected the ancestral firm, business, the whole world of Lübeck; his revolt has been successful and, outwardly, not very difficult, but a sense of guilt and remorse remains. The reckoning is unusually gentle, as such things go; the rejection reluctant. Sympathy and admiration for the father's world persist, and with them the chronic bad conscience of the Mannian hero. Without this ambivalence toward the burgher, so different from the harsh singlemindedness of Heinrich Mann, Mann's view of the world would be clearer and sharper, but his books cooler and less felt. As he states in *Tonio Kröger,* the problematic love for the bourgeois world represented by his father (and arbitrarily called the "normal") was one of the strongest forces impelling him to write. The same emotion must have produced the psychological tension, the "charge," which saves *Buddenbrooks* from being only another family novel.

*Buddenbrooks* then is profoundly autobiographical, but it stands also in a European literary tradition. Mann had a great debt to his predecessors in the novel of the nineteenth century—Scandinavian, French, and Russian. From German writers, with one or two exceptions, he took little. Theodor Storm attracted him by a certain dexterity in the creation of a mood of sentimental reminiscence, and in a not unskilful use of the leitmotif. Theodor Fontane, the most distinguished figure in the German novel of the Eighties and Nineties, had more to offer: a dryly realistic style, a benevolent irony, a flair for social nuances, understatement, and civilized conversation. An aristocrat by temperament, Fontane found the bourgeoisie problematic as well as comic. But what was Fontane compared to the Goncourts, Zola, or Tolstoi; what was Berlin to Paris or St. Petersburg?

Yet Mann's most immediate indebtedness was to less spectacular figures, to Scandinavian writers like Alexander Kielland and Jonas Lie, whose subject matter was allied to his own. Lübeck, as a Hanseatic city, was in a sense spiritually closer to the North than to Munich or Berlin; and since Ibsen, the Norwegians had enjoyed a great and often inflated reputation in the Reich. Lie and Kielland were both men of solid, unspectacular talent. The former's *The Family at Gilje* (1883), a novel dealing with the middle class, concerns itself largely with the lot of women who have to make marriages of convenience; the frustrated love between Inger-Johanna and the student Grip, a somewhat advanced and unconventional person, may have served as a model for the far more moving idyll between Toni Buddenbrook and Morten Schwarzkopf. Lie's genre pictures, the Christmas scene at Gilje, for instance, may have given Mann some useful hints, but one should not overstress the value to Mann of this rather undistinguished book. Alexander Kielland had more to offer. He was an elegant, cultivated, and rather complicated figure, who combined naturalistic seriousness with irony and self-irony, and democratic tendencies with pride in his upper-class background. "He had himself sprung from one of these rich ship-owning, patrician families . . ." and it seems clear that Mann must have felt a considerable affinity with him. The "Hanseatic" side of Kielland is obvious in his *Garman and Worse* (1880), which might well have been subtitled "Decline of a Family" or "Decay of a Shipping Firm." His short stories, like Mann's, show a double heritage: the *Novelletter* (1879—translated as *Tales of Two Countries* in 1891) are located partly in Norway, partly in Paris. The protagonists in *Two Friends*, a *novella* of the love-hatred between a responsible burgher and a ne'er-do-well, afford a certain parallel to Thomas and Christian Buddenbrook.

The analogy between *Buddenbrooks* and Zola's *Rougon Macquart*, "Histoire d'une famille sous l'Empire," has been noted; and surely Mann's novel would have been very different—less solid, detailed, and documented—without the French precedent. There is no reason to question Mann's statement that he had not read Zola at the time he was composing *Buddenbrooks;* it was not necessary—Zola was in the air. (It was M. G. Conrad, one of Zola's major followers in Germany, who had published Mann's first *novella* in his *Die Gesellschaft,* a leading naturalistic journal.)

Yet Mann's debt to the "more artistic" Goncourt brothers was greater as well as more direct. For all of its naturalistic touches, *Buddenbrooks* is not intended as a "slice of life," but as a carefully arranged composition. Mann read *Renée Mauperin,* he tells us, "again and again, with delight in its lightness, successful execution, and precision . . . ," with "admiration which became productive." As originally planned, *Buddenbrooks* was to have been in scope and in manner much closer to the examples of the Goncourts than was the book that was actually written: a tightly organized novel of barely three hundred pages, centered on the last two generations. Something intervened. Mann speaks of the sheer

mass of material furnished by a faithful Lübeck friend. More fundamental no doubt were his characteristic desire to get at the bottom of
things, to go back as far as possible behind the coulisses of time, and his
equally characteristic conviction that "only the thorough is truly interesting." This was not the only time in Mann's career that a relatively
modest plan was to eventuate in a monumental book; the work, as he
put it, showed a will of its own. *The Magic Mountain* and *Joseph* were
to be even more strikingly transformed in the process of composition.

To return to the Goncourts—Mann intended, at one point, to emu-
late even their process of fraternal collaboration; his brother Heinrich
was to take over the historical aspects of the novel. This notion was of
course abandoned, but *Renée Mauperin* did provide insights into middle-
class psychology which proved really useful, in its stress on the "reign
of money," on business "ideals"—one thinks of the "practical ideals" of
the second Johann Buddenbrook—and on the pride of bourgeois families. The skilfully distressing account of the heroine's prolonged illness
may have strengthened Mann's inclination to treat scenes of disease,
death, and decay.

Mann's debt to Tolstoi is more difficult to describe. He has testified
that *Anna Karenina* "strengthened" him while he was writing *Buddenbrooks*. It would be difficult to think of two novels more different in
spirit; very likely it was precisely the dissimilarity of the Russian work
which he found helpful. Mr. André von Gronicka has argued that Mann
learned the technique of the leitmotif in part from Tolstoi through
Merezhkovski. Aside from this point, it is not tangible "influences" that
are important here; one may speak rather of a certain affinity in Mann
to Tolstoi's epic breadth and unhurried pace, of another "admiration
which became productive."

To deal with the fortunes of four generations of Buddenbrooks, Mann
found that he needed over seven hundred pages, divided among a host
of chapters which are organized into eleven parts. For all its bulk, the
novel has structure: the prestige and power of the family rise, reach
a sort of plateau, and then imperceptibly slip into a decline which gradually gathers a terrifying momentum. It is Thomas, the central figure of
the third generation, on whom the welfare of the family comes essentially to depend, so that the crisis of his life is also the crisis of the
novel. The failures of his brother and sister, both obvious by the center
of the work, isolate him increasingly, and the slow erosion of his strength
makes inevitable the fall of the whole group.

This group does not exist in a vacuum; Mann shows its life against
the background of the city-state of Lübeck, in whose oligarchic government the Buddenbrooks play a considerable role. Farther in the background, we are aware of the evolution of Germany from 1835 to about
1878: the emergence of German unity, prosperity, and material power
as reflected in the customs union among the German states, the victorious

Prussian wars with Denmark, Austria, and France, and the sharp rise of commerce and trade. The broader developments are briefly mentioned without didactic digressions; the focus is always upon the Buddenbrooks as a particular group of very special individuals. Mann did not intend to write a symbolic novel of the German middle class, which was rising to new heights of prosperity during the period he describes, but rather to represent the decline of cultivated patricians, pushed to the wall by the new bourgeoisie. The testimony of his brother Viktor shows how Mann "stylized" the history of his family to heighten the impression of decadence. Yet the European reaction to *Buddenbrooks* suggests that his interpretation was by no means a merely arbitrary one but illuminated a very real social process.

*Buddenbrooks* is a novel of tradition as well as of decadence; the one implies the other. For the tradition of the patrician burgher, quite different from that of the "ordinary" middle class, Mann has profound respect. It stands for activity, energy, a degree of cultivation, and certain not too rigorous ethical standards, for "life" in a good sense. Despite ironic indications—fewer than one would expect—that the burgher's devotion to money is extreme, Mann is clearly on his side. There is no implication that the Buddenbrooks have amassed an undue amount of wealth; on the contrary, when the family bank balance sinks, we feel that the world is out of joint. Before their decline begins, the Buddenbrooks accept the business world in a robust, unquestioning way. Only in the third generation, with Thomas, do they become too delicate for the ethics of competition; only the sick Buddenbrook questions a laissez-faire capitalism. (Thomas, after a business reversal, perceives that his "best friends" react not with sympathy but with frigid distrust; he is weary and sensitive enough to consider this a personal injury.) Before that point, the Darwinian struggle for survival is taken as a matter of course. Not that the Buddenbrooks are Nietzschean buccaneers. "My son, engage joyfully in business during the day, but make only such deals that we can sleep well at night" is their motto—a very bourgeois code, but still a code. Without hypocrisy, one must be deeply concerned in preserving the appearance of solidity and respectability. Bankruptcy is the unforgivable sin. Thomas' feckless brother, Christian, can be excused for his failures, his sexual divagations, even his idleness; but when he remarks that every businessman is "really a swindler," no pardon is possible; his brother, a person by no means given to melodramatic gestures, is driven to pronounce a downright curse on him. The ideal Buddenbrook is a nonreligious churchgoer whose ethic might have served as an instance of the inner bond between Protestantism and capitalism argued by Max Weber and Tawney. Religious fervor is suspect—it is not "solid"—music is still more so, and Thomas' taste for French novels and habit of citing Heine are clearly indications of danger.

Occasionally, Mann does treat his worthy patricians ironically, as in the repeated accounts of their fabulous meals, but his identification with them is too close to allow him to depart often from the tone of respect. His most ironic pages deal with the liberal bourgeoisie and the hopelessly docile working class. Thus the young student, Morten Schwarzkopf, believes ardently in the ideals of the ill-fated German liberal revolt of 1848—abolition of class distinctions, academic freedom, freedom of the press, and all the rest. He is a charming fellow, but clearly naïve; we cannot take him seriously. When the "revolution" breaks out in Lübeck, the novel enters the realm of farce. The "people" break a few windows, demonstrate aimlessly for some hours, and then are sent home in good humor after some friendly words of paternal advice by the younger Johann Buddenbrook. Undoubtedly this account has a good deal of historical validity. One is reminded of Trotzky's remark that the German workers would not seize a railway station unless they had bought tickets first. In any case Mann's personal sympathies are clearly with the conservative side, where they remained until after the defeat of 1918.

Yet despite this affectionate respect for the patrician tradition, the theme of decadence clearly predominates. Decay is considered as an inevitable spiritual and biological process, not as an occasion of moral reproach. It is most strikingly shown in the succession of four male Buddenbrooks, three of whom are heads of the ancestral firm. Johann Buddenbrook, Sr. is a type of the eighteenth century as popularly conceived—rationalistic, optimistic, skeptical, and of uncomplicated, single-minded energy. His son, the younger Johann, is an excellent businessman and devoted to money; but his sentimental religiosity causes a split in his nature which leads to unconscious hypocrisy and "practical ideals." The Buddenbrooks are on the way to becoming problematic. With Thomas Buddenbrook they have become so. Thomas is the most appealing and impressive of the line. Cultivated, able, and enormously conscientious, he guides the family to its greatest successes, but he has no real belief in the value of his enterprises; his energies are eaten away.

Despite all his efforts, he cannot overcome the somehow innate tendency to dissolution which has overtaken the family like a sort of fate. At one point (VIII, 4)[1] he violates the traditional ethics of the firm in a desperate effort to recoup its fortunes, but the maneuver fails. After long and bitter struggles, he is utterly defeated. Yet his prolonged endeavor gives him stature: he has much of that "heroism of weakness" which Mann so greatly admires, and which he was to represent later in the more impressive figures of Schiller, in *A Weary Hour,* and of Gustave von Aschenbach. In Aristotelian terms, Thomas' flaw may be

---

[1] References to *Buddenbrooks* are to part and chapter.

said to lie in his externality, evident in his sacrifice of human values to the welfare of the firm, and in his supreme concern for maintaining appearances. As his vitality decreases, he is forced more and more to mask his actual condition. Only Hanno, the most sensitive of the family, fully perceives this.

Shortly before his death, Thomas has an experience which could have saved him, spiritually speaking, but he lacks the force and courage to hold it in his grasp. More or less by chance he comes upon a volume of Schopenhauer and finds in it a source of metaphysical ecstasy. His cares suddenly appear unspeakably petty and indeed irrelevant; his own individuality and even that of his son seem unimportant.

> Have I hoped to live on in my son? In a personality yet more feeble, flickering, and timorous than my own? Blind, childish folly! What can my son do for me—what need have I of a son? Where shall I be when I am dead? Ah, it is so brilliantly clear, so overwhelmingly simple! I shall be in all those who have ever, do ever, or ever shall say "I"—*especially, however, in all those who say it most fully, potently, and gladly!*
>
> (X, 5)

Schopenhauer—or better, Schopenhauer modified by Nietzsche—could then have freed him from the tortures inflicted by the will. But he lacks the intellectual energy to maintain himself on these philosophical heights. He never opens the book again. One feels that this failure, like the others, is due less to any tangible defect in Thomas than to that inner weariness which, Mann implies, must be taken as given and lies beyond explanation.

Mann has made no secret of the fact that he has attributed to his not very intellectual hero a metaphysical experience of his own. One admires all the more the tact and skill which make the episode credible, and the control which keeps ideology in its place. *Buddenbrooks,* in this regard, is more of a work of art than most of the later novels.

While Thomas, in his way, is a tragic figure, his son Hanno is pathetic. He is possessed of some musical talent but lacks the strength for any sort of career, let alone that of restoring the shaken fortunes of the family. He is phenomenally sickly, and dies while still a schoolboy, physically of sickness but essentially of decadence. With him the family comes to an end. The theme of successive and cumulative decline is repeated in a number of lesser figures.

What happens to the Buddenbrooks is a decline only from the point of view of normality. As always, Mann shows the opposite aspect: in terms of "the spirit" the process is one of ascent to greater awareness and intellectuality, to art, and to—death. Life and the spirit are irreconcilable foes; there is no hope, in Mann's early thought, of a possible synthesis, and the suggestion of a possible *juste milieu* would have been rejected as childishly optimistic. Mann clearly implies in *Buddenbrooks* that the game of the spirit is not worth the candle. Not until *Tonio Kröger* does he reach a rather wry acceptance of the life and the role of the anormal, artistic person.

Decadence then is inevitable and has a potentially creative aspect, but it is greatly to be feared. Mann devotes all his powers of naturalistic description and all his psychological subtlety to develop the theme. It is with the sentimental religiosity of the younger Johann Buddenbrook that feelings "other than the normal, every-day sentiments proper to good citizens" enter the family tradition and begin to alienate it from life. From this point, early in the novel, until the horrible death of the adolescent Hanno, the process takes its inexorable course. (At times Mann implies a dubious biology: decay would seem to be in the blood.) Largely it is seen as a physical development: all the later Buddenbrooks are labile, they tend to migraines, carious teeth, premature aging, and "bluish shadows below the eyes." The terms "nervous" and "exhausted" occur again and again. But primarily the evolution is psychological: with greater self-consciousness come extreme subjectivity and introversion. Energy, and finally the will to live itself, fall away; it is Hanno's lack of *élan vital* that makes him succumb to typhus. In him, as earlier in Christian, the "death wish" becomes dominant. Loyalty to the family and the firm gradually becomes a problem, and then an insoluble one. Artistic, and above all musical endowment is not merely a symptom of the decline; it is a causal factor. Christian, the artist *manqué*, is merely grotesque, but Gerda and her son Hanno are mortally threatened. In Gerda's affair with Lieutenant von Throta, music is linked, as so often in Mann, to illicit love; for Hanno, it is his chief solace, but also his greatest danger. The cumulative effect of the workings of the forces of decay is such that one welcomes Hanno's death as a release too long withheld.

Looking back on the novel, we realize with what careful persistence Mann has developed the theme of death as a force possessed of an uncanny fascination. This note is first sounded briefly, without apparent emphasis, during the last illness of the wife of the elder Johann Buddenbrook. "Something new, alien, extraordinary seemed to have entered the house, a secret which they read in each other's eyes; the thought of death had gained admission and ruled silently . . ." It is struck again and again, with increasing frequency and force. Schopenhauer makes death seem a boon to Thomas in his worst days; and Hanno's boyhood is so filled with funerals that it is almost an education for dying. The smell of death, "the alien and yet so familiar odor," repels and yet attracts him, as it was later to attract Hans Castorp.

That death should play a part of central importance in a story of decline is hardly surprising, but Mann elaborates on the theme in a way which goes far beyond what the inherent logic of the situation or

the tenets of naturalism could demand. It becomes increasingly obvious
that he found death (or what the Germans curiously call the "problem"
of death) more important, more interesting, more germane to his talents
than life. It is here above all that he appears as the heir of German
romanticism. Not that he indulges in any facile raptures; he is far too
much the conscientious observer for that. One needs to recall only the
famous chapter on typhus (XI, 3), or the picture of Thomas Buddenbrook after his collapse on the street:

> Since the street sloped sharply downwards, the upper part of his body
> was quite a bit lower than his feet. He had fallen on his face, from under
> which a pool of blood at once began to spread out. His hat rolled down
> a way on the road. His fur coat was spattered with filth and melting snow.
> His hands, in their white kid gloves, lay outstretched in a puddle. (X, 7)

As the novel of the eighteenth century tended to end in a marriage or
series of marriages, *Buddenbrooks* draws to its close in a succession of
deaths. At the beginning of the last section, four minor characters are
dispatched on a single page (XI, 1) The development of the theme
reaches its climax in the chapter which recounts Hanno's death of
typhus. This follows immediately, with all the shock of suddenness,
upon an ironic, in part almost comic account of Hanno's day at the
gymnasium. "A case of typhus takes the following course." Picturing the
disease as a general force strengthens its impact by making its power
more impersonal, greater, and more ghastly. Mann withholds no clinical
detail, but he has given these pages an eloquence and rhythm of their
own. Hanno's illness is transformed into a drama; the crisis is dramatic
as well as medical; and it is a psychological force, not the illness as such,
that prevails.

The account of the onset of typhus is one of the high points of
German naturalism, and it is only one of many passages in *Buddenbrooks* which demonstrate that Mann had little more to learn about
exact observation and description. Whether or not the story that Mann
once scrutinized a departing friend through opera glasses is true, it is
highly credible; when one reads that Grünlich had put "a little powder
on the wart on the left side of his nose" on the day of his wedding
with Toni Buddenbrook (III, 14), one thinks of Zeiss glasses and tele-
scopic lenses. Permaneder, who succeeds him in Toni's affections, is
described (VI, 4) with equal accuracy but less malice. One notes also,
especially in the first part, the careful documentation to give historical
flavor. Mann's method is phonographic as well as photographic, employing Bavarian dialect as well as *Plattdeutsch,* and reproducing even the
curiously modified vowels of Sesemi Weichbrodt's dialect.

But there is much more here than naturalistic reproduction. As so often, Mann displays his flair for giving the effect of a musical work; above all in his account of Hanno's composition. (VIII, 6)

> Soft and clear as a bell sounded the E-minor chord, tremolo pianissimo, amid the purling, flowing notes of the violin. It swelled, it broadened, it slowly, slowly rose: suddenly, in the forte, he introduced the discord C-sharp, which led back to the original key, and the Stradivarius ornamented it with its welling and singing. He dwelt on the dissonance until it became fortissimo. But he denied himself and his audience the resolution; he kept it back. What would it be, this resolution, this enchanting, satisfying absorption into the B-major chord? A joy beyond compare, a gratification of overpowering sweetness! Peace! Bliss! The kingdom of Heaven: only not yet—not yet! A moment more of striving, hesitation, suspense, that must become well-nigh intolerable in order to heighten the ultimate moment of joy.

His use of light and his feeling for subtle gradations of color as well as for brilliance, relate him closely to the impressionist school. Thus, in description of a warm January day:

> The pavement was wet and dirty, and snow was dripping from the gray gables. But above them the sky stretched delicate blue and unmarred, and billions of atoms of light seemed to glitter like crystals in the azure and to dance. (X, 7)

The scene around the Buddenbrooks' Christmas tree (VIII, 8) is a Manet in words: the whole picture is constructed of a multitude of lights—the countless flames of little candles, the larger lights, the reflections. Mann is equally successful with softer tones, as in this sentence describing an interior just before a storm.

> The colors in the room, the tones of the landscapes on the walls, the yellow of the furniture and the curtains had faded, one could no longer see the play of nuances in Toni's dress or the brightness in people's eyes. (IV, 11)

The leitmotif is employed prodigally in *Buddenbrooks,* and put to a variety of uses, from the rather trivial to the broadly symbolic. It can emphasize a purely physical characteristic, like Toni's "somewhat prominent upper lip" or Gerda's dark-red hair. More importantly, it can pick out a physical trait which has psychological significance: Tom's nervousness, either explicitly stated or implied by repeated mention of his Russian cigarettes; or the bluish shadows below Gerda's eyes. The extension of such a motif from one character to another of course establishes a bond between the two: thus Toni later shares in Tom's nervousness, and Hanno "inherits" his mother's bluish shadows. (That he possesses this sign of weariness at the age of four weeks [VII, 1] would seem to be an instance of the triumph of theory over artistic judgment.)

A repeated word or phrase can of course characterize the speaker: thus the insuperably childish Toni never outgrows the word *vornehm* (upper-class; "Ritzy"); or a motif can be used with humorous intent or for a dozen other purposes. It is most successfully employed, however, as a device of reminiscence; this sort of leitmotif can call up a whole cluster of associations and psychological subtleties. To have its full, "musical" value, the associations evoked must be emotionally charged; the motif with purely descriptive or ironic intent, like "who associated with the best families," has a far less powerful appeal, and its repeated use tends more easily to tire the reader. Broadly speaking, the motifs of *Buddenbrooks* do not have as much emotional content, so to speak, as those of later works, notably *Tonio Kröger* and *The Magic Mountain*. There is one very striking exception: the phrase "to sit on the stones," ultraprosaic though it seems, is used both subtly and movingly. Toni's first lover had been obliged to sit on a pile of stones while she chatted with upper-class friends; then the phrase came to mean, to the two of them, "to be neglected and lonely"; after giving up her lover, Toni uses the phrase again and again, in all sorts of contexts, sometimes without herself remembering, apparently, the whole richness of association. But the alert reader does remember, and the five words revivify a whole series of recollections, causing the story of Toni to "be all there in a given moment."

This economy of means, which makes the leitmotif a sort of shorthand for the emotions, is perhaps its chief merit. When used too often, as occasionally toward the end of *Buddenbrooks,* the device can very easily become as boring as an old family joke.

The manipulation of a variety of other techniques shows how far from the novel of naturalism *Buddenbrooks* really is. For example, the use of contrast: after telling of a particularly depressing incident in the life of Thomas Buddenbrook, Mann shifts quickly to the music of Bach; it is no accident that the discussion centers on counterpoint. (VIII, 6) A similar contrapuntal effect is produced by the introduction of the Christmas festival as a pleasant interlude within the sordid story of Herr Weinschenk's troubles with the law. (VIII, 8) Musical also is the effect of acceleration gained at the end through the rapidly repeated blows of death and disaster and the accumulation of the evidences of decay. Probably Mann gives us too much of a good thing—that the Buddenbrooks' dentist, for instance, is decadent too would seem to be a clear case of piling Ossa on Pelion; it may be that the influence of Wagner has something to do with this tendency toward excess. Possibly Mann's later device, so notable in *Joseph,* of repeating a whole incident, or introducing, under another name, a character who is "archetypically" the same as one who has preceded him, is foreshadowed in his first novel. Thus Toni's first husband, Grünlich, turns out to be a swindler, and the marriage ends in divorce; her daughter Erika goes through fundamentally the same experience with Hugo Weinschenk.

*Buddenbrooks* is an end and a beginning. After writing incomparably the best of German "family novels" Mann abandoned the genre, and never again was he to come so close to the pure epic. *Buddenbrooks* is obviously the least problematic and complex of his major works, but it is not without its paradoxes: realistic in manner, it is romantic in spirit; abundant in Dickensian *Gemütlichkeit*, its essence is the mood of "the cross, death, and the grave"; apparently unilinear in its treatment of time, it uses the leitmotif on occasion to give the effect of emotional simultaneity. From the perspective of half a century, one can see how the technical innovations of the novel point forward to more experimental works to come.

# Tonio Kröger: An Interpretation

## by E. M. Wilkinson

### I. Themes

*Tonio Kröger* occupies a central position in Thomas Mann's spiritual and artistic development. But a work of art must contain its own justification, and to appreciate the story there is no need to know anything of the author's physical or literary antecedents, nor to have read anything else he has written. Taken in and for itself, *Tonio Kröger* is many things—above all a tender study of youth, of its yearnings and sorrows and its soaring aspirations, of the incredible bitterness of its disillusion. Herein lies, perhaps, its widest appeal. But it is also the story of the growth of a man and artist into self-knowledge, while yet another major theme is an account of the process of artistic creation. Much of this process, its later stage of shaping and craftsmanship, lies outside our actual experience. Even these the poet may enable us to experience imaginatively, so that under his spell we embrace even the alien and unknown. But in one vital aspect of artistic creation, its early phase of "seeing" as distinct from "shaping," we share directly.

This, the aesthetic experience, is a special kind of awareness of the universe. It comes in those moments when we experience things and people, not in their bearing on our own needs and affairs, but for their own sake. They are then no longer simply particular people, things, or events. We see through their accidental bounds and discover immense vistas beyond. Such moments of profound recognition are often the moments of "idle tears" which well up "from the depths of some divine despair"; idle in the absence of personal-practical cause or end, tears not for sorrows but for Sorrow. "What business of yours is the king who weeps because he is lonely?" Tonio asks with tender irony. And Hans could but have answered "What indeed?" Yet this power to weep with the king implies knowledge of a kind that Hans will never have, "star pupil" though he be. For it is not the result of gifts or

*"Tonio Kröger: An Interpretation,"* by E. M. Wilkinson. From *Tonio Kröger,* ed. E. M. Wilkinson. Copyright 1944 by Basil Blackwell. Reprinted, with slight modifications, by permission of the author and Basil Blackwell, Publisher.

ability, but of an inner relation to events. Tonio converts the "continual impact of external event" [1] into real experience, endows fortuitous happenings with pregnant meaning and reads the pattern out of life. For him the walnut tree and the fountain, his fiddle and the sea, are more than themselves. Into them he sees "contracted" the "immensities" of beauty and art. Above all he possesses a Hamlet-like clairvoyance about his own reactions to people. He despises his teachers for their rejection of his verse-making. Yet he cannot help seeing their point of view too, so that, "on the other hand," he himself feels this verse-making to be extravagant, and "to a certain extent" agrees with them. These qualifying phrases haunt him painfully early. He is poignantly aware of this complexity in his relations to his parents. The contrast between them is more than just a contrast between two individuals. It is evocative of deeper issues, a symbol of the dualism in his own nature. His relation to Hans is equally complex. Tonio knows well enough that it is a relation which can never bring fulfilment, a love in which all the longing and burning, all attempts at closeness and all torture at their frustration, will be on one side. But he knows far more than this. And it is just in this *more* that the quality of awareness emerges most clearly. For even at fourteen he senses the universality held within this personal experience. Anyone so aware of life as he, cannot help being open and vulnerable to literature too, where the art of the poet underlines the universal within the particular. But this again cuts him off from Hans, for whom bangs and explosions are associated with fireworks, but scarcely with thrills over *Don Carlos!*

In this story Thomas Mann dwells mainly on the pain which awareness brings, on the separating effect of this kind of knowledge. Its compensations are ignored. Yet they are very real, as Tonio must ultimately have known. The joy it brings outweighs the pain. And even though awareness may make the pangs of suffering sharper, it yet removes from it the destructive quality of blind sorrow. To be so involved that we can see nothing beyond ourselves, to be so completely sufferer that light is shut out, and we grope along in the darkness of almost animal pain, is a deadening experience. *"Dumpfheit,"* mere hollow existence, Goethe called such blind living, and preferred "a life eternally resonant," whether it brought him joy or sorrow.

This awareness, the power of being absorbed in something beyond oneself, of responding to the essential quality of a thing or event, the artist shares with others. But in him the mood is more intense and more permanent. The differentiation within the self is such that he more continuously perceives meanings which are hidden when we are absorbed in our own affairs. Of him it is especially true that "there is one man in us who acts and one who watches." Thomas Mann holds

[1] T. S. Eliot, *The Family Reunion* (London, 1939).

fast for us the very moment when this watching trembles on the brink of becoming literature, the transition from awareness to the communication of it through the medium of words. We can distinguish four phases in Tonio's love for Hans; not in time, for they may have happened in one single illumination, but in quality and depth of experience. First he loved Hans and suffered much on his account. That is a purely personal experience expressed in particular terms. Then he was so organized that he received such experiences consciously and recognized the hard fact that he who loves more must suffer more. That is a general human experience expressed in universal terms. But now—and this is the transition from "watching" to "shaping"—"he wrote them down inwardly," that is, the experience became formed, a kind of blueprint of a poem. Finally we get the hallmark of the artist, the pleasure in the experience, with all its bitter knowledge, for its own sake, without any thought of its practical value for his living: "to a certain extent he took pleasure in these experiences, without indeed adjusting his personal life to them nor gaining practical advantage from them."

Much of Tonio's delight in his beloved "fountain, walnut tree, his violin and, far away, the sea, the Baltic," is due to the music of their names, "names which can be included in verses, with good effect." It is the delight the poet takes in calling "the bright, unshadowed things he sees by name." When Lisaveta speaks of the "redeeming power of the word," she surely means that through his medium the artist's insight becomes manifestly fruitful. But again Tonio chooses to ignore the rewards and to dwell rather on the toll which the artist must pay for having surrendered to the power of his medium, a toll paid in sterility and isolation. Even as early as his love for Inge, Tonio realized that he must be in some sense remote from an experience in order to be able to "form" it into literature, remote, not in space or time, but in attitude. Later his joy in the world and the need for "distance" took such possession of him that he became merely an onlooker of himself and others. The roots of such an artist's loneliness lie deeper than is normally supposed. The restlessness which chafes at domesticity, the need to conserve his energy, these are only the more superficial aspects of the problem. His inner loneliness springs rather from his deep sense of failure as a human being. At some point in an experience words become more exciting to him than the experience itself. Even in an intimate relationship he fears he may be sidetracked by his artist's eye, his urge to form may suddenly "see" it, crying out to be shaped by his hand into a work of art. Tonio gives utterance to this sense of failure: "To see clearly, even through a cloud of tears and emotion, to recognize, notice, observe . . . even in moments when hands clasp each other, lips meet, when man's eyes are blinded by feeling."

Tonio has nothing but scorn for the dilettanti, those spare-time artists, who make the mistake of thinking they can pluck "one leaf, one single little leaf" from the laurel tree of art without paying for it with life itself. "The sterile branch" from Goethe's *Tasso* might serve as a motto to this whole conversation with Lisaveta. So humanly impotent does the artist seem to Tonio that he even questions his virility, and again a remark of Goethe's: "Every poem is, as it were, a kiss, which one bestows on the world; but children aren't born from mere kissing," might well complete the sentence he leaves unfinished: "We sing so beautifully that it's really moving. However. . . ." It is the serene finality of art, its contrast with the deadly earnestness of all actuality, which tortures Tonio, as it tortured Nietzsche when he spoke of the flame of genius, "from whose bright circle everything flees, because, lit by the flame, it seems so like a Dance of Death, so foolish, thin as a lath and vain."

Just because Tonio feels equally strongly the pull toward life, he carries within him the possibility of harmony. But Hans is represented as completely lacking in imagination, and we cannot help wondering whether this must always and inevitably be so. Will Tonio's language never be, in part at least, his language? Will he forever be saying resignedly to the Hansens of this world: "Do not trouble to read *Don Carlos*"? We know that it need not be so, that, though it seems likely that this Hans will remain all his life what he is, there is also Hans Castorp, who begins as one of the "innocent, unseeing ones," but ends by discovering that the germs of imagination, which are in all of us, must not be surrendered, must be tended and harnessed in the service of life. When Tonio stands lost in window-longing, unable to join in the dance, he needs some friendly hand to help him out of his lonely introspection. But even more do Hans and Inge need a push in the opposite direction, need jolting out of the confident assumption that they are the hub of the universe. For only a balance between these two ways of experiencing can bring maturity: doing and seeing, being one of the crowd and being an onlooker. The important thing is that life should not only be lived in and for itself, but that it should also be known.

Tonio does go a considerable way toward maturity. By bringing his problem into the light, he rids himself of much of the bitterness which had been accumulating while he pursued a way of life so alien to one side of his nature. This clearing away of the old is essential if new values are to be born: "Die and be born again!" The irony of his final remark: "That settles me!" symbolizes the destruction of a former self. Soon after this self-confession, he feels the need to go back to his beginnings. As in a dream, he revisits his childhood, passes in review figures which have become symbols, and re-estimates their value for him. Despite his apparent emancipation, the influence of his father had been at work underneath, as his dreams betray clearly enough, secretly sapping his energy and undermining his confidence in himself and his calling. When now, in his dream return, he sees the old house, symbol of the burgher's way of life, filled with books, children begotten of the spirit, what a revelation it must seem of the way he ought to go! What an indication that the "toughly persistent diligence" of the burgher can play its part just as effectively in his own realm of the spirit. The tenderness with which the whole incident is suffused is a sign that the bitterness has been eased and the tensions relaxed.

An artist cannot fence off his living from his creating. They must run fluid one into the other. But he has also to learn not to let his entity as an artist be disturbed by the life he lets in. And he can only achieve this security if he accepts his art, if he believes in his mission of making life expressive for the inarticulate. Then he need not fear lest his art be shaken by rich, vital experience, nor lest his human relationships suffer because of the artist in him. Tonio comes to maturity when he accepts himself as an artist, an artist "from the very beginning, born and fated to be one," and repudiates that aestheticism which, through fear and insecurity, takes flight from the spring into the rarefied atmosphere of the coffeehouse! It remains eternally true that "What is to live in song immortal, Must be destroyed in mortal life"; but equally true that "one must first *be* something, if one is to create something." "To have died" is only one stage in the process of artistic creation; and for the artist to cut himself off from life altogether means going out into the waste land of pure form and art for art's sake.

As a man, too, he matures. The journey to self-knowledge has brought him the courage to face the isolation of personality, and he is now content to leave those he loves in their "otherness" without wishing to possess them. Out of the growing acceptance of himself, the longing for what he is not is eased, and he can watch with tender understanding their small intensities which are none of his intensity, and love them with the love which is extolled in the thirteenth chapter of St. Paul's First Epistle to the Corinthians.

## II. *Artistry*

The art of story-telling, that is quite simply the art of compelling people to listen, even if one disregards the content.

No analysis of the artistry by which Thomas Mann compels us to listen to his story can ever take the place of direct appreciation. Criticism is never a substitute for the aesthetic experience. After—and only after—we have been exposed to the direct impact of a work, analysis can perhaps help us to further deepened and enriched experience of it. But there remains always the task of synthesizing what has been analyzed, and this cannot be done by a simple process of adding parts. The whole is always greater than the sum of the parts, and different. Synthesis can only be achieved by surrendering again to the power of the story itself.

The architectonic outlines of this *novella* grow naturally out of the requirements of the story. Its mixture of epic and dramatic, the absence of connecting links, justify Thomas Mann's own description of it as a prose ballad. Two brief episodes give the essence of the youthful Tonio. There follows a short narrative passage leading to the central reflective part, where all that was implicit is made explicit. It is a commentary on those dramatic scenes which were directly presented to our imagination, but there is nothing artificial about it. It is natural that Tonio, caught at a turning point in his life, should render account to himself of all he has been and is becoming. This is the critical turning point of the *novella,* and it occurs simultaneously on three planes. In the outer world of space and time the turning point is marked by his decision to leave Munich. In the inner world of the spirit it is a moment of rebirth, marked by his wholehearted affirmation of life. And in the timeless world of form the ballad-style here gives way to long monologues of introspective reflection. The final part is again dramatic, but in a different way. In revisiting his past Tonio trails behind him the cloak of all that has happened in between. There is consequently a large measure of introspection to this second drama. Not only are the episodes of the first part fused into one experience, but the conversation with Lisaveta vibrates beneath. With the final admission that his deepest love is still for the "blond, the blue-eyed," the *novella* returns to its beginnings.

The perfect symmetry is achieved by the skilful weaving of the strands, backwards and forwards, so that the past fulfils the future as surely as the future fulfils the past. The Hans and Inge *motifs,* announced separately at first, are loosely intertwined as Tonio paces the streets of Lübeck. But in Denmark these strands are pulled taut and woven together with symbolic value. How subtle are the variations in this disturbingly familiar quadrille scene! There is no M. Knaak, but the directions are in French all the same and with "nasals"! The second confession to Lisaveta, this time in letter form, rounds off the whole. Nothing is lacking to complete the symmetry. Even the short epic transition leading to the scene with Lisaveta finds its echo. For, as Tonio lies in bed after his encounter with Hans and Inge in Denmark, his thoughts run back to those years of "rigidity, desolation, ice. . . ."

The two first episodes are brilliant illustrations of the choice of a "pregnant moment." Each, the walk and the dancing lesson, occupies at most an hour. How in so short a time does the author manage to convey a relationship so that we breathe its very essence? He does it by skilful choice of time and place, catching the relationship at flood tide and in a situation calculated to reveal all the pull and thrust of tensions. The books we like, the people we admire, the activities we pursue, are eminently revealing, and Thomas Mann makes full use of this fact. Hans loves horse-riding, and the contrast between his "books about horses, with snapshots" and Tonio's *Don Carlos* brings out strikingly the incompatibility of their natures. When Mann introduces Erwin Immerthal we experience directly the ease of Hansen's manner with his own kind, and his awkwardness with Tonio is thereby thrown into greater relief. In the Inge episode the contrasts are between the sheer physical delight in the dance and Tonio's escape into the imaginative world of *Immensee,* between Inge's admiration of M. Knaak and her scorn of Tonio's clumsiness. Despite the unmistakably different atmosphere of these two stages of adolescence, there is a marked parallelism which gives a satisfying sense of form.

Just as the symmetry grows naturally out of the requirements of the story, so too the ironic style is the ideal form for a hero who stands between two worlds and for a situation in which the artist admires and needs the burgher, and the burgher replies by arresting him! As long as spirit (*Geist*) and life remain unreconciled in Thomas Mann's work, they are treated with irony, "something in between, a neither-nor and both-and." Hence those qualifying phrases so akin to our English understatement and derived no doubt from that Low German parentage which we and he have in common. The style of a writer, he declares, is ultimately, if one listens closely enough, a sublimation of the dialect of his forefathers: "and I make no secret of the fact that . . . in its absence of passion and grandiloquence, in its proneness to mockery and pedantic thoroughness, my style is a typical Lübeck mode of speech." His dry humor often results from an aside which jerks the reader out of his absorption in the story, inviting him to study the character with detachment: "for he played the violin"; "for he often said. . . ." Understatement has the special virtue of arousing interest while leaving scope for the imagination to complete the picture. How effectively it is used here to convey that moment when some ordinary and familiar object or person is suddenly illumined by a new and unearthly light: "He had seen her a thousand times; on one evening however he saw her in a *certain* light, saw how she . . . laughing, threw her head to one side in a *certain* proud manner, in a *certain* manner raised her hand . . . to the back of her head . . . heard how she accented a word . . . in a *certain* way. . . . That evening, he took her image away with him." The repetition of "certain" implies far more than is actually said and sends our imagination in pursuit of what Tonio saw.

Ideas are but the raw material of art, and only by taking on body can mind become spirit. Thomas Mann, being first and foremost an artist, expresses his thoughts naturally in images. His are not the primordial, universal images we find in poetry. They are suggested by figures and events of his immediate surroundings: father and mother, the friends and loves of his youth, a criminal banker he has known, a lieutenant he has met, a prince in civilian clothes, a young businessman, an actor without a part. Everything is presented in sensuous form rather than in concepts: not sterility, but the laurel tree; not separateness, but the mark on his brow; not responsibility, but immaculate sober dress; not Bohemianism, but a ragged velvet jacket and a red silk waistcoat; not art versus life, but "fixative and the odor of spring," "the perilous knife-dance of art and life's sweet, banal waltz time." The names are symbolic, too. Why is Lisaveta a Russian except that she acts as confessor to Tonio's introspection in the manner of Turgenev? Or M. Knaak so typically Low German except to emphasize the spuriousness of his French pretensions? Why Magdalena, except that in some obscure way intimate associations had formed in the author's mind between this name, moral- or physical-falling, and those early Christians "with clumsy bodies and fine souls?" Or take the ring of Tonio's own name, upper-middle-class like the cuisine of his Lübeck home, and derived from *Krog,* which occurs so frequently in Low German place names, signifying an inn! How it contrasts with the exotic Tonio, clearly his mother's choice, so that the very title announces the theme of the story!

An image becomes a symbol when it is remembered for the sake of some special significance it had for us. It is then stripped of irrelevant and extraneous detail, and details from other images of similar significance are often superimposed on the first and become part of the symbol. The episode of the lieutenant was clearly an actual incident in Tonio's experience. But we know at once that it has more than anecdotal significance for him, because it is related to the other anecdotes he tells solely by the accident of its connection with his own problem. This is the only thread on which all these stories are strung. Sometimes we can trace the development of an episode into a symbol. At first the girl "who often fell down while dancing," is a real person, and we are told details about her; her surname, her father's profession, that she asked Tonio to dance and to show her his poems, even that she asked him to do so twice, a detail quite irrelevant for the meaning of the symbol. Of all this he remembers only the connection between physical clumsiness and love of poetry, and in the conversation with Lisaveta makes the generalisation: "people with clumsy bodies and subtle souls, people who are always falling down, so to speak." The actual experience has become symbol. Later this symbol is transmuted into art. Magdalena is brought to life again, but no longer as an individual person. There adhere to her traits derived from his other experiences of people with spirit. She has become the symbolic peg on which to hang such associations.

Nowhere is the poet's power "to ring up the curtain for us" more evident than when, in Tonio's dream return to his home, he conveys the bittersweet melancholy of the days that are no more. The problem here is to raise an idea from the level of a mere concept to that of an emotional experience. The idea to be conveyed is a familiar one. When we relive something in the memory, everything happens much more quickly. The whole experience is telescoped. We do not have to take Tonio's word for it that this is what happens now. We got through the experience itself.

Tonio lives his early life again, but we relive the first part of the *novella*. We do this because memory permeates the language and sets it vibrant, because the words are similar enough to awaken in us the same reminiscent melancholy which stirs in him. Yet there is that slight difference which is always there when we revisit a familiar scene or dream about it. We, too, feel that quality of pastness which is inseparable from memory. Hans and Tonio watched the train go by and, with the trustful confidence of children, waved to the man perched up on the last coach. The grown man, less spontaneous and more circumspect, merely gazes after him. Without any comment, merely by means of this slight alteration, we feel the whole weight of the intervening years. Similar variation is used with twofold effect at the gate of Hansen's old house. No mention of sedateness or of the time that has passed, but the same weight of years comes across merely because he swings the gate with his hand instead of riding on it. And here we see very clearly the telescoping effect of recollection. It all happens more quickly, detail and dialogue fall away. And whereas the first time we had the simple statement: "their hands, when they shook them, had been made quite wet and rusty by the garden gate," now Tonio's mood of pensive reflection is conveyed by the addition of: "Then for a while he examined his hand, which was cold and rusty." This is enough, without any direct reference to his emotional state.

The trance-like quality of this return is suggested by the magic use of words connected with *sleep* and *dream,* by the hypnotic effect of "Where was he going?" thrice repeated at regular intervals to mark the stages in this progress between sleeping and waking, by the tenderness with which he perceives that the narrow-gabled streets have become poignantly small! How directly we share in his experience when it says: "He would have liked to have kept going for a long time. . . . But everything was so cramped and close together. Soon one was at one's destination"! We, too, are brought up sharply, because we have arrived sooner than we expected.

The same dream light shines on his experiences in Denmark. Now that Hans and Inge have become symbols, they have the strangeness of all dream figures. In masterly fashion the uniqueness, the personal immediacy of this experience is preserved, while at the same time it is lifted beyond the particular to the typical. That they are not the old Hans and Inge, but figures on to which he has projected all his own imaginative yearning, is brought out by the significant little phrase: "who was perhaps his sister." This is indeed the Inge Holm he—and we—knew, and this the same little Hans Hansen grown up; the same and yet different, for she is every Inge, and he is every Hans.

In a purely artistic sense, Thomas Mann suggests, it was probably its musical qualities which most endeared his "lyrical *novella*" to its readers. "Here for the first time I grasped the idea of epic prose composition as a thought-texture woven of different themes, as a musically related complex—and later, in *The Magic Mountain,* I made use of it to an even greater extent. It has been said of the latter work that it is an example of the 'novel as architecture of ideas'; if that be true the tendency towards such a conception of art goes back to *Tonio Kröger.*" When he speaks of a musical structure in his works he does not mean, like so many modern poets, that he is more concerned with the rhythmical arrangement of words than with their sense. The meaning of poetry is much more than that conveyed directly to the intelligence; far more is conveyed indirectly by the musical impression upon the sensibility. But, even so, this musical impression of poetry is never the same as that conveyed by music itself, for words have a meaning before they are rhythmically arranged in poetry. Thomas Mann is passionately concerned with the meaning of words, and the musical quality of his prose does not lie so much in their rhythmical arrangement, as in the repetition of certain phrases in different contexts, phrases which call up a whole world of associations as a snatch of song might do. This is the leitmotif technique which he adopted from Richard Wagner.

In *Buddenbrooks* the linguistic leitmotif was handled on an external and naturalistic basis. A descriptive phrase was attached to a character, a label, which usually called up some outward and accidental aspect of him rather than his essence. In *Tonio Kröger* the leitmotif is transferred from the outward to "the more lucent medium of the idea and the emotions, and thereby lifted from the mechanical into the musical sphere." From being a mere label each leitmotif now bears a strong emotional content arising from the central problem of the story, and they are woven into the texture with contrapuntal effect, each theme being pointed against another to express the fundamental opposition between art and life. Nowhere is this method used more skilfully or with greater effect than in the conversation with Lisaveta. Art and life run parallel throughout, both in theoretical formulation and in symbols ranging from one single word ("fixative" and "odor of spring") through phrases ("who are always falling down") to symbolic anecdotes (the lieutenant and the banker). First one voice announces the theme, then another takes it up. A contrasting theme is announced, and they are played off against each other as in a Bach fugue. Our delight is in tracing the emergence, the blending, the dividing and dying of the themes.

The reason for the effectiveness of the verbal leitmotif, when used in this way, is that we remember not only in images, but also emotionally. When a pregnant phrase is repeated, chords of remembrance are struck, which go on echoing in us long after the notes have died. Instead of recapturing only Tonio's remembrance of the past, we recall the whole emotional aura of our own original reaction to the phrase, a whole train of personal associations for which the author is not directly responsible.

Even when a leitmotif in Tonio is of a descriptive nature, it is nevertheless not used in the same way as in *Buddenbrooks*. Tonio's father is first described by a phrase which is little more than a label giving the essence of the burgher. But the context in which it occurs endows it immediately with emotional quality, for we connect Herr Kröger's concern at his son's bad report with his formal correctness. The next time this motif appears, the descriptive element recedes (his blue eyes are omitted); the appearance of the father is becoming symbolic of one side of the conflict in Tonio's breast. People see his way of life as an outward sign of the decay of the family. "The tall, thoughtful gentleman," his father, dies—that is, one side of himself dies, or goes into abeyance. The third time the symbolic aspect entirely predominates: "perhaps it was his inheritance from his father—the tall, thoughtful, cleanly dressed man, with a wildflower in his buttonhole, which made him suffer so much down there." Is the variant "cleanly" introduced as a kind of contrast to his own feeling of being sullied through his adventures of the flesh? It is as if the same theme were given out by another instrument. The fourth time it is modulated into a minor key. Time, by removing all non-essentials, has brought mellowness. Tonio's understanding of his father is growing, although he has long been dead. With deepened insight he sees through the impassive mask and knows that behind the immaculate gravity there lies something of wistful melancholy: "the tall, correct, rather melancholy and pensive gentleman with a wildflower in his buttonhole." Each time the father motif is repeated, it is pointed against that of the mother, for together they symbolize the theoretical formulation of the problem: life—spirit, burgher—artist, North—South. Finally, in the letter to Lisaveta they are no longer used merely as leitmotifs, to evoke associations. Tonio now analyzes the significance of these symbols, thus fusing thought and emotion, idea and image.

But most of the leitmotifs in *Tonio Kröger* are not descriptive at all. It is fascinating to trace the development of a motif such as "to give form and shape to something, and in serene aloofness to fashion a complete whole out of it," to note how its emotional connotation varies each time it appears. It is first repeated twice within a few lines, so that we know at once that symbolic value is attached to it. Then it is blended with "effective *pointe*," thereby establishing the symbolic significance of this alternative motif for shaping and forming. Henceforward they can be used, either separately or together, to call up the same associations. When they are played off against life within Tonio himself, against his love for Inge, for the spring or the walnut tree, these symbols of craftsmanship fall in the scale of values. But when they are contrasted with life outside him, with the slightly ridiculous figure of the blunt policeman, they rise. For then the shaping impulse is not pulling against his own urge to life, and he can note with satisfaction the "effective *pointe*" he has made. Finally, with increasing harmony, a balance of values is achieved. The sea inspires him to poetry, but he is too much under the stress of emotion to shape it. Yet he accepts this knowledge without impatience, content to wait for the "serenity" which will surely alternate with intensity of living. "It was not complete, not formed and shaped and not serenely fashioned to something whole. His heart was alive. . . ." These simple, independent statements are free of all the fret, the pull and thrust, of the two dependent clauses in which the motif first made its appearance.

It is no accident that three great influences in Thomas Mann's life were Schopenhauer, Wagner and Nietzsche, all passionate lovers of music. It was the symphonic music of Schopenhauer's thought which appealed to his very depths, and of Nietzsche he wrote: "his language is itself music." His apprehension of things was aural rather than visual, and it is little wonder that he paid such enthusiastic tribute to Schiller's *Spontaneous and Sentimentive Poetry,* in which the distinction between musical and plastic poetry was first made. This accounts for the criticism so often levelled against his work, that there was no landscape in it. In his defence he urges firstly that his is an urban scenery, to be more precise, the characteristic Gothic setting of his native Lübeck, with its tall towers, pointed gables, arcades and fountains, its grey skies and the damp wind whistling down the narrow streets which wend their crooked way from the harbor to the market square. And then, much more important, the sea beyond, Travemünde, the town he knew from boyhood. "The sea is no landscape, it is the vivid experience of eternity, of nothingness and death, a metaphysical dream." It is the solace for all who have seen too deep into the complexity of things. Looking at it Tonio experiences "a deep forgetting, a free soaring above space and time," thereby anticipating Mann's absorption with the problem of time in *The Magic Mountain.* The sea, its rhythms, its musical transcendence, vibrates in the language of all his books, even when there is no talk of it. And no German since Heine, whom he idolized in his youth, has written of it so that we not only hear its rush and roar, but feel the spray and the salt tang on our lips and crush the shells beneath our feet.

Thomas Mann speaks of certain lyric poems by Theodor Storm which, "however old one becomes . . . cause this tightening of the throat, this being seized by an implacably sweet and sad sense of life; it was for its sake that one was so devoted, at sixteen or seventeen, to this cadence." One can say the same of his own *Tonio Kröger.* If we are young we experience this tightening of the throat because Tonio is part of all of us; as we grow older, because he is what we were and because, like him, we too have to come back to our beginnings and recognize that it could not have been otherwise, that it all had to happen thus. Like him we hope to be able to accept this knowledge.

> We shall not cease from exploration
> And the end of all our exploring
> Will be to arrive where we started

And know the place for the first time.
Through the unknown, remembered gate
When the last of earth left to discover
Is that which was the beginning.[2]

[2] T. S. Eliot, *Little Gidding*. In *Four Quartets*. Reprinted by permission of the publishers, Harcourt, Brace & World, Inc. and Faber and Faber, Ltd.

# Thomas Mann's *Royal Highness* As
# Symbolic Autobiography

## *by Hermann J. Weigand*

In his brief essay "On *Royal Highness*" (1910) Thomas Mann wrote:

The ruler whom I really had in mind is the one of whom Schiller's Charles the Seventh* says: "Thus the minstrel should be at the king's side. Both of them dwell on the pinnacle of humanity." The allusive analysis of the existence of the sovereign as a formal, unreal, superreal one and the salvation of "highness" through love: that is the theme of my novel. Full of understanding sympathy for every sort of "special case," it preaches humaneness (*Menschlichkeit*).

Here Thomas Mann states with complete clarity that it was the parallel between the life of the ruler and his own mode of life as an artist which attracted him to this particular subject matter. Thus he portrays a human type with the autobiographer's intimate, expert knowledge. Near the end of the same essay he writes that the professional critics had racked their brains to discover how in the world he might have hit upon this remote and resistant subject—

just as if I had ever been concerned with any "subject" other than my own life. Who is a poet? He whose life is symbolic. In me lives the belief that I only have to tell tales about myself in order to speak for the age, the generality of men; and unless I cherished this belief I could rid myself of the toil of production.

The life of the sovereign—to reverse the parallel—is also symbolic. Indeed, this is one of the most significant axiomatic truths which Dr. Überbein imparts to the young prince Klaus Heinrich:

What am I? An assistant teacher. Not a completely ordinary one—all right —but still nothing more. A very definable individual. But you? What are

* [*In The Maid of Orleans.*]
"Thomas Mann's *Royal Highness* As Symbolic Autobiography," by Hermann J. Weigand. *PMLA*, XLVI (1931), 867-879. Copyright 1931 by *PMLA*. Reprinted by permission of the author and the editors of *PMLA*. Translated by Henry Hatfield.

you? That is harder to say . . . Let's say an essence, a sort of ideal. A
vessel. A symbolic existence, Karl Heinrich, and therefore a formal existence.

The "very definable individual" stands for himself; the "symbolic existence" on the other hand is representative, and Überbein says:

> To be representative, to stand for many, while playing one's own role, to
> be the heightened and disciplined expression of a multitude—represent-
> ing, of course, is more and higher than simply being. . . .

With these words the creative writer proudly and openly declared his
faith in his high rank in the scale of human types and in his dignity.
Although representative, formal existence is really "of course" larger and
higher than the simple way of life, he elsewhere justifies its pre-eminence
by his express indication that the demands of formal accomplishment
are much more searching than those of a solid, practical (*inhaltlich*) sort.
Klaus Heinrich experiences this himself when he plunges into the study
of the elements of government and economics, and when Thomas Mann
informs us of this incident, the symbolic reference is obvious:

> Moreover, he found that it was not difficult to comprehend all that, if
> one really applied oneself. No, this whole earnest reality in which he
> now participated; this simple-minded, coarse structure of interests, this sys-
> tem of obvious if logically arranged needs and necessities, which innumer-
> able young people of ordinary birth had to get into their cheerful heads,
> so that they could pass their examinations in the field—it was far less
> difficult to control than he, on his heights, had believed. Representing,
> he found, was more difficult.

In this passage then, the symbolic and autobiographical nature of the
work is clearly established by the author himself; in broad outline it is
shown in the work itself. Since, however, the "professional" critics at the
time of publication (1909) showed not the slightest inkling of what the
work was really about, and since the novel was also monstrously mis-
interpreted when it appeared in an American translation,[1] it is a rewarding task to investigate this "allusive" work further, with reference to the
relations which connect the life-style of the poet and artist with that of
the sovereign. Needless to say, in this discussion, that part of Thomas
Mann's life work which must be consulted as a basis of comparison is
that which had already been published when *Royal Highness* appeared;
I shall refrain from mentioning the further formulations and variations
of the artist's style of life which Mann's last two decades have presented
to us.

Anyone who has absorbed, with alert mind and senses, *Tonio Kröger,*

---

[1] In the review by Joseph Wood Krutch, *The Nation*, April 21, 1926, p. 454.

Mann's first extensive work of fiction to treat the nature and the problems of the modern artist, would probably understand the few direct hints in which the author of *Royal Highness* indicates that the existence of the sovereign, in our novel, possesses a symbolic meaning along with a literal one. In the first conversation between Grand Duke Johann Albrecht and the Jewish physician Dr. Sammet, the existence of the sovereign, so sharply segregated from the norm of ordinary life, is contained in an extensive frame of reference which includes the exceptions and special cases in a sublime as well as a disreputable sense. "Sublime-disreputable" —does not this double predicate circumscribe the artist's hybrid nature, as it appears and becomes aware of itself in the personality of Tonio Kröger? Yet one must read between the lines, I suppose, to take Dr. Sammet's words as a reminder of this theme. We are given a second, quite casual but more direct hint when we, along with Klaus Heinrich, see his photograph in a shop window, "next to those of artists and great men, whose eyes gazed out from the loneliness of renown." For the initiate, Thomas Mann speaks more clearly when he has the assistant declare to his princely pupil that the latter "walked on humanity's heights"; for everyone who remembers Schiller's *Maid of Orleans* from his school days supplies the missing line about the minstrel.[2] When finally Klaus Heinrich and a real poet meet, face to face, the prince gains insight into a strictly ascetic existence, wholly focused on form, which he himself feels to be related to his own. "He doesn't have a comfortable or easy time of it," Klaus Heinrich tells his sister the princess, after the audience. "And that's what matters, Albrecht, that one doesn't have a comfortable time of it"— those were the words with which he had vindicated the dignity of his own purely formal profession against his brother's disdainful attitude.

In the person of Axel Martini, to be sure, the disreputable aspect of the poetic calling is strongly emphasized. This somewhat veils the fact of the intrinsic affinity, for the prince's utterly naïve ignorance about matters of poetry provokes the writer (who had been summoned to the audience) to self-revelation of a comical, ironic hue. The ethos of his disclosures, after all, differs markedly from the type of questionableness which is inherent in the Prince's empty, unsubstantial style of life. Evidently Thomas Mann was concerned, in contrast to the carefully benevolent irony and delicate consideration with which he treated the very questionable strain in the nature of his allegorical twin, to draw the actual poet with all the more bold and vigorous strokes, so to speak as a figure of disenchantment.

Once one has noticed the equation of the formal, representative existence of the ruler with that of the poet, the parallels become completely clear. The individual points may be conveniently grouped around four problems, which, in their totality, express the essential presuppositions

[2] See above, p. 35.

of Thomas Mann as artist and creative writer. These are 1: the heroic-ascetic ethic of an existence focused on the achievement of exemplary form; 2: the questionable nature of a human type in which all content is volatilized into form; 3: the path of development to a full humanity, to synthesis of the values of form and content—redemption; 4: the tie to the community; popularity and representation as a calling.

## I. *The Heroic-Ascetic Ethic*

The effect of a folk tale on Klaus Heinrich's psyche, when he was a child, is symbolic of the renunciation of the "raptures of ordinary life"—to quote *Tonio Kröger*—as the correlative of a lofty, exceptional position. When listening to the adventures of fairy princes and princesses, other children feel a heightening, an elevation of their natures above actuality and ordinary life, whereas Klaus Heinrich and his little sister regarded "those figures as their own sort, with a relaxed sense of being equally highborn." Carried over to the sphere of art, this means: the person who belongs to this sphere and has his home in its high regions is denied the easy heightening and elevation above the everyday level which the average person feels when occasionally, for moments or hours, he abandons himself to the magic spell of art. Also symbolic is the vivid experience of terrible loneliness, which swept over the thirteen-year-old Klaus Heinrich in the midst of the bleak magnificence of the "silver hall," of which Mann states: "And it was cold in the silver Hall of Candles, as in the hall of the Snow Queen, where children's hearts freeze stiff." That art is a sphere of coldness Tonio Kröger had learned quite well enough. Indeed he too characterizes the act of artistic creation not so much as a liberation and redemption as, rather, a "chilling of emotion and placing it on ice." The whole atmosphere of the Hall of State, a concentrated emblem of severely formal existence, is a symbol of the artist and his passionate and exclusive endeavor to create form: "Severe and empty splendor prevailed here and a formal symmetry of arrangement which presented itself, self-contained, unconcerned with purpose or comfort—a high and zealous service no doubt, which seemed far removed from relaxed lightheartedness, which obligated you to decorum and discipline and controlled self-abnegation." "Loneliness and being shut off from happiness, from a happy-go-lucky life" as one's destiny; "an exclusive and severe focusing on creative achievement"—an achievement which must give the appearance of easy mastery and spontaneity though it is the product of the most disciplined exertion of one's energies; giving up "spontaneity" and the "joys of intimate confession": these are indeed the principles which put their stamp both on the pedagogy of the Prince's tutor and on the self-education of the artist. After all, part of the artist's manner of working, as Thomas Mann relates from his own experience,

is "a sort of patience—no, far more! a doggedness, an obstinacy, a discipline and enslavement of one's own will which are hard to conceive of;
and which often strain the nerves, believe me, to the breaking point."
And if he ever succumbs to the temptation to let himself go and, with
the cover of a punch bowl [3] on his head, perhaps, to share in the delights
of ordinary life, he must pay a bitter penalty.

The poet Axel Martini, too, who praises the full enjoyment of life in
such fiery words, has a tale to tell about that: "Renunciation is our pact
with the Muse; our strength and dignity is based upon it, and life is our
forbidden garden, our great temptation, to which we yield at times, but
never to our own good." And later: "For living hygienically—that is our
whole ethic." We are reminded of Tonio Kröger's bitter question whether
the artist is a man at all: "Ask 'woman' about that!" Related in its severe,
ascetic fulfilment of duty to the ethic of the categorical imperative, and
owing much both in ascetic severity and in the lofty, confident sense of
being chosen to Nietzsche's inspiration, the existence of the sovereign and
of the artist is of markedly aristocratic nature; with proud contempt it
puts the merely human in its place. For the merely human means good
nature, relaxation, lack of dignity, putting up with mere attempts instead
of severe achievement; in a word, it is the human-all-too-human. Therefore Dr. Überbein reverses the eighteenth-century paradox: "He is a
prince! . . . He is more than that; he is a human being!" By now the
paradox has degenerated to a flabby untruth, and he states emphatically:
"That is mere humanity, but at heart I'm not very much for humanity;
I take the greatest pleasure in speaking disparagingly about it!" And
Thomas Mann has the same pedagogue utter, in its most extreme form,
the credo of the artist, creating, in full awareness, on the lonely heights:
"Spirit (or intellect-*Geist*) is the tutor who insists implacably on dignity,
yes, who actually creates dignity; he is the archenemy and aristocratic
antagonist of all humane and humanitarian good nature (*Gemütlichkeit*)."

## II. *Questionableness*

But now the seamy side of this severe self-discipline intent on form
alone. Even as a small child, Klaus Heinrich has the experience that his
mother—she too achieves virtuosity in her own specialty—saves up all
her tenderness and motherliness for public occasions. Within the intimacy
of the family, on the other hand, she displays very little of this warmth;
and the "proud" insight dawns on the little, pitiably docile prince: "that
in accordance with the nature of things it was not fitting for us to feel
simply and thus to be happy, but rather that it was our lot to make our
affection vividly clear and to display it at court functions, so that the

---

[3] [A reference to a scene in the novel. The young prince, a bit tipsy, crowns himself with this article; but fraternization leads only to humiliation.]

hearts of the guests might swell." When every energy is expended on "making clear" and display, what is left for emotion per se? Is not this whole cult of form calculated to volatilize all sense of essential substance and make an expression which has no corresponding content become rigid, empty form? How frighteningly empty an education during whose course the pupil grasps the fact that every objective element of instruction is basically a sheer pretext, that the dignified and courteous gesture of shaking hands with the teacher was really "more important and essential than all the lessons that came between handshakes." How systematically mendacious is a type of coaching which encourages the student, after he has reached a perfidious secret understanding with his teacher, to simulate, by raising his hand, a knowledge which he does not possess! Thus bluffing is an axiom of life! And all his development is shaped in accordance with this principle: his year at the preparatory school, his year at the university, his year in the army and his so-called grand tour (*Bildungsreise*). His sphere of activity is similarly constructed when his destiny involves taking over his brother's "representative" duties, the journeys and official speeches and layings of cornerstones, the open audiences in the castle, which, with their emphasis on meticulous observation of etiquette, are primarily devoted to the purpose of diverting the petitioner from the real point of his request. One thinks also of the questions apparently inspired by the most pertinent interest—words of praise, of encouragement, which make a fool of the unsuspecting burgher—except for cases when an artful fellow, a man whose nature is related to the ruler's, a sovereign of the spirit, is summoned to one of these audiences and gives vent to his irony —which leads to a priceless situation.

Let us confirm, by quoting a confession of Tonio Kröger, that in this semblance of an existence, in this systematically cultivated falsity of feeling, the whole problematic nature of the artist is symbolically reflected. Tonio's language is clear:

> One works poorly in the spring, surely; and why? Because one feels. And because whoever believes that a creator is allowed to feel is a bungler. Every genuine and honest artist smiles at the naïveté of such blunders— perhaps sadly, but he smiles. For what one says must never be the main thing; it is rather raw material, neutral in and of itself. From it the artist must put together the aesthetic structure, with easy, calm superiority. . . . Emotion, warm, heartfelt emotion is always banal and unusable; worthy of art are only the irritations and cold ecstasies of our corrupted, our artistic, nervous system.

In Tonio Kröger's case the problematic nature of an existence entirely focused on semblance reaches its height in the remark that in the realm of art "it is perhaps a matter of a gift with extremely evil preconditions, extremely questionable in itself"; and in his personal confession that he felt—"transferred into the intellectual sphere—all the suspicions about the artist-type" with which his honest ancestors had confronted jugglers and roaming acrobats. In Klaus Heinrich's case the analogous state of affairs is formulated as a question, decisive in his relations to Imma, which he himself expresses as a humbly hesitant supplication: "Couldn't you put a little trust in me?" Trust, that is the essential point. A personality whose every fiber is in the grip of the service of form; which habitually "works up" everything substantial and essential, treating it as mere neutral raw material; which—to use Tonio Kröger's words again—is subservient to artistic aims even "when hands clasp each other, lips meet, when man's gaze is blinded by feeling,"—is it at all possible, in human terms, to feel trust in such a personality? At first Imma's answer—though she does regard the Prince with some warmth—must be: "It is quite impossible to have any trust in you." "To be a poet means to sit in judgment on oneself"—Thomas Mann is one of those artists whose conscience subscribes to this motto of Ibsen's.

### III. Redemption

And yet the antinomy between formal and essential existence is not Thomas Mann's last word. That the opposition of form and essence is not an absolute but a dialectic one, which can and must be reconciled in a higher synthesis—Thomas Mann professes this conviction at the end of *Tonio Kröger,* by letting the hero of his *novella* find his way back from emotional torpor to humanity. Chilling and slaying emotion with the purpose of refining it into sheer form is a process of artistic development which must inevitably be undergone, so that artistry may grow into full humanity. If the artist has attained mastery of form through the passionate yet ascetic sacrifice of all his humanity, he must then find again the road to ingenuous emotion, to being a human simply and unpretentiously. Otherwise artistry cannot mean a general heightening of innate human talents but only the variation of a special endowment—subtly interesting to be sure, but incapable of really living. Of the "artist," love for the human, the living, the ordinary, makes the "poet."

Tonio Kröger finds the way back to humanity; Klaus Heinrich first has to find that there *is* a way. For from the cradle his life has lacked any true content, and his education has systematically frustrated all his capacities of becoming substantial. Surely these were latent in him, for he had the urge to "rummage about." Thus an extraordinary, fortunate chance must intervene in his life, so that the vessel of his life, having been shaped as sheer form, may be filled with substance. Love for a woman who is equally marked, remote from life, and lonely, builds a bridge for him. A kindly providence arranges that the fulfilment of his longing for his own happiness is made to depend on his learning to devote a real, sympathetic interest to the cares of his own people and of the individual. He took his first step on his new path when he began to subject Dr. Überbein's ascetic, "antihappiness" ethic, his provocative insistence on achievement, to muted criticism. He calls this ethic decent but profoundly unfortunate, and sinful into the bargain, "for it is a sin against something more splendid than his severe decency, this I now realize, and he tried to educate me to this sin too, for all his fatherliness. But now I've outgrown his guidance—in this point I really have." Here it is a matter of the concept of humility, of accepting fate, whether it bring us pleasant or harsh experiences, of redemption from the stiff, obstinate pride of individualism. When he becomes aware of the actual state of his country's finances, he starts zealously to study economics; and his personality is gradually freed, during his common studies with Imma, of its chilling air, its insistence on decorum. The eccentric countess may let herself go in his presence, and Klaus Heinrich, with kindly indulgence, agrees to call her "Frau Meier" for the time being. Thus, symbolically speaking, Klaus Heinrich is gradually redeemed from the state of being merely an artist and becomes a poet; thus he vividly experiences the synthesis of form and essence. Both "perceptively observing and playing his role," he will henceforth live at Imma's side, uniting humaneness with decorum. Mann's final formula is: "Highness and love—a severe happiness."

## IV. *Popularity and Representation as a Calling*

The form of life and the development of the protagonist have appeared, in all their basic aspects, as a metaphor, in which Thomas Mann is actually telling of his own nature as artist and poet, with all its problems. The metaphor, however, has a further range: it concerns not only the sovereign, but also the complementary concept, the people, and the mutual relationships which tie the people and the sovereign together. If we pursue the interpretation of this side of the metaphor, we arrive at insights which are important and in part downright surprising.

A political scientist who happened to read *Royal Highness* in a leisure hour might well reach the conclusion that this work was devoted to an ingenious philosophical justification of monarchy as the form of government which most appropriately expresses the essence and will of a people. In fact, Thomas Mann does not tire of pointing out that basically the people glorifies itself at festivals when apparently it is celebrating its sovereign, that it cries "Long live the king!" and really means itself, that in the sovereign it is searching for the "heightening" wish-picture of its own being. Granted that the author's actual liking for the monarchical form of government—in the abstract—plays its part, it is still important to note that the people's demonstrations of affection towards other, quasi-public personages is based on the same suppositions. Why does it wildly cheer the soubrette Mizzi Meyer, who is not beautiful, barely pretty, and sings with a shrill voice? Because as long as this blond, thickset person with her blue eyes, her broad cheek bones set a bit too high, her healthy, gay, but also often sentimental air, stands bejeweled, rouged, illuminated from all sides, on the stage before the crowd, it finds its own type, glorified, in her. "Yes, the people applauded itself when it applauded her."

But what else is the poet's significance but a similar glorification of the people, higher to be sure? "The people wishes to see its best, its higher nature, its dream, yes, something like its soul represented in its sovereign," we read in the very first chapter. If we substitute the word "poet" for "sovereign" in this passage, the statement clearly contains the formula for the representative calling and the lofty task of the creative writer. It is this calling, this task of which Mann gives an accounting here.

The poet's acknowledgment of his representative character and his fitness for this task imply two presuppositions. The first is the abandonment of a purely individualistic attitude. The concept of autonomous genius à la Nietzsche, which is responsible only to itself and knows no law but the heightening of its own personality and cares only for itself, is replaced by the idea of obligation to the whole and responsibility towards the cultural community. The poet feels that he is the highest member of that community. What the poet expresses is not only his own subjective feeling but the urge to higher things which slumbers even in the dull crowd and appears, transmuted to clear self-awareness, only in him, the most refined distillation of the "popular soul," as it were. Wherever Klaus Heinrich went, colorless life was transfigured and became poetry; "the dull burgher, in frock-coat and top hat, became aware of his own worth and was moved." That is the poet's effect: he redeems the longing of the "popular soul" from its dullness by helping it to become conscious.

The second point: so that the poet may actually have this elevating, redeeming effect of bringing happiness, there must be a living sense of intimate kinship and reciprocal affinity between the people and the poet. When it is absent, this fortunate effect does not exist. In Albrecht II, the sickly, neurasthenic, overbred aristocrat, whose body and instincts do not reflect the nature of the people in any way, it does not find its "heightened" wish-picture. It cannot shout "Long live Albrecht" and mean itself, and for his part, he finds representation a ridiculous calling. He describes it with the revealing term "monkey business." On the other hand, Klaus Heinrich with his broad cheek bones,[4] characteristic of the nation, and his broad hand—and his correspondingly simpler psychological make-up —rejoices in his "representative" calling and enjoys the happiness of popularity. That is a not very profound but splendid and inclusive sort

[4] I have found this point used seventeen times as a leitmotif.

of intimacy, which to some extent compensates both the sovereign and the poet for the fact that their private lives are exposed to all the world.

The reference to Thomas Mann's own situation is obvious. He has himself so often and so clearly stressed his love for the burgher's way of life, his psychological affinity to the class from which he sprang, that it would be redundant to discuss the point at length. He achieved the happiness of popularity early in life, as the tremendous success of *Buddenbrooks* bears witness. That, on the other hand, he does not fail to recognize the danger which popularity implies for the man of exceptional talent is made clear in Klaus Heinrich's youthful experience when he behaves in all too ordinary a fashion at the "citizens' ball" and thus unleashes drives which find satisfaction in dragging down the high, the elite, to the level of vulgarity. Further evidence is his elder brother's serious admonition, contained in his congratulations when Imma becomes Klaus Heinrich's fiancée: "I wish you happiness, but not too much, and hope that you will not bask too much in the love of the people."

I shall leave it to Thomas Mann's biographers to comment on the well-known fact that his wooing of the lady who became his wife and the happiness of his young marriage are reflected in *Royal Highness*. But we cannot ignore another personal relationship here, one which has nothing to do with the general public's habit—which Mann has sharply criticized—"of sniffing about in the author's personal affairs when confronted by his absolute achievement." For me there is no doubt that Klaus Heinrich's relation to Albrecht corresponds essentially to Thomas Mann's relation to his elder brother Heinrich. Heinrich Mann, the overrefined, neurasthenic individualist, is related to Albrecht's type. Far removed from any sense of solidarity with the burgher sphere, he has coined this formula to express the idea of the burgher: "So I call all those who have ugly feelings and moreover lie when they express their ugly feelings." There is a further affinity in the fact that Heinrich Mann's coldly controlled, sophisticated art of the grotesque has not made contact[5] with the general public. It is Heinrich who turns over to his brother Thomas the dignified task of representative achievement; Heinrich who warns his brother of the dangers of popularity and admonishes him not to take things in too relaxed a way. Presumably the remark which follows Albrecht's congratulations, spoken when he raises his lids from his blue eyes with their lonely expression, refers to Heinrich: "And in this moment it became clear that he loved Klaus Heinrich." And we hear Thomas Mann paying ungrudging tribute to his brother's aristocratic genius in Klaus Heinrich's words to Albrecht: "I have always looked up to you, because I have always felt and known that you are the more aristocratic, the higher of us two, and I am only a plebeian compared to you." It is

---

[5] Needless to say, I am not referring to the development of Heinrich Mann's work during and after the first World War.

amazing, by the way, that such an abundance of parallels in problems, matter, and motifs joins the creative work of the two brothers, despite the most distinct difference in their temperaments. It is reasonable to expect that this complex of intellectual relationships will be subjected before long to the most thorough investigation.

In this essay the symbolic and autobiographical elements of *Royal Highness* have not indeed been exhaustively treated, but their basic features have been elucidated. Everywhere this novel has turned out to be a variation of the same theme which Thomas Mann had already treated very searchingly in *Tonio Kröger*. A variation, not a repetition, for the intellectual features of *Tonio Kröger* and of the work devoted to Klaus Heinrich differ as do those of the youth from the man's. Thus Tonio is a person torn apart, not really at home in either of the two worlds to which his service and his love are devoted, and only at the end does he dimly sense the resolution of the antinomy of his nature. In Klaus Heinrich's case, on the other hand, the ethical character of formal achievement is much more strongly emphasized from the very beginning; and the concept of the poet's tie to the community, which gives his calling its representative value, is the foundation which supports the whole structure of the work. A decisive difference in mood and tone corresponds; while a painfully emotional pathos colors the style of *Tonio Kröger,* this "didactic fairy tale" is recounted in the mood of benevolently smiling, warily kind irony.

It is impossible to end this essay without referring to a third dialectic variation of the theme of the problematic nature of the vocation of artist and poet, with which Thomas Mann surprised the public only two years later. Symbolically, *Death in Venice* is also autobiographical, even though Mann was only thirty-six years old when he conceived of the figure of Gustave Aschenbach, who is at the height of his fame and already over fifty. For the figure of Aschenbach, the hero of creative work, who creates the illusion of strength and health (though he is laboring on the brink of exhaustion) until he suddenly and completely collapses, implies an anticipation of tragic possibilities which are inherent in the artist of his own type. Aschenbach's fate signifies a projection summoned up by the author as a warning to himself, like the aging Ibsen's Solness, Allmers, Borkmann, and Rubek. And thus the classically severe "master style" of this *novella* harmonizes with the process of dissolution which it describes. Its uncanny, horrible tragic nature is of a precipitous sublimity which excludes any expression of banal compassion.

# Myth Plus Psychology:
# A Stylistic Analysis of *Death in Venice*

## by *André von Gronicka*

### I

In an exchange of letters with the Hungarian anthropologist Karl Kerényi, Thomas Mann has pointed to a basic quality of his writings by revealing that he had early recognized "mythos plus psychology" as his natural "element" and that he had been for a long time "passionately fond of this combination." [1] Mann's formula calls for a brief amplification. "Myth" as used in it stands for rather more than the term conventionally defines. It encompasses legend, history, and the literary traditions of the more recent past; it calls for a language that is cleansed of the colloquial and the commonplace, is marked by lyric pathos, or evokes the monumental and the statuesque. "Psychology," on the other hand, implies a penetrating analysis and a carefully controlled statement in an all but naturalistic idiom, of the reality of the psychophysical world. The "plus" in the formula does not represent simple addition but a most subtle combination and permutation of disparate elements resulting in a unique *"Steigerung"* [heightening and intensification].

When we examine Mann's *oeuvre* with this revealing statement in mind, it is not difficult to detect this "combination" even in the very early works in which the author time and again bursts through the predominantly realistic, even naturalistic theme and style, transcends psychology, and confronts the reader unexpectedly with the surreality of the demonic and the diabolic by way of caricature and the grotesque

"Myth Plus Psychology: A Stylistic Analysis of *Death in Venice*," by André von Gronicka. (Original title: "Myth Plus Psychology.") *Germanic Review*, XXXI (1956), 191-205. Copyright © 1956 by Columbia University Press. Reprinted by permission of the author and Columbia University Press.

[1] Karl Kerényi, *Romandichtung und Mythologie; ein Briefwechsel mit Thomas Mann* (Zürich, 1945), p. 82.

(*Little Lizzie*),[2] with apocalyptic visions (*Gladius Dei; Fiorenza*). Or else he leads us in a manner at times reminiscent of Hoffmann, at times of Andersen, into the magical fairy-tale world (*The Wardrobe; Royal Highness*), only to bring us back to reality, rarely with a jolt, mostly by way of gentle transition, or to leave us suspended in the ambivalence of reality and make-believe inextricably fused. This bifocal view of life that encompasses both the transcendent and the real develops steadily to reach, in the masterly *novella Death in Venice,* a degree of perfection which Mann has rarely if ever excelled.

To be sure, he coined the formula "myth plus psychology" with explicit reference to the *Joseph* tetralogy. However, in this relatively late work the effect of the "combination," though it has gained in sophistication and finesse, has lost something of its unbroken vitality and immediacy, and this for three basic reasons: first, because the very plot and locale of the tetralogy are drawn from myth, legend, and ancient history, not from the palpable reality of the "here and now" and their realization is a deliberate act of "deception," a "game";

> Accuracy, making things real is a deception, a game, artistic semblance, a realization and bringing things home to the reader achieved by main force, by using all the instruments of language, of psychology, of representation, and of probing commentary whose essence, however serious on a human level, is humor.[3]

Secondly, because of a programmatical purposefulness in the rationalization and humanization, reversing the function of myth with the help of psychology:

> In the last decades myth has been so often misused as an instrument of obscurantist counterrevolution that a mythical novel like *Joseph,* when it first appeared, necessarily stirred up the suspicion that its author was swimming in this muddy stream. The public has had to give up this suspicion, for on closer examination it perceived a reversal of the function of myth of which one would not have thought myth capable. Readers observed an event comparable to capturing a cannon in battle, turning it around, and aiming it at the enemy. In this book the myth was taken from the hands of Fascism and *humanized,* down to the last linguistic detail.[4]

---

[2] An interesting corroboration of this early tendency is offered by Thomas Mann's sketches in the *Bilderbuch für artige Kinder,* esp. the sketches "Lawyer Jacobi and his Spouse," "Mother Nature," and "Life (*Das Läben*)," reproduced in V. Mann, *Wir waren fünf* (Konstanz, 1949), pp. 56 ff.

[3] Cf. Th. Mann, *The Theme of the Joseph Novels* (Washington, 1942), p. 6.

[4] Cf. ibid., p. 21, cf. also *Romandichtung und Mythologie,* p. 82. The italics are Mann's.

And finally, because of a sharply increased irony, a playfulness in the author's attitude toward his material:

> Discussion is part of the game here . . . it is oblique, a humorous rhetorical device, a contribution to pseudoexactitude, very close to persiflage and certainly to irony; for the scholarly manner, applied to what is entirely unscholarly and fabulous, is sheer irony.[5]

In the *novella,* on the other hand, everything springs with a surprisingly unbroken vitality and directness from that bifocal view of life: the locale, the plot, and especially the characters. Here everything is rooted both in this-worldliness and in the realm of myth and legend. Here Thomas Mann lays hold of life in all its concrete outer-inner, psychophysical reality, while reaching deep into the rich storehouse of myth and legend, as well as of modern literature. He does this with an uninhibited creative energy that informs reality with myth's timeless grandeur, while rescuing myth from abstract remoteness and endowing it with a vibrant immediacy far removed from "persiflage."

In the "Sketch of my Life," written in 1930, Mann recollects that he had never before or since the composition of *Death in Venice* experienced "such a splendid sensation of uplift." [6] Of the hero of the *novella,* of Gustav von Aschenbach, he says: "His spirit struggled to give birth, his memory flung up primal thoughts inherited in youth, but never before made vivid by his own fire." We are safe in reading this characterization of Aschenbach's creative state of mind as a fragment of self-revelation on the part of the author. It was surely in a similar state of supreme creative élan that Mann achieved the well-nigh miraculous, and could write both as the soberly meticulous analyst and delineator of physis and psyche[7] and as the inspired recreator of the world of myth. Thus, in this *novella* Mann's cultivated mind, oriented Janus-like toward the past as well as the present, becomes a potent synthesis of the meticulously observed and recorded world of contemporary, bourgeois civilization and the timeless and measureless vistas of man's cultural heritage. It creates a unique work of art, suspended in an unceasing tension between the poles of psychological realism and the symbolism of myth, which we now propose to examine in some detail.

## II

We know from Mann's autobiographical sketch that a trip to the Lido in the spring of 1911 had furnished him "all the materials for his

[5] *Theme,* p. 6 f.

[6] *A Sketch of My Life* (New York, 1960), p. 46.

[7] D. E. Oppenheim, *Dichtung und Menschenkenntnis* (München, 1926), p. 142.

*novella*": "The wanderer by the North Cemetery in Munich, the gloomy ship from Pola, the old fop, the ambiguous gondolier, Tadzio and his family, the departure frustrated by missending the baggage, the cholera, the honest clerk in the travel bureau, the malevolent street singer and whatever other element might be mentioned—everything was given," and—significantly—"showed its interpretability and usefulness as an element of composition in the most astonishing way." [8] The above enumeration is its own best proof that the "interpretability" did not reside in the raw materials per se, but rather was a characteristic of the artist, of this particular artist, who seized upon them and had the intellectual equipment and the genius to transform them into the stuff of art:

> The glance which one casts as an artist on external and internal things is different from the one with which one regards them as a human being: it is colder and at the same time more passionate, . . . your demon forces you to "observe," to perceive in a flash, with painful malice, every detail which is characteristic in a literary sense, has typical significance, opens perspectives, marks distinctively the racial, social, or psychological element . . .[9]

and again, he asks, "But what is raw material?" to answer with all possible emphasis, "The personal element is all. Raw material is only the personal." [10] and sums up: "Whether he [the creative artist] fills an inherited tale or fills a piece of living reality with his breath and his being, it is the bringing to life, the penetrating and filling the material with the artist's own personality which makes it his own," that is, a unique work of art.[11]

The central locale of the *novella,* Venice, "the sunken queen" is caught by Mann's bifocal vision as the "flattering and dubious beauty . . . half fairy tale, half tourist trap," in its sordid reality and mythical splendor. We are not spared the oppressive sultriness and fetid stench of its alleyways, nor the garbage floating on its canals with their evil exhalations; yet above these very waters there rises the "graceful splendor" of its palaces, bridges, churches, of its "fairy tale temples," rendered in a rhythmical prose of exquisite limpidity and grace. This *ambiente* is done with the most painstaking precision of detail, yet not in order to produce a naturalistic picture of the city, but to create, by way of an ever alert selectivity, a highly stylized composition characterized by a tense equilibrium of realism and idealization. There is modern Venice drawn in a decidedly up-to-date idiom, liberally sprinkled with tech-

[8] *A Sketch of My Life*, p. 46.
[9] "Bilse und ich," *Rede und Antwort* (Berlin, 1922), pp. 13 f.
[10] *Pariser Rechenschaft* (Berlin, 1926), p. 119.
[11] *Rede und Antwort*, p. 23.

nical terms and with foreign loan-words and entire phrases, particularly French:

> The waves beat against *concrete* (*betonierten*) walls of the narrow canal, which takes its course through the island to the *Hotel Excelsior*. An *automobile omnibus* awaited him there as he returned . . . His room, to be sure, had been taken, but another one, not inferior, was at his disposal at once. *"Pas de chance, monsieur,"* said the Swiss *lift*-boy, smiling, as they glided upward. And thus the fugitive had again been given *quarters* . . . (*italics mine*).

And next to, superimposed upon, and integrated into this modern Venice is the timeless, exotic city par excellence, the "very seat of all dissoluteness," [12] the perfect stage for the "noiseless and criminal adventures in the plashing night" as fashioned by the imagination of Elizabethan poets and dramatists and by the Italian novelists, Venice of Oriental "fabled splendor," Romantic Venice risen from the dreams of Byron, Platen, Wagner, and Nietzsche, that magical city of ruthless passions, of passions-unto-death, of the *Liebestod*. And on this complex *montage*,[13] this subtle composite of reality and literary tradition, Mann superimposes the world of classical antiquity,[14] its scenery, historical figures (Socrates, Phaedros, Critobolus)[15] and the gods of Olympus:

> The goddess approached, the seductress of youth who stole away Cleitos and Cephalus and defied the envy of all the Olympians in enjoying the love of handsome Orion. A strewing of roses began there at the edge of the world, an ineffably lovely gleaming and blossoming, infant clouds, radiant, flooded with light, hovered like attendant amoretti in the rosy, bluish haze, deep crimson fell upon the sea, which seemed to wash it along on its billows, golden spears darted from below up to the zenith, the gleaming light became a conflagration, noiselessly with overwhelming divine power, glow and heat and blazing flames streamed upward, and with rapid hooves her brother's sacred steeds rose above the sphere of the earth. Struck by the rays of the god's magnificence he sat, lonely and awake, he closed his eyes and let his lids be kissed by the radiance.

[12] Cp. Lord Byron, as quoted by W. Pabst, "Satan und die alten Götter in Venedig," *Euphorion*, XLIX (1955), p. 337: "That is, been at *Venice*, which was much visited by the young English gentlemen of those [Elizabethan] times, and was then what *Paris* is now—the seat of all dissoluteness."

[13] Mann's definition of this "montage technique" is: "Arranging factual, historical, personal, even literary events in such a way that, almost as in the 'panoramas' of my youth, tangible reality flows, almost imperceptibly, into the illusion produced by painted perspectives." Cf. *The Story of a Novel* (New York, 1961), p. 32.

[14] Cf. Fr. H. Mautner, "Die griechischen Anklänge in Th. Manns *Tod in Venedig*," *Monatshefte*, XLIV (1952), pp. 20-26.

[15] Cf. L. Gustafson, "Xenophon and *Der Tod in Venedig*," *Germanic Review*, XXI (1946), 209-214.

One need but compare the imagery and rhythm of this passage with the word-choice and general tone of Mann's description of modern Venice to be at once impressed by the amplitude of this style, by its skilful exploitation of the devices of contrast and counterpoint. This style has developed into a perfect vehicle of Mann's formula, of his "combination." From its wealth of realistic detail it extracts the maximum of symbolical meaning, weaves a rich pattern of fact and fancy, modernity and myth and lends to the reality of life a new dimension in depth.

## III

Turning from the locale of the *novella* to its characters, we shall limit ourselves to three prominent figures, to the "stranger" in his various guises, to Tadzio, and to Gustav von Aschenbach. The bifocal vision of Thomas Mann is clearly at work when the stage is set for Aschenbach's fateful meeting with the stranger. Time and place are stated in an exact factual manner which could well serve to open a realistic, even naturalistic tale, yet the apparent realism of the "English Garden" and the "busy garden restaurant next to which some cabs and carriages were standing," of the Ungerer Strasse with its streetcar tracks, is subtly modified by interwoven elements of description: the "more and more quiet paths," the sinking sun, Aschenbach's "way home across the open meadow [!]," his tiredness and the thunderstorm that broods threateningly over Föhring, are elements which charge this realism with a significant *Stimmungsgehalt* [mood content] and lend it a symbolical quality which gradually becomes dominant. Our attention is drawn to the desolate "stonemason's yard, where crosses, commemorative tablets and monuments, displayed for sale, form a second graveyard," to the "cemetery chapel, a building in the Byzantine style . . . in the reflected light of departing day," to a setting which causes Aschenbach's inner vision ("geistiges Auge") to lose itself "in the translucent mystic meaning [of the inscriptions]."

When the stage is set in this manner, the stranger makes his unobserved, uncanny entrance to stand-elevated-at the portals of the funeral hall: "Whether he had come out of the hall through its bronze gate or had climbed up there from outside, unnoticed, was uncertain." Here, surely, is more than a suggestion of the mysterious and eerie which, however, is at once counteracted by the very next sentence: "Aschenbach, without devoting particular thought to the question, inclined to the earlier assumption." Both the content and tone of this sentence, especially the matter-of-fact, off-hand phrase "inclined to the earlier assumption" are calculated to break or at least weaken the spell of spectral other-worldliness that might have been worked by the description of the cemetery, the funeral hall with its "hieratic paintings" and "apocalyptic beasts," and of the "not quite ordinary appearance" of the stranger.

The manner in which the stranger's appearance is characterized reminds one at first of an official identification, abrupt, curt, exact in its phrasing: "moderately tall, spare, beardless, and strikingly snub-nosed." Suddenly, however, we become aware that the figure is raised above commonplace reality, acquires a statuesque quality, a striking monumentality. No longer merely a Bavarian tourist, the stranger has grown to the stature of a mythical figure. He *is* the archtempter Satan, he *is* also the imperious, ruthless liberator from life's toil, Death with his characteristic mask: "his short turned-up nose," with lips "completely drawn back from his teeth, so that they, exposed down to his gums, appeared white and long between them," the skull as it appears in many a Dance of Death. To be sure, in this composite figure the hoof of Satan is decorously hidden. Yet the stranger's long, scrawny neck with its starkly protruding Adam's apple, red eyelashes over pale eyes, would amply identify the Lord of Hell even if it were not for the two "vertical, energetic furrows" etched on his forehead and drawn down between his eyes, which—ever since Dante's day—have served to symbolize the devil's mythical horns.[16] But while shaping this mythical figure, Mann is ever intent to justify and explain its existence on realistic and psychological grounds. "Perhaps his elevated and elevating position contributed to this impression . . ." he ventures to suggest, and again, in explanation of the mask of death and the marks of the devil, he offers as the realistic cause, the sun's blinding rays which may well have forced the stranger to grimace.

The effect of the stranger upon Aschenbach, though powerful, is rendered in a pointedly realistic manner. The bellicose gaze of the stranger, "so militant . . . so straight into his eye, so obviously intending to drive the matter to the extreme . . ." causes no sudden surrender, no petrifaction nor casting down upon bended knees with head thrown back and arms spread wide. To suggest such a typically expressionistic gesture is to point up the absurdity of all excess and eccentricity and sudden "break-through" within the context of Thomas Mann's worldview and corresponding style. His Aschenbach is merely "painfully moved," turns away, and "had forgotten him [the stranger], the next minute." It is difficult to imagine a more sobering denouement of a highly charged situation.

But then the author switches to the psychological plane and here unfolds a masterful analysis of the effect of the meeting upon Aschenbach's psyche, his "imagination," shows how the indefinable "physical or psychic influence . . . of the stranger" releases a flood of long and ruth-

16 Cf. Pabst, *op. cit.*, p. 348.

lessly repressed emotions[17] which crystallizes into a waking dream of such poignancy as to leave Aschenbach shaken, his heart throbbing "with horror and enigmatic desire."

Yet is this transfer to the realistic plane of psychoanalysis complete? Does the mythical figure of the stranger vanish altogether in the light of this analysis? Are his "not quite ordinary appearance and enigmatical influence really "explained" on rational grounds? Can we agree with Aschenbach when he attempts to rationalize the encounter as the upshot of a sudden onset of "desire to travel, nothing more"? By no means. It is precisely the paradox of Mann's style that, despite its thorough realism, it leaves myth and legend in their very palpable existence. The mythical figure of the stranger will return in the mythico-realistic forms of the Gondolier-Charon, of the lewd and lascivious old fop, of the goatee'd captain of the "ship from Pola," to weave its enigmatical spell, to sell Gustav von Aschenbach a first-class ticket to Venice, and, on the mythical level, to draw up a first-rate devil's pact: ". . . he wrote big scrawling letters, strewed blue sand on the paper, out of a box, let the sand run off into a clay dish, folded the piece of paper with his yellow, bony fingers and wrote again . . ." while his "empty talk seemed to indicate that he was trying to stun and divert the traveler, as if he perhaps feared that Aschenbach might still change his mind about going to Venice." The choice of vocabulary and the resultant slight but significant exaggeration and "focusing" of reality are such as to make the suggestion inescapable: Aschenbach is here being lured, hypnotised into a contract, the terms of which are final and fatal.[18] And once again the stranger appears as the mendicant singer of crude and vulgar ballads, who is marked by the selfsame death-devil features and becomes, moreover, associated in Aschenbach's mind with the symbol par excellence of death, the hourglass. The "street singer" had just made his grotesque exit amidst diabolically derisive laughter of triumph over his victim:

> The night strode ahead, time fell apart [!]. In his parents' home, many years ago, there had been an hourglass—he suddenly saw the fragile yet meaningful little object again, as if it were standing before him. Soundlessly, subtly the rust-red colored sand ran through the narrow glass passage; and as it was running out in the upper chamber, a small, yet powerful whirlpool had been formed.

The motif of the inexorably vanishing sand [life] acquires a particularly ominous and sinister effect through the adroitly selected detail of the

---

[17] Cf. H. Hatfield, *Thomas Mann* (Norfolk, Conn., 1951), p. 61: "Too great a devotion to the Prussian ideals of duty and discipline brings him to the point of collapse; the 'death wish' rebels against the categorical imperative of his conscious mind."

[18] A theme which was to become central in *Dr. Faustus*. See *The Story of a Novel*, p. 30. Cf. also A. von Gronicka, "Th. Mann's Doktor Faustus," *Germanic Review*, XXIII (1948), esp. pp. 211 f.

down-sucking whirlpool of passion. The passage is a perfect example of a meticulously observed, realistic description charged with an atmosphere of the numinous.

All these figures stand in the realm of the possible, do not strain unduly our sense of the real, yet—at bottom—they are spectral. "Without raising difficulties for reason they are nevertheless of a profoundly miraculous nature." They are creatures both of this world and not of it. Emissaries of the beyond, they move in the bright light of day, upon the firm ground of reality. Their existence within space and time, in the here and now, is guaranteed, as it were, by the realism of their surroundings, yet they, in turn, impart to the world in which they move an air of mystery and magic, a strange and dreamlike quality: "It seemed to him [Aschenbach] . . . as if a dreamlike sense of alienation were setting in, rendering the world distorted and strange"; and "Aschenbach looked darkly at him [the old fop], and again a sense of dazedness came over him, as if the world were revealing a barely perceptible yet irrepressible tendency to render itself distorted, strange, and grotesque." Moreover, the surrealistic quality of these encounters is enhanced by their very repetition which soon impresses as being preordained, inexorable. Thomas Mann was to elaborate the view of human life as a repetition and recurrence of mythical constellations, of protopatterns, "images of the circling cosmos" into a life's philosophy and was to give this deeply romantic *Weltanschauung* its fullest artistic expression in the *Joseph* novels.[19] Yet even in this relatively early *novella* (1911) we find this view creating in Aschenbach's encounters with the life-death symbol, the stranger in his various guises, a striking prefiguration of the "mythic pattern," of the "repetition and return of the primeval form," of the "mythic return" so basic to the tetralogy.

## IV

The figure of Tadzio is also the creature of the two worlds of reality and myth, a creation of Mann's bifocal view. We see him, almost exclusively through Aschenbach's eyes, both "at the most advantageous distance, aesthetically," as a "statue, imaging and mirroring intellectual beauty" as well as from close range. We see him as the little Polish boy of pale complexion, with carious teeth, we hear his high-pitched voice, observe a fit of his high-strung temper. But we also behold him as the paragon of beauty whose flawless profile awakens in Aschenbach memories of "Greek statues of the best period," "mystical concepts . . . of primeval times, of the origin of form and of the birth of the gods." In fact, Tadzio's shortcomings serve to support rather than weaken in

[19] Cf. P. Heller, "Some Functions of the Leitmotif in Thomas Mann's Joseph Tetralogy," *Germanic Review*, XXII (1947), 126-141.

Aschenbach's mind the ideal qualities of his figure. The pallor of Tadzio's cheeks enhances the boy's resemblance to the "Boy with the Thorn in his Foot"; the collar of his sailor suit, precisely because of its poor fit, serves to set off all the more effectively "his flower-like head in its incomparable charm . . . the head of Eros, with the yellowish glow of Parian marble . . . ," and the fit of uncontrollable temper acquires, in Mann's carefully stylized description, the quality of myth, and calls to mind the image of a young god in rage: ". . . a storm of angry scorn came over his face. His brow darkened, his lips curled; on one side of his mouth a grimace of bitterness distorted his cheek, and he knit his brows so fiercely that his eyes seemed to have been drawn in under their pressure; dark and angry, below them, they spoke the language of hate."

This "intensification" of the realistic figure into a figure of myth is carried out with the greatest circumspection. Nowhere is the reader required to relinquish reality in favor of myth. To be sure, Tadzio is set apart from his sisters, he is "desired, courted, admired." That in itself, however, would not lift him above the plane of reality. Only in Aschenbach's inflamed imagination is the figure likened to or identified with the immortal beings of Greek mythology. Even Tadzio's final appearance as Hermes in that impressive setting of complete isolation on the sea-encircled sand bar as a "figure most isolated and apart . . ." is at once rationalized as a vision of the dying poet: "But to him it seemed as if the pale and lovely psychagogue out there were smiling, beckoning to him, as if, lifting his hand from his hip, he were pointing ahead, flying before him into the realm of promise and tremendousness (*ins Verheissungsvoll-Ungeheure*)." Analysis, then, proves psychological realism unbetrayed. Tadzio's identification with figures of myth can in every instance be explained on solidly rational grounds as a figment of Aschenbach's overwrought imagination.

And yet, such is the vividness of Mann's evocation of the mythical figures and their identification with Tadzio that we experience their fusion as palpably real and must exert a conscious effort to disengage in our imagination the "real" boy from the mythical overlay of the divine figures. Here Mann achieved a truly perfect *montage,* a splendid example of what Vernon Venable aptly calls his "new technique for the exploitation of poetic meaning . . . in which no symbol is allowed unequivocal connotation or independent status, but refers to all the others and is bound rigorously to them by means of a highly intricate system of subtly developed associations." Neither Tadzio as the Polish boy nor Tadzio-Hyacinthus, nor Tadzio-Narcissus,[20] nor even Tadzio-Hermes[21] are "al-

---

[20] Cf. T. O. Brandt, "Narcissism in Thomas Mann's 'Der Erwahlte,' " *German Life and Letters,* N. S., VII (1954), 233-241.

[21] Cf. Th. Mann in *Romandichtung und Mythologie,* p. 83, where he writes that Kerényi's and Jung's interpretation of Hermes Psychopompos as an "essentially childlike divinity" reminds him of Tadzio.

lowed independent status" but they "are identified with each other and
finally fused into the single, nuclear, paradoxical meaning which Mann
wishes to emphasize":[22] Tadzio as the embodiment and symbol of beauty's
fatal fascination for the endangered artist. And even this "single, nuclear . . . meaning" does, in fact, remain "paradoxical." For, though
Tadzio *is* Aschenbach's tempter into the "limitless intermingling" of
sexual frenzy, the "stranger god," another Dionysos, who leads the "frenzy
of degradation," [23] though he *is* Aschenbach's guide into the limitless,
formless vastness of the sea, that symbol of the "perfection of nothingness," of the "disorganized, measureless, eternal," the guide into the
bliss of Nirvana,[24] he *is*, at one and at the same time, the very antithesis
of this rôle and this realm. For he is also the "statue," the paragon of
measured, perfectly articulated form. With the regularity of a leitmotif
he is contraposed to the measureless, shapeless void of the ocean as the
supreme articulation and embodiment of Apollinic plasticity, harmony,
balance. A well defined vertical, he cuts boldly across the sea's limitless
horizontal: "But as he [Aschenbach] was dreaming so deeply, gazing into
emptiness, the horizontal line of the shore's edge was suddenly cut across
by a human figure; and when he retrieved his gaze from the limitless
element and concentrated it, it was the beautiful boy, approaching from
the left, who walked past him on the beach." Thus Tadzio is, paradoxically, the inspiration and challenge to the artist's creative urge that
measures and molds and bodies forth, and is its nemesis, the tempter to
lassitude, stupor, and final disintegration of body and mind.

When Aschenbach first catches sight of the youth, he is at once impressed by his beauty as a magical combination of a uniquely personal
charm, of the "purest perfection of form." He is stimulated to musings
on the secret of the "mysterious union which the normative must form
with the individual element, so that human beauty may be born . . ."
It is this "mysterious synthesis" which Thomas Mann has achieved in
his figure of Tadzio. He has created in him the human being of flesh
and blood with its unique charm, with its flaws and failings that bring
him close to us and rouse in us the compassion which goes out only
toward our fellow men; and he has raised this "real" being into a com-

[22] Vernon Venable, "Death in Venice," *The Stature of Thomas Mann*, ed. Ch. Neider
(New York, 1947), p. 131. Unfortunately, Venable's interpretation of examples in
support of his definition greatly weakens it. Thus, he maintains that ". . . in the first
episode, the symbols were for the most part unambiguous: the stranger meant life
and life only; the cemetery death and death only . . ." etc.; certainly a simplistic
interpretation in flat contradiction of his own theoretical position.

[23] Tadzio is identified with the "stranger God" by means of the orgiastic cry "made
up of soft consonants and a drawn-out, sounding 'u' at the end, sweet and wild at
once," which is the very pattern of the boy's name in the form of address: Tadziu;
Mann describes its sound in the same terms.

[24] Cf. Mann, "Lübeck als geistige Lebensform," *Die Forderung des Tages* (Berlin,
1929), p. 47, "The sea is not a scenic view; it is the vivid experience of nothingness
and death, a metaphysical dream."

plex symbol whose existence is beyond time and space in the realm of eternal myth. In sum, he has achieved in Tadzio a perfect combination of "psychology plus myth."

## V

It is not at all surprising to find in Mann's portrayal of Gustav von Aschenbach his skill of psychological analysis and realistic description at a high pitch of perfection,[25] for Aschenbach is, to a significant degree, a self-portrait and is the representative of a way of life, the artist's life, which Mann has explored with such uncompromising, sharp-eyed penetration. What is more impressive is to find the author able to maintain in his portraiture of the protagonist the same subtle balance and tension between reality and symbol, psychology and myth which we had found in the other characters of the *novella*, Mann's delineation of Aschenbach oscillates tensely between the poles of apotheosis and deflation, of idealization and searching analysis touched with gentle irony, between grandiloquence and understatement, between rhetorical flourish and sober naturalistic prose,[26] without, however, ever quite touching either extreme.

The dialectical polarity of style is rooted in Mann's attitude toward his hero, which is at once detached and empathetic, marked by an urge to elevate to the prototypical and to deflate to the problematical, characterized by sincere admiration, even adulation and by that smiling irony that has discovered the Achilles' heel. This double-visioned manner of portrayal is also predicated upon Mann's basic concept of the protagonist as an "unheroic" hero, as the "hero of creative work" par excellence. This heroism is a heroism of weakness, a heroism of the "despite" *despite* frailty of body, *despite* a problematical, overfastidious, quickly exhausted mind. Such heroism cannot be conveyed except by way of realistic description and searching psychoanalysis, while at the same time the urge to ennoble must also be operative. Thus, Mann's favorite combination of "psychology plus myth" proves to be the perfect means to body forth such a "heroic" figure. Gustav von Aschenbach is raised upon a pedestal as *the* poet-laureate of exemplary achievement, but he is also examined as a "case" on the psychiatrist's couch. He is associated in the reader's mind with figures of the glorious Grecian past and of Christian legend,

[25] Cf. D. E. Oppenheim, loc. cit.

[26] Cf. the opening sonorous, grandiloquent sentences of the biographical section II: "The author of the lucid, powerful epic treating the life of Frederick of Prussia . . . " with such a sober, pointed description of Aschenbach as "Gustave Aschenbach . . . was born in L., in the capital of a district of the province of Silesia, as the son of a high official in the judiciary . . . " or with the following passage: "Gustave von Aschenbach was of somewhat below medium height, brunette, clean-shaved. His head appeared a little too large, relative to his person, which was almost delicate."

with Socrates and Saint Sebastian.[27] Yet these figures are themselves
brought down from their lofty plane. To be sure, Socrates is shown
as a man of mature wisdom but he is also characterized with quite
unGrecian pathos as the human-all-too-human mark of youth's seductive
beauty, and the figure of Saint Sebastian is introduced, significantly, by
a "clever analyst"—none other, of course, than the "analyst" Thomas
Mann himself—who proceeds to modernize the figure by way of an
analysis which is both "brilliant" and "precise" into the representative
of an "intellectual and youthful manliness, which clenches its teeth in
proud bashfulness and stands quietly while the swords and spears transfix its body." It is interesting to note how this passage in its choice of
descriptive vocabulary holds the finest balance between the elevated
and the realistic style, moving closer to the former in such a traditionally
"heroic" phrase as: "while the swords and spears transfix its body,"
tending toward the realistic in the expression: "clenches its teeth" which
serves to render a carefully observed physiological detail from the work-
aday world. Unquestionably, the sacrosanct figure of the Saint loses some
of its patina in the hands of the "analyst." In fact, it may be argued
that the very opposite of "myth-building" is taking place, that it is not
Aschenbach who is elevated, by the process of association and approximation, to the Saint's immortal plane, but rather that it is the figure
of saintly legend that suffers a loss of imposing other-worldliness in
changing into an "unheroic" hero of our times. The juster view would
seem to be that of a well-nigh perfect ambivalence with the patina lost
by the Saint being transferred to the figure of Mann's hero.

Aschenbach's way to his doom is traced with extreme economy on the
level of plot, in keeping with the demands of the *novella* genre and,
more significantly, with Mann's view of the highest function of narrative
art. With Schopenhauer he holds that the epic writer's aim should be
to conjure up the richest possible inner life by means of a minimum of
external action: "Art consists in the writer's affecting our inner life most
strongly with the least display of outer life; for the inner is essentially
the object of our interest." [28] Thus every detail of Aschenbach's outward
life is so chosen as to illuminate the deepest recesses of his mind and to
furnish the richest symbolical meaning. Aschenbach is drawn, on the
psychological level, as the aging man whose rational, disciplined self is
overwhelmed by a late and sudden eruption of emotional drives which
had been all too long and ruthlessly suppressed; he is also the artist
"who, sacrificing in the spirit, engenders beauty." This delineation is
most searching in its statement of the unique case, yet at the same time
it is most effective in raising the unique to the typical. Aschenbach
transcends the individual, his fate too is set up as the symbol and mirror

---

[27] Also with Xenophon, as shown very convincingly by L. Gustafson, *loc. cit.*

[28] "Die Kunst des Romans," ("The Art of the Novel") *Altes und Neues* (Frankfurt
1953), p. 396.

of the lot of creative man who follows the danger-beset path, that "erring and sinful way" which leads by the senses toward the goal of ultimate cognition and beauty. In fact, Aschenbach's figure gains its importance precisely by transcending the unique and individual "case" and rising to the typical and the eternal. Thus *Death in Venice* is once again seen to be an important step in Mann's reorientation, with growing maturity, from the "middle-class and individual" to timeless myth: "It is probably the normal course that in certain years one gradually loses one's taste for everything merely individual and special, the special case, the "middle class" in the broadest sense of the word. Instead, the typical, always-human, always-returning, eternal, in a word, the mythic takes the center of the stage." [29]

It is but natural that Aschenbach's figure and fate, being central to the *novella,* would have received extensive and intensive treatment. To enter upon a full-scale analysis would be to move along well-beaten paths. Nevertheless, one important theme seems to have received no more than passing mention[30] and deserves elaboration. It is the typically Romantic theme of the fatal fascination held by the sunlit, idyllic South for the denizen of the mist-shrouded North. The *locus classicus* of this theme in the *novella* is that seemingly realistic description of Aschenbach's summer place in the mountains and the subsequent passage quoted all but verbatim from Homer's *Odyssey.*

Just prior to complete surrender to the lure of Venice and his long yearning for "freedom," Aschenbach thinks back to the place of his creative toil in the North: "He remembered his country place in the mountains, the scene of his creative struggles in the summers, where the low clouds passed through the garden, frightful evening storms put out the lights of his house, and the ravens which he fed swung in the tops of the spruce trees." Surely, on the level of realism, it is rather startling to have Aschenbach keep "ravens" for pets. Yet this eccentricity of description with its attention-provoking "cue" is, of course, intentional. It serves to switch the mind of the reader attuned to the "combination" of realism and myth to the mythological plane. With a start one becomes aware of Aschenbach's approximation to Odin-Wodan whose mythological bird was, in fact, the raven. Now the other elements of the montage fall neatly into place and reveal their full significance: the mountainous setting, the low-hanging clouds, the terrifying storms that extinguish the lights of the house, the ravens swinging in the wind-tossed "tops of the spruce trees." With what calculated effect the words are chosen to conjure up the mythological setting without entirely cancelling out reality! We see Aschenbach's "country place" but at the same time we see, as if superimposed upon it, mighty Thor in his ram-drawn

[29] *Neue Studien,* p. 166; cf. also *Romandichtung und Mythologie,* p. 19.
[30] Cf. Pabst, loc. cit., p. 349.

chariot laying about him with hammer and lightning, threatening the home, extinguishing the hospitable fire of helpless mortals; we see the typical setting which Romantic imagination has formed into the timeless abode of the Nordic gods, especially stark and forbidding when contrasted with the idyllic shores of the Mediterranean and the sunlit heights of Olympus.

It is precisely this Romantic antithesis that patterns Aschenbach's feelings and thoughts. As he recalls his Northern home, his present surroundings turn into a veritable Elysium: "Then it would seem to him as if he had been transported to the land of Elysium, to the limits of the earth, where the lightest of lives is granted to men, where there is no snow nor winter, no storm nor streaming rain, but Oceanos ever sends up the gently cooling breeze and in blissful idleness the days slip by without effort, without struggle, and entirely devoted to the sun and its festivals."

This is the passage from the *Odyssey*[31]—slightly revised so as to point up the theme of leisure and feasting of foremost importance in Mann's antithetical structure—in which Proteus, "the unerring old man of the sea" informs the demigod Menelaus[32] that:

> it is not ordained that thou shouldst die . . . in horse-pasturing Argos, but to the Elysian plain and the bounds of the earth will the immortals convey thee . . . where life is easiest for men. No snow is there, nor heavy storm, nor ever rain, but ever does Oceanos send up blasts of the shrill-blowing West Wind that they may give cooling to men. . . .

Here we have a supreme example of sophistication in Mann's composition, which the cultivated reader should relish. The quotation from the classical source is used to develop most effectively a deeply Romantic theme. It serves, at the same time, to furnish another link between Aschenbach and Greek mythology. The informed reader acquainted with the general context in which this passage occurs, will recognize Mann's intention to identify the hero of his *novella,* admittedly by way of hidden inference, with Menelaus, the demigod, and to underscore the mythical quality of Aschenbach's death by associating it with Proteus' prophecy of Menelaus' apotheosis. Though on the level of realism Aschenbach suffers an all but sordid collapse, ravaged by an unnatural passion and the onslaught of cholera, on the level of myth he does not die "in horse-pasturing Argos" but is conveyed by the "immortal" (Tadzio-Hermes-Psychopompos) "to the land of Elysium, to the limits of the earth," "to the realm of promise and tremendousness." Thus, Aschenbach's psychophysical disintegration is informed with the dignity and the beauty of

---

[31] Cf. also Franz Mautner, *loc. cit.*
[32] So regarded as the husband of Helena, the daughter of Zeus.

apotheosis by being linked with the "mythic pattern," the "mythic return" of a demigod's entrance into the bliss of Elysium.[33]

In the supreme achievement of his master *novella* Thomas Mann draws equally from both fountainheads of truly great art, from the immediate, sensible present and the endless vistas of the past, from the fleeing reality of life and the timeless reality of art. Throughout he maintains, with an unerring touch, a unique equilibrium between the realism of coldly controlled observation, of self-critical analysis and that Dionysiac intoxication, that inspired creative élan, that "splendid sensation of uplift" capable of infusing the specters of a mythical past with a new vibrant vitality and thus creates what must be adjudged a masterpiece of "psychology plus myth."

[33] Cf. Fritz Martini, "Der Tod in Venedig," *Das Wagnis der Sprache* (Stuttgart, 1954), p. 202, on the psychological and mythical aspect of Aschenbach's fate.

# Conversation on the Magic Mountain

## by *Erich Heller*

The dialogue as a form of critique stands in need of only one apology; not, as it may appear at first glance, for frivolity and playfulness but, on the contrary, for the semblance of presumption: it seems disastrously immodest to provoke memories of Plato or Dryden or even Friedrich Schlegel. But it is with no thought of emulating them that I have decided to break the monotony of a monologue which has all the time, and no doubt noticeably, been a disguised conversation—a conversation with myself, with fellow critics, and not least with Thomas Mann. In a letter written exactly one year before his death he said that 'Thou com'st in such a questionable shape' had been 'only too familiar to me as a manner of addressing myself.' It seems appropriate, then, that questions should be asked.

A critic is well advised to heed Goethe's impatient words: "If I am to listen to the opinion of another, then it must be expressed positively; I have enough problems in myself." Yet we may be allowed a few experiments with contraries when the subject of the discourse is an author who has given so positive expression to the belief that everything is problematical. It might be helpful then to clear the ground for affirmation by letting someone else gather up the questions. The performers of the following dialogue are Q, standing for the questionable and the questioner, and A, standing for an answer and an affirmation.*

"Conversation on the Magic Mountain." From *The Ironic German* by Erich Heller, pp. 169-214. Copyright © 1958 by Erich Heller. Reprinted by permission of Little, Brown & Co. (Atlantic Monthly Press) and Martin Secker & Warburg Ltd.

* Many friends and colleagues have, without knowing it or perhaps even, mercifully, without recognizing their shares, contributed to this dialogue. Q in particular is a highly complex personality. For his existence I have certainly to thank more critics than I can with certainty relate to the troublesome Questioner. I should, however, be very much surprised if some of the more recent books on Thomas Mann have not helped to form Q's, and no doubt also A's, critical opinions: for instance, Bernhard Blume's *Thomas Mann und Goethe* (Bern, 1949), Louis Leibrich's *Thomas Mann* (Paris, 1950), E. M. Butler's *The Fortunes of Faust* (Cambridge, 1952), Henry Hatfield's *Thomas Mann* (London, 1952), Jonas Lesser's *Thomas Mann in der Epoche seiner Vollendung* (München, 1952), Hans Eichner's *Thomas Mann* (Bern, 1953), Roy Pascal's

*Q:* At the end of his essay "Dostoevsky—within Limits," Thomas Mann tells us that a friend, who knew of his plan to write a short introduction to the Russian writer, had warned him: "Be on your guard! You will write a book about him." And half apologizing for the brevity of the essay, half pleased with himself for having been brief at last, Thomas Mann adds: "I have been on my guard." [1] Admirable warning, admirable obedience! I wish he had listened more often to the voice of caution. Am I not right in thinking that both *The Magic Mountain* and *Joseph* grew from very modest conceptions?

*A:* Yes. *The Magic Mountain* was to be no more than a sequel to *Death in Venice,* a caricature of the fascination with death so seriously treated in that *Novelle,* and *Joseph* merely the biblical section in a triptych of religious stories of which the second would have been about Luther, and the third about a Spanish theme from the Counter Reformation. [2] We may even add *Buddenbrooks* to your list of mountains magically made out of molehills. Originally Thomas Mann thought only of the short life of Hanno. The attempt to "sketch in" the boy's ancestry led to a novel of two volumes. The author himself tells us that he found some comfort in remembering a tetralogy which had once grown from the plan for one opera, *The Death of Siegfried.* It became *The Ring of the Nibelung.* [3]

*Q:* Six massive volumes instead of three short stories! Germanic thoroughness indeed! It is a thin line which divides conscientiousness from pedantry. For me it is often rendered invisible by Thomas Mann's work.

*A:* He himself once said that only that which is thorough is truly entertaining. In that he is the very opposite of Nietzsche, whose ambition it was to say in three sentences what others say in a book—"and yet do not say." But is there not also high intellectual pleasure, almost a fairy-tale pleasure, in discovering the inner riches of a modest-looking idea? Or in exploring the potential range of a thought? And how rare are truly expansive thoughts in an age whose ideas, if they move at all, move usually by a series of mechanical explosions—jet-propelled. Thomas

*The German Novel* (Manchester, 1956), R. Hinton Thomas's *Thomas Mann* (Oxford, 1956) or, of course, Hermann J. Weigand's several recent articles. But for particular, and to me particularly interesting, points Q is indebted to H. E. Holthusen's *Die Welt ohne Transzendenz* (Hamburg, 1949), Peter Heller's 'Versuch über Thomas Mann' in *Forum* (Vienna, May 1957), and to a very relevant aside in Harry Levin's altogether very relevant essay *Symbolism and Fiction* (Charlottesville, 1956).

I should like to repeat here the warning that the references, maintained even in this conversation for scholarly (or perhaps pedantic) reasons, merely locate quotations. Unless he wishes to make sure of these, the reader is asked not to let the numbers trouble him.

[1] *Neue Studien* (Stockholm, 1948), pp. 101-102.
[2] *Altes und Neues* (Berlin, 1953), pp. 310-311, 678-679, and *Joseph and His Brothers* (Foreword to the edition in one volume, p. vi).
[3] *Altes und Neues,* pp. 567 and 295.

Mann's ideas grow smoothly and "organically," like seeds into trees.
They need no pushing or kicking. There is pedantry and pedantry. The
one is the tedious conscientiousness of a trivial mind, the other——
*Q:* —the not necessarily less tedious conscientiousness of a sophisticated
mind. I think I have good reason not to be entertained by Thomas
Mann's excesses in thoroughness. Pedantry is incompatible with form.
Therefore it is the enemy of art. A sculptor's workshop is strewn with
chips—matter lightheartedly sacrificed to shape. Thomas Mann's aesthetic
sin is a sin of nonomission. He spoils his shapes by working the chips
back into them. His workshop needs no dusting. His works do. You have
talked at some length about his irony. He himself once defined it as the
inability to make up his mind. "Maybe," he said, "it is good to be resolute. But the really fruitful principle, the principle of art, is . . . reserve," namely "that irony which plays subtly and undecidedly . . .
among the opposites, and is in no great hurry to join issue . . ." [4] As a
"principle of art" this strikes me as calamitous, indeed as the very calamity of his writing. If I were in a mood to evolve principles of art, I should
opt for resolve. Aesthetic decisions are resolute. Things are either formed
or left in abeyance. They cannot be both. You will, of course, protest
that the "reserve" he means is an intellectual attitude towards the *material* of his art, and need not affect its *aesthetic* form. You will, of course,
accuse me of confusing content and form—
*A:* Of course?
*Q:* I say "of course" because this is what you are bound to say at some
point, just as at another you are bound to say that there is no such
distinction. Not because this is you, but because this is a discussion about
literature; and in a discussion about literature someone simply *must* be
told that he confuses content and form, and *must* be told a little later
that the two are really one. I like literary debates. They are full of such
magic. If then I may for a moment avoid the confusion of what at all
costs must be kept apart, and cannot possibly be confused because it is
the same, let me quickly say that Thomas Mann's irony brings into
question the very possibility of art. I admit that his pedantry is the conscientiousness of a highly ironical and highly sophisticated mind. He dare
not leave out anything because anything may be of unsuspected importance and therefore any choice and decision premature. Hence the in-
ordinate length of his works. I once heard you describe the artist's mind
as occupying some kind of halfway house between the saint's and the
anarchist's. The saint, you said, sacrifices most human potentialities to
one supreme idea of truth, while the anarchist is reluctant to pay with
any of the riches of life for the advantage of order. The artist, between
the two, desires both: profusion *and* order, abundance *and* form; and
so he goes out at night, equipped with his workshop lantern, picking up
every particle which has been thrown out for the sake of order and tidi-

---

[4] *Essays of Three Decades* (Stockholm, 1945), p. 173.

ness, inspecting it carefully and compassionately, and asking: "Poor thing, have you really got to be abandoned for the sake of form, order, and artifice?" Through such salvage the great conquests of art come about, such as Shakespeare's poetry or Renaissance painting. Imagine, you exclaimed, how much of the hitherto unruly world they have brought under their artistic rules! The seemingly impossible is attained: form is enriched and yet the chaos outside diminished; the tribe speaks more clearly and more courteously without increasing the sphere of the unsayable and of the menacing silence. This is what you said, and it may be so. But surely, your salvager artist must stop somewhere. He must not pick up too much. The constant suspicion that *anything* may be important will in the end persuade us that *nothing* is. Irony? It is the irony of "everything" on the verge of "nothing," and of art on the verge of its own impossibility. This is what I meant.

*A:* This is what *he* means too and has never ceased meaning since he wrote *The Magic Mountain.* You remember he once said that there was nothing left for art to do except become its own parody? "Art on the verge of its own impossibility"—it is the main theme of *Doctor Faustus,* and in the diary he kept while writing the novel, he quotes Harry Levin's observation that Joyce's *Ulysses* is "a novel to end all novels"; and himself adds: "This is no less true of *The Magic Mountain, Joseph,* and *Doctor Faustus. . . .* Would it not seem that only such novels can still be written which, strictly speaking, are no longer novels?" [5] And as for form—"the form of the novel!" Dear me! The air thickens with tedium at the mere approach of the question, and all about us is the dry rustle of papers written for literary societies. A great Viennese satirist and poet confessed that he was unable to read novels: "I once opened a book," he said, "which they had told me was a great work of art, and I saw the following sentence: 'Had Napoleon not ridden out to the village on the evening of the 24th, and had he not then ordered an immediate attack on the redoubt but begun the attack next morning, no one would have doubted that the redoubt was the left flank of our position, and the battle would have taken place where we expected it.' I closed the book again wondering what sort of art it was in which such a sentence could find a place." This may strike you as capricious, but is it not perhaps true to say that the novel, as a literary medium, is the great concession art has made to the age of spiritual informality?

*Q:* Flaubert. What about him?

*A:* Yes, Flaubert: the aesthetic frenzy against the heaviest odds ever. And what remains in the end is the unconquerable odds: *Bouvard et Pécuchet.* How to make prose yield to an aesthetic rigor as exacting as that of the traditional forms of art—this is the besetting problem of the artists among novelists. And by "prose" I mean not only a manner of writing. I mean life experienced in the mode of prose—prosaically. Our salvager

[5] *Die Entstehung des "Doktor Faustus"* (Amsterdam, 1949), p. 83.

artist with his lantern has certainly had rather troubled nights of late. The world, littered with utterly prosaic stuff, has sorely tempted him either to leave out everything—everything except the purest words cleansed from their content—or else shamelessly take in everything, lock, stock, and barrel: blotches, scratches, freckles, obscenities, muddy streams of consciousness. Thomas Mann is one of the very few who has neither given in nor given up. And apropos form, do you know that the most thorough reviewer of *The Magic Mountain,* Hermann J. Weigand, in his book on the novel, comes to the conclusion—after a very close scrutiny— that it is "the most highly integrated" of all novels conceived on a large scale? [6] Everything I said about the strict organization of *Death in Venice* is true of the much, much longer work. And the irony of it all is that the danger of formlessness of which we spoke is not only one of the main themes of the book, but is actually "used" as a means of enriching its form. May I read to you a conversation from *The Magic Mountain?* It is between Hans Castorp, the "simple young man," the "problem child of life," who has by then travelled a considerable distance towards becoming "educated," and Hofrat Behrens, the jovially melancholy and medically straightforward ruler of the sanatorium. It is a lesson in physiology. Hans Castorp, seized by a rapture of curiosity, rhapsodically bursts forth: "What is the flesh! What is the human body! Tell us, Herr Hofrat, tell us this afternoon, tell us exactly, so that we know once and for all!" "Mainly water," says Behrens, and then goes into scientific detail. "And what is death?" "Dissolution."

> "Dissolution, putrefaction?" said Hans Castorp. "They are the same as combustion: combination with oxygen—am I right?"
>
> "I couldn't agree more. Oxidization."
>
> "And life?"
>
> "The same. Indeed, the same, young man. Life is principally oxidization of the cellular albumen. That's where the agreeable animal warmth comes from, of which we have sometimes more than we need. Yes, living is dying, no use mincing the matter—*une destruction organique,* as some Frenchman has called it with his native levity. It smells like that, too. Whenever it affects us differently, our judgment is corrupted."
>
> "And if one is interested in life, one must be interested above all in death, mustn't one?"
>
> "Oh, well, after all, there is some sort of difference. Life is where form is maintained throughout all changes of substance."
>
> "Why maintain form?" said Hans Castorp.
>
> "Why? Now listen, young man! What you are saying sounds far from humanistic."
>
> "Oh, but form is so finicky." [7]

---

[6] Hermann J. Weigand, *Thomas Mann's Novel "Der Zauberberg"* (New York, 1933), p. 159.

[7] *The Magic Mountain* (London, 1927), pp. 265-267.

May I bore you with a little exegesis?

*Q:* You may. But not too much. For I fear you might stretch the meaning of the passage beyond its natural elasticity. I have yet to meet a literary analyst who is not a stretcher. Certainly, the passage contains the very theme of *The Magic Mountain*: the juxtaposition of "dissolution" and "form." I should say there is hardly more in it than this: Hans Castorp, whose newly awakened intellectual curiosity is a kind of inflammation of the mind caused by his passion for Clavdia Chauchat—his judgment concerning the human body is indeed "corrupted"—is in danger of abandoning himself to disease, death, Dionysian chaos. Form is sobriety, discipline, clarity, and is "so finicky" because it somehow goes together with being restrained, polite, and industrious—in short, with being a shipbuilding engineer in Hamburg, a rather unattractive career for young Tannhäuser if the alternative is life with Madame Venus in her mountain. Is it not just the old story again of Aschenbach's Greek hexameters unsteadied by the long-drawn-out *u*-sounds of the Venetian beach?

*A:* Not quite. It would be entirely as you say if *The Magic Mountain* were, as was originally planned, the mere foil to *Death in Venice*. As it is, it has moved on to yet another level of irony: the Dionysian intoxication is, as you have correctly observed, productive of learning. Hanno Buddenbrook, similarly inspired, was a bad pupil. Hans Castorp becomes a very good one. His soul bursts forth rhapsodically, while his mind patiently learns all about the oxidation of cellular albumen. I wish I were that excellent reader of whom Friedrich Schlegel said that only his voice could do justice to the subtle irony with which the whole work is irradiated.[8] If that voice were mine, you might even allow me to read to you the whole chapter entitled "Humaniora."

*Q:* Friedrich Schlegel taught you how to read *The Magic Mountain*? Haven't you got your dates wrong?

*A:* Of course. Yes, I have. Friedrich Schlegel meant Goethe's *Wilhelm Meister*. But as a reader of *The Magic Mountain* you should know what tricks Time is apt to play on us when we happen not to be in the mood for playing on it our trick of objective measurement. It is one of the pervasive themes of *The Magic Mountain* that clocks and calendars are both imprecise and dull ways of registering the movements of the elusive river—as imprecise and dull as everything that disregards the human soul. And to the human soul time does not flow evenly, either in retrospect—three weeks of travel seem longer than three months of routine life—or in anticipation—that lecture I have promised to give eight months hence appears to be as distant as the Future Life, and deceptively leaves me with as immeasurable an amount of time in which to prepare myself. And while time actually passes (and we pass the time—so that Heaven only knows who or what it actually is that passes what or whom)

---

[8] Friedrich Schlegel, *Kritische Schriften*, ed. Wolfdietrich Rasch (Munich, 1956), p. 274.

there are time's all but stagnant pools when it appears not to flow at all, and there are its Niagaras; and there is a state of the soul when it has no time.

*Q:* A *state* of the soul? Well, I agree that nowadays nobody ever has any time.

*A:* Because we have nothing but time.

*Q:* Are you being paradoxical?

*A:* With your permission. There are two reasons for not having time. You meant the first: having too much to do. Why have we too much to do? Because nothing counts except what we do in our time and with our time, because we have nothing but time. What I meant was the other reason for not having time: because the soul enjoys the timeless state, and has, as it were, God's good time. An age which has so little of this must find its dealings with time exceedingly problematical. *The Magic Mountain* is a great novel of the epoch in nothing so much as in its preoccupation with Time. Thomas Mann was a contemporary of Einstein's.

*Q:* I am very doubtful of such facile offerings of the *Zeitgeist*.

*A:* I deeply respect your scepticism and shall not mention Time and Bergson, Time and Proust, Time and Heidegger. But it so happens that both Einstein's Relativity and *The Magic Mountain* are concerned with a concept of time rendered problematical by the absence of a valid standard of measurement, the absence of an Absolute; and if the *Zeitgeist* can be defined by what it lacks: this is it. Perhaps the jam jars in the larder of Hans Castorp's childhood home have got it.

*Q:* The jam jars? Have got what?

*A:* Have got the Absolute. I mean the airtight glasses full of jam, fruit, or meat, which Hans Castorp suddenly remembers as Naphta, his gravest educator on the Magic Mountain, instructs him in the Hermetic Philosophy. "Hermetic—what a lovely word, Herr Naphta!" Hans Castorp exclaims, "I have always liked the word hermetic"; and then interrupts his mentor's learned discourse with the homely memory of the conserves: "What struck me always as magical," he says, "was their being withdrawn from time, they were hermetically sealed off from it, time passed them by, and there, shut away from time, they stood on their shelves." [9] This is a typical example of the occasional *Alice in Wonderland* touch of *The Magic Mountain*. But it is, as I said, the chapter "Humaniora" which I should like to read to you in the voice prescribed by Friedrich Schlegel.

*Q:* What is it about?

*A:* About the rhapsodic and the scientific, and how both are facets of one passion; about Hans Castorp's discovering the high comedy and the high seriousness of the "Humanities." Hofrat Behrens, an amateur painter, has painted a portrait of his patient Clavdia Chauchat. Hans Castorp, already secretly in love with Clavdia, persuades Behrens to show him and cousin Joachim his works. Joachim is a passive victim of the occasion,

---

[9] *The Magic Mountain*, p. 511.

cunningly used by Hans as a kind of chaperon to lend the appearance of innocence to the adventurous enterprise. The episode begins in the garden of the sanatorium—"it was yet another of those incomparable alpine October days: bright without being heavy, hot and yet with a tang in the air"—and ends in the living quarters of the Hofrat. The epithets given to the October day describe the mood of the whole chapter. Hans Castorp grows ever more exuberant, almost inebriated as he is by the portrait of Clavdia—a very bad likeness "which he ought not even to have recognized" but distinguished by an exceedingly faithful, scientifically minute, and unusually "concrete" rendering of the *décolleté* (*"anschaulich"* is the Goethean adjective Thomas Mann parodistically uses in a situation teeming with parodistic Goethean associations). For the first time Castorp uninhibitedly displays, to the amazement of the doctor and the embarrassment of the cousin, the interests he has developed, and the extraordinary knowledge he has acquired during his febrile stay on the mountain. His exchanges with Behrens bring into ironical, and often very comic, play the variety of angles under which man can see himself and his works. "If a man knows a little about what goes on under the epidermis," says Behrens, acknowledging the praise he receives from Hans for the masterly execution of Clavdia's skin, "if he can paint a little below the surface, . . . and stands in yet another relation to nature than just the lyrical, . . . it all comes in handy. . . ." [10]

*Q:* It sounds like an apologia for the literary method employed in *The Magic Mountain*.

*A:* An ironical reflection on it, not an apologia. For it is the unashamed intention of *The Magic Mountain* to bring together the lyrical and the prosaic modes. Read once again the chapter "Research," not because it is the best, but because it carries out the intention most resolutely. You will then soon notice very much subtler ways of handling the theme throughout the book.

*Q:* Is it about Hans Castorp's studying biology and physiology?

*A:* Yes, Hans Castorp's reading about life and the mystery of its origin, and reading about it by the light of the dead moon and the red-shaded glow of the table lamp. And as he lies in his deckchair on the nocturnal balcony above the glittering valley, the image of life, left rather vague and abstract by the scientific books, assumes an imaginatively concrete shape which resembles Madame Chauchat. I have often heard literary critics say in praise of what they take to be particularly happy specimens of literary creation, that in them language "does" what it describes. I am never quite sure what they mean; I only know that they are after something less simple than the onomatopoetic use of words. But whatever they mean, Thomas Mann's language "does" it in the chapter "Research." It positively "does" science, and it "does" poetry. [11]

---

[10] Ibid., pp. 251 ff.
[11] Ibid., pp. 276 ff.

*Q:* I remember that spirited flirtation between the rhapsodic and the scientific vocables, the lyrical and the prosaic modes.

*A:* Flirtation? A consummation—the consummation of German romanticism.

*Q:* Of German romanticism? I always believed German romanticism was the organized *avoidance* of the prosaic mode—something like the cultivation of raptures and ecstasies, the contemplation of splendid agonies and exemplary Middle Ages, or, in its homelier form, the elegiac intimacy with babbling brooks, moonlit woods, and wild roses. I shouldn't have thought cellular albumen and the epidermis came into it very much.

*A:* Wild roses *and* cellular albumen, rhapsody *and* physiology—perhaps this is one way of hinting at one of the many varieties of romantic irony. Nocturnal solitudes and the pining spirit and the quest for the blue flower—yes, it is all there; but the bluest of flowers searched for by the first German romantics, that amazing group of people around Friedrich Schlegel, is a "synthetic" one: the flourishing synthesis—how Friedrich Schlegel loved the prefix *syn!*—of the poetic and the scientific. It is not for nothing that the Romantic Movement can be said to begin with the publication in 1794 of a book called *The Scientific Doctrine*: Fichte's *Wissenschaftslehre*.

*Q:* Well, scientific . . .

*A:* You need not think of Newton. But what you are asked to think of seems "unromantic" enough: systematic rationality. What a strange mind was Friedrich Schlegel's! Profound, superficial, brilliant, awkward, crazy, reasonable—all in one: self-appointed commander in chief to maneuver the poetic spirit over that zero point of rationalistic depression which, a little later, Hegel declared to be the end of all art. Schlegel tried to believe that it also marked a climax of intellectual freedom at which man was able freely to choose, and knowingly to create for himself, the good life of poetry which until then had been a dark compulsion of the imagination. "A wholly free and educated person," he wrote, "must have the power to attune himself at will to philosophy or philology, to criticism or poetry, to history or rhetoric, to the ancient or the modern—just as one tunes an instrument." [12] It is a method which Thomas Mann has raised to the level of genius. Remarkable, isn't it, how much both Joseph and Felix Krull have of this infinite adaptability? And in the night of the Mardi gras even the linguistic ignoramus Hans Castorp speaks fluent French.

*Q:* "Just as one tunes an instrument?" It sounds to me like an apotheosis of charlatanism.

*A:* It is. Of the serious charlatanism of absolute self-awareness. This is the more surprising as our "romantic" idea of the artist is of a man who, like Luther, "cannot do otherwise." He is at the mercy of a demon, an instinct, an inspiration, and knows not what he does. This, we are some-

[12] Schlegel, *op. cit.,* p. 12.

how accustomed to believe, is his "integrity." In contrast to this, Schlegel's romantic artist does *know*. He is supremely conscious—so much so that, while he does what he does, he can at the same time do something else: for instance, "from the height of the mind smile down upon his masterpiece," as Schlegel believed Goethe did in *Wilhelm Meister*.[13]

*Q:* Did Goethe smile down upon *Wilhelm Meister*?

*A:* Perhaps not quite as broadly as Thomas Mann upon *The Magic Mountain*. Even if Friedrich Schlegel had been a still more voracious reader than he was, he would hardly have found in the literature available to him more classical examples than Thomas Mann has since produced of this particular brand of romantic irony. For instance: "Like everyone else we claim the right to our own private thoughts about the story we are telling." [14] This is how he introduces a reflective passage, ironically apologizing for it—to readers who, I presume, have somewhat naïve ideas about the proper relations between "creation" and "reflection." Or again: "At this point the author feels it would be advisable for him to express his surprise at what is coming next, or else the reader might try to do it for himself and overdo it." [15] Or, when he says of the word "relationship" he uses in describing the feelings, as yet silent, undeclared, and distant, which Hans Castorp has for Clavdia Chauchat, that "it is Castorp's term, not our own; we disclaim responsibility for it." [16] This, by the way, is one of the many passages which floor the translator. The German *"Verhältnis"* means not only "relationship" but also "love affair."

*Q:* If you go on like this, you will soon reduce me to the status of those comfortable Platonic dummies who keep on saying "That would be but natural," or "True. I had forgotten."—Still, I see your point; and even if, measuring "the height of the mind," we may not arrive at precisely the same figures, I too can see the smiling down. It is broad enough. No doubt in German it is still broader.

*A:* You sound cross.

*Q:* Perhaps because the "somewhat naïve ideas" are mine. For I do believe that creation and reflection are different activities of the mind, and that it is one of the weaknesses of Thomas Mann's that he cannot keep them apart.

*A:* Who, at this time of day, can? A few talented simpletons—and they succeed because they have precious little reflection to keep apart from precious little creation. For the rest any attempt to cultivate nowadays "pure creation" in literature leads to affectation or obscurity or alcoholism.

*Q:* Why nowadays?

[13] Ibid., p. 270.
[14] *The Magic Mountain*, p. 229.
[15] Ibid., p. 183.
[16] Ibid., p. 140.

*A:* I wish I knew the answer. From Hegel to Spengler many answers have been suggested. They are all uncertain. Only the symptoms are certain. Friedrich Schlegel already took these symptoms for granted and tried hard to convince himself that they meant the approach of "masterpieces of romanticism" in which creation was suffused with reflection, and reflection was released with the spontaneity of the creative imagination. What he obviously "divined" was the emergence of the European novel, which you, insisting so much upon the "two activities of the mind," seem still to judge by the standards of the epic. Schlegel was much more up to our date. Hence it is not surprising that he gave what almost amounts to an anticipatory definition of the literary art of *The Magic Mountain* when he described romantic poetry as "progressively universal"—"*progressive Universalpoesie.*" Its task is, he said, "to reunite the separate genres of literature and to bring together poetry and philosophy," to mix and mingle "the poetic with the prosaic, creative spontaneity with critique," to "satiate the medium of art with solid learning of every kind and to animate it with the vibration of humor." Such a writer, he continues, "may so lose himself in what he portrays that he appears to be concerned with nothing else but the characterization of imaginary figures, and may yet at the same time, and as if unwittingly, completely portray himself." Only then will his work have a chance "of becoming the image of the age," while he himself remains contemplatively aloof, "multiplying reflection as if in an infinite series of mirrors" and "infusing every single part of his creation with the identity of the whole." [17] It is amazing how well this fits *The Magic Mountain*—in fact, much better than the work on which Friedrich Schlegel was in the habit of calling as the main witness to his conception of "*progressive Universalpoesie.*"

*Q:* Goethe's *Wilhelm Meister*? I seem to remember that Schlegel's friend Novalis—and he was what Schlegel was not: a poet—spoke rather unkindly of it. Did he not call it "The Pilgrim's Progress towards a Knighthood"?

*A:* He did, and said even worse things of it: that it was a satire against poetry, a "Candide aimed at poetry," that from it "the economic nature of man emerged as his only true nature," that it was "a divine image made of straw and wood shavings," and a "piece of poetic machinery to deal with recalcitrant material." [18] You can see that it is all much to the point.

*Q:* To which point?

*A:* To my point. For elsewhere he calls Goethe "the true vicar on earth of the poetic spirit," and *Wilhelm Meister* "the novel *per se,*" a work which comes close to the greatest literary achievements of antiquity.

*Q:* A moody fellow.

*A:* As moody as the poetic spirit in a prosaic age. For he too regards the

[17] Schlegel, *op. cit.,* p. 37.
[18] Novalis, *Fragments,* ed. Ernst Kamnitzer (Dresden, 1929), pp. 632-633.

history of literature from the ancients to the moderns as a dialectical quarrel between poetry and prose, with Goethe as "the nucleus of a synthesis." Therefore he feels his way into *Wilhelm Meister* dialectically: now he allows it to affect him as "prose against poetry" and now again as "prose resolved in poetry." [19] May we now look once more upon our passage from *The Magic Mountain* in the light of Friedrich Schlegel's *Universalpoesie*?

*Q:* I am not so sure if "light" is not a euphemism. I am still in the dark.

*A:* Like Hans Castorp. I wish I could be Settembrini for a moment, the man of the Enlightenment. You recall his first visit at Hans Castorp's bedside? The young man, until then a mere visitor in the sanatorium, the guest of his sick cousin Joachim Ziemssen, had contracted a cold and was sent to bed by Hofrat Behrens. There he spends three weeks, if "spending" is the right word for his passive dealings with time and the time-devouring monotony of the daily routine. He eats at midday, always the same midday, his "soup everlasting," and thinks of Clavdia Chauchat at nightfall, always the same nightfall. But one evening there is a knock on the door, and in comes Settembrini, "and instantly the room was flooded with light. For the visitor's first motion, while still on the threshold, had been to turn on the electric light." [20]

*Q:* Rather obvious.

*A:* Because I have made it so. Besides, everything he does is obvious. He is without mystery.

*Q:* Who?

*A:* Well asked! I meant Settembrini. But in a sense it could also be said of Thomas Mann. Yet if it was well asked it was also asking too much. True, there are writers—or had we better say: there *were* writers?—whose works have the ineffable quality of a primitive mystery, like the sea, or a landscape, or a truly loved person. Yes, such works do exist—although much of modern literary criticism seems systematically to exploit the assumption that they don't. But they do. We may read them time and again, and at each reading they will be different, mysteriously different, revealing something new and veiling something new. With Thomas Mann's works we feel that their secret, which is not a mystery, is, at least in theory, discoverable.

*Q:* Well answered! So they are not art. Except, perhaps, *Buddenbrooks*.

*A:* If you are not careful, you will soon understand Friedrich Schlegel. From *The Magic Mountain* onwards, Thomas Mann's novels move towards that farthest point of art, its *ne plus ultra*, where it yet defiantly asserts itself in the face of its ultimate deprivation. Art tragically laments the loss of its own mystery in *Doctor Faustus*, and gaily reports it to the cosmic police in *Felix Krull*. Friedrich Schlegel, like a complex simpleton and profoundly prophetic fool, believed that precisely this would be art's

[19] Ibid., pp. 652-656.
[20] *The Magic Mountain*, p. 192.

supreme triumph, and read *Wilhelm Meister* as if it were *The Magic Mountain*. It is a book, he said, which "saves the critic the trouble of judgment." And why? Because it holds no mystery: "it judges itself. And not only does it judge itself, it also represents itself"—together with the story it purports to represent.[21] For "everything that can be done so long as philosophy (which for Schlegel is only another name for systematic rationality, self-awareness, and critique) exists apart from poetry (by which he means all the literary genres) has already been done. Therefore it is time that they should come together." [22] He thought they had done so in *Wilhelm Meister*. By a mere whim of history Thomas Mann had lost his most enthusiastic critic. May we now look at *The Magic Mountain* in the light——

*Q:* Yes, I think I am beginning to catch a glimpse of Schlegel's meaning. He thought, did he not, that *Wilhelm Meister* was the first great literary work produced by a mind in the state of perfect critical awareness concerning the nature of literature, and who produced it not despite such awareness, but, on the contrary, entirely by virtue of it?

*A:* That is more than a glimpse of Schlegel's meaning.

*Q:* How unromantic!

*A:* I have been trying all the time to disillusion you concerning the "romanticism" of the first German romantics. However, I ought to remind you that Shakespeare and Cervantes belong to Schlegel's history of romanticism as the first great writers who were also conscious *actors* of the spirit of poetry and literature—and therefore great *ironical* writers. Do you know Schlegel's *Lucinde*?

*Q:* Almost. I know it superficially, and wonder whether this is not the proper way of knowing it. I found it constrained, affected, and intolerably self-conscious.

*A:* Exactly. He certainly wasn't the writer to practice his theory. But you can see what he was aiming at. His theory was that "construction," if only it was carried to its utmost limits, would finally re-enter, on a higher level, the sphere of organic growth, while self-consciousness, mounting higher and higher, would ultimately transcend itself in a reasoned ecstasy of spontaneous creation.

*Q:* And all this happens in *The Magic Mountain*? Small wonder it is so long.

*A:* Of course it does not happen in *The Magic Mountain,* and is not likely to happen anywhere; for it is the great romantic dream of irony enthroned as the first principle of all literature. But it is only because the great romantic dreams are unrealizable that *The Magic Mountain* is not its fulfilment. It achieves as much of it as can be achieved, and renders the rest undreamable. Maybe this is the nature of all great

[21] Schlegel, *op. cit.,* pp. 270-271.
[22] Ibid., p. 98.

achievements. Let us at last look at *The Magic Mountain* in the light of Schlegel's theory.

*Q:* I am sorry. I seem to have succeeded in holding up your exegesis of Hans Castorp's lesson in physiology. Now it is no longer necessary. Our romantic ramble has not wasted *my* time. I can see now: the rhapsodic *and* the prosaic, the poetic *and* the scientific . . . "to mix and mingle creative spontaneity with critique," and "to satiate the medium of art with solid learning of every kind." Yes, there are, in *The Magic Mountain,* pages and pages of critique, science, philosophy, without, I should say, much noticeable admixture of "creative spontaneity." There are, believe me, whole chapters where I feel that not only "the medium of art" is "satiated with solid learning." I am too.

*A:* I doubt the solidity of the learning.

*Q: You* doubt it?

*A:* Of course I do. Can any one person have a solid knowledge of all the sciences that come into *The Magic Mountain*? Anatomy, physiology, pathology, pharmacology, radiology, psychology, engineering, philosophy, theology, meteorology, political theory . . .

*Q:* You are right. Nobody can have a solid knowledge of political theory. But you are confusing me: surely, *I* ought to have said all this?

*A:* Forgive me. I was only prompting. I know the list of grievances against *The Magic Mountain.* But *had* you said that you doubted the solidity of Thomas Mann's learning, I should have agreed. It is *startling* enough; it is even said that doctors marvelled at *The Magic Mountain,* just as egyptologists marvelled at *Joseph in Egypt,* and musicologists at *Doctor Faustus.* And although Thomas Mann could certainly not afford to be blatantly misinformed concerning their subjects, it cannot be the point of a work of literature to amaze the experts.

*Q:* I couldn't agree more. But what *is* the point of all that learning in *The Magic Mountain*?

*A:* Must I repeat myself and Friedrich Schlegel? I must not. May I therefore ask why you think it should *not* be there?

*Q:* Because a novel is neither a dissertation nor a scientific textbook.

*A:* Please make it more difficult for me. You know yourself that *The Magic Mountain* is neither.

*Q:* But long passages in it read like passages from a scientific textbook. They are dead matter in an artistic organization of which we are entitled to expect an aesthetic rendering of human experience.

*A:* I know *that* textbook all right. Human experience . . . I suppose you mean love and hatred, war and peace, adventure and death, gain and loss. There is plenty of all that in *The Magic Mountain.* But is not learning a human experience?

*Q:* Not the kind of human experience which can be rendered aesthetically.

*A:* "Yet for he was a scholar, once admired
For wondrous knowledge in our German schools. . . ."

What about Faustus?

*Q:* That's different. Both Marlowe and Goethe, in so far as "learning" plays any real part in their works, give us the poetry of the *passion* for learning. Thomas Mann gives us the stuff itself.

*A:* The "real stuff." Just as Clavdia Chauchat is more "real" than Helen of Troy. For we are dealing with a "realist." But Clavdia is not only "real"; she is also, like Helen of Troy, the object of passion. And what is true of Madame Chauchat is true of the learning. Hans Castorp is in love with both. And as it is the convention of realism to show us the objects of passion not only in their passionate and poetic aspects but "as they really are," there is no reason—unless we reject the realistic convention—why Thomas Mann should not show us the learning, pursued with passion by Hans Castorp, as realistically as he shows us the woman. But this apologia, addressed as it is to a blind spot in your comprehension, also misses the point of *The Magic Mountain,* which is to present the experience in both its passionate and sober aspects, as "poetry" and as "prose," as "lyrical" and as "scientific," and to reflect upon it from a multiplicity of angles. Yet of all the demands made by Friedrich Schlegel upon "universal poetry" none seems to have been as conscientiously and successfully fulfilled by *The Magic Mountain* as the one asking that every single part of a literary creation should be "infused with the identity of the whole."

*Q:* Do you mean to say that Thomas Mann consciously constructed his novel to fit Friedrich Schlegel's design?

*A:* Certainly not. I even doubt that Thomas Mann was at any point of his work conscious of the prophetic definition. Schlegel was simply a great diviner of the historical probabilities of literature, and Thomas Mann was possessed of a sensibility which functioned as the *Zeitgeist's* most reliable seismograph.

*Q:* I am not sure whether I understand what is meant by "every single part of a literary creation being infused with the identity of the whole." Does it imply more than a certain unity of style?

*A:* We cannot be quite sure what Schlegel meant. Had he thought of *The Magic Mountain,* he would have meant a great deal more than you suggest, unless the term "unity of style" covers such radical attempts at perfect integration as whole chapters once again telling in their own terms the whole story of the novel.

*Q:* A rather boring device. Or, to be just, it would have bored me had I noticed it.

*A:* I said, "in its own terms." The chapter "Snow," for instance—

*Q:* In which it happens that Hans Castorp defies the rules of the sanatorium and goes on his lonely skiing expedition into the mountains?

*A:* Just as he once defied the rules of burgher life in Hamburg and climbed the Magic Mountain. He soon reached regions "which filled his heart with sensations of wildness, strangeness, and extreme danger."

*Q:* In the sanatorium?

*A:* In the snow. He "struggled up ever paler heights and knew not whither. It seemed to him they led nowhere. Their upper reaches blended with a sky which was as misty-white as they, and it was hard to tell where it began. No summit, no ridge was visible—Hans Castorp strove towards haze and nothingness. The world behind him, the inhabited valley, fell swiftly away from view. No sound was to be heard. In no time at all, it seemed, he had become as solitary and as lost as heart could wish. His loneliness was deep enough to call forth that terror which is the condition of courage." [23] Metaphorically, this is a description of the first steps of Hans Castorp's education on the Magic Mountain. Literally, it is only about this particular adventure in the snow. You may even go further, leave this particular Hans aside, and read both book and chapter as a parable of Man, man lost and saved—or perhaps not quite as much saved as he is lost.—Or do you remember "the ethics of sin and self-abandonment" on which Clavdia enlightens Hans? This is its version in the snow: "He rejoiced in his inspired freedom and abandon. Before him stretched no path, none lay behind him to take him back whence he had come. At first there had been posts, set up as guides through the snow—but he had soon cut free from their tutelage . . . because they seemed incongruously to intrude into his relations with the great wintry wild." [24]

*Q:* I believe you. Yes, the chapter "Snow" is a synopsis of the whole book. Yes, the whole book aspires to, and perhaps, achieves, a formal unity unparalleled by any other novel. It weaves and interweaves its motifs and arabesques into a pattern which, despite its endless variations, seems yet complete on every single page. And if I can find a few more phrases of praise for the formal excellence of Thomas Mann's art, you shall have them all. But you yourself said that analyzable formal excellence does not necessarily establish the quality of a work of art.

*A:* I did say it. Yes, form may be dumb. It may have nothing to say. But *The Magic Mountain* says as much through its form as it says through its content. The two are really one.

*Q:* I know, I know, they are one and therefore must not get mixed up. And what does it say through its form? That "form is so finicky"?

*A:* The whole book is about form and dissolution, the disciplined effort of living and the relaxing lure of death, the honors of achievement and the advantages of dissoluteness. It is about the civilized shape of Europe on the verge of its disintegration. Thomas Mann's insistence on literary form is a parodistic response to his own theme in so far as he treats of the temptation, delight, and danger of disorganization in the most elaborately organized prose. But it is also a militant measure in defence of form.

---

[23] *The Magic Mountain*, p. 478.
[24] Ibid., pp. 480-481.

*Q:* Whichever it is, it is overdone.

*A:* As overdone as the white blood corpuscles around the center of an infection.

*Q:* Except that it cures nothing. On the contrary, form overdone may itself be a symptom of death.

*A:* Abstract form. This too Thomas Mann knows. You remember Hans Castorp's learned speculations in the snow—on snow crystals? It is a very good piece—despite its learning, as you no doubt wish me to add. The last sentences of the piece say of those crystals: "They were far too regular for any substance meant to live. Indeed, the blood of life seemed to run cold at the mere suggestion of anything so precise. The secret of their precision was the secret of death, and Hans felt he understood the reason why the builders of antiquity were in the habit of purposely and furtively breaking, with minute deviations from symmetry, the rigid rule of their structures of columns." [25]

*Q:* Oh, he is so maddeningly circumspect and has the cowardice of a scholar who enjoys nothing more than frustrating by clever anticipation Professor X's attempt to catch him out! All right, form is death, and form is life, and *The Magic Mountain* is about life and death, and therefore doubly formed.

*A:* You are unjust. It is not Professor Q's criticism against which he guards. He is considerably subtler than that. He guards against the voice within, the Janus voice, the voice of absolute irony.

*Q:* The exasperating voice which makes it so difficult for me either to admit or to deny even to myself what I know to be a high probability: that *The Magic Mountain* is, by any available standard, one of the greatest novels ever written.

*A:* I understand why you cannot deny it. What prevents you from admitting it?

*Q:* The sun and the moon and the curse of modern literature. I remember a passage from *The Magic Mountain,* the first book of Thomas Mann's I ever read. Even in translation I was struck by the lyrical beauty of the piece: Hans Castorp's remembrance of a lonely boat ride one evening on a lake in Holstein. I could feel the coolness of the late summer air, and hear the splashing of the water against the boat, and smell the meadows stretching from the bank where the grass was cut for the second time. I don't know whether all this is actually in the passage, but I am sure it was all around me when I read it. But the sun and the moon are certainly there, the almost full moon rising above the bushes that border the lake, and where the moon is, there is night, while the sun still dominates the west with the broad, sober, glassy light of day. I can still see Hans Castorp, sitting in his boat and turning his eyes in amazement from

[25] Ibid., p. 480.

east to west and back again, from night to day and back to the moon. I liked it.[26]

*A:* I can see the sun and moon. I cannot see the curse.

*Q:* The curse is that it is a sort of allegory. Hans Castorp remembers the lake, the boat, the sun and moon, while, stirred by Settembrini's account of his family history, he contemplates the difference between his own grandfather in the medieval garments, and Settembrini's ancestor fighting the battles of Reason against the darkness of the past. Perhaps I feel less strongly about it now. But at the time I felt that it was the desecration of a summer evening through unholy literature. The summer evening is too true, too good, and too real, to serve as a mere visual accompaniment to the imaginary family squabbles taking place in Hans Castorp's mind.

*A:* It is strange that the summer evening, which you find so true, good, and real, is the work of the same writer who so tactlessly relates it to what you call the family squabbles.

*Q:* It is the terrible compulsion to relate everything to everything, this relentless obsession with the cross references of the universe, which is the curse of our godless but oh! so "religious" literature. If you believe in God as the creator of the world, then go and try to decipher His often illegible hand in the scrolls of His creation! But what, I ask you, is gained by relating one sadly meaningless thing to another, sun and moon to two grandfathers, or the superstitious number seven to almost any arrangement on the Magic Mountain? Oh, for those healthy times when metaphors were ornaments of language, not revelations of spurious meaning! There is, believe me, method in those Symbolists unaccountably electing the American Edgar Poe their master. Their whole school is one of the first manifestations of Americanism in Europe: more and bigger and better correspondences, all quivering with vitally appealing intimations of sense and senses, instead of one clear and sensible truth. Summer evenings and grandfathers and crisscross references galore—and when all the relating, referring, and corresponding is done, we are left with a number of types which are given a violent sort of "significance" within a contrived aesthetic pattern, but are divested of the independent and individual existence they once had in the eyes of God. Did I call them allegorical? No, they are not even that, for allegories live entirely by the faith of writer and reader in an ultimate meaning. Yet everybody and everything in the novel "represents" something: Hans Castorp represents Germany, Settembrini the West, Clavdia the East, the song of the linden-tree death, but what is represented is certainly not more significant, and is only bigger, than its representatives, who in their turn have acquired "typicalness" at the expense of their uniqueness.

*A:* Your arguments are formidable and would be devastating if they were themselves less "typical"; and by this I mean that they bring into question

[26] Ibid., p. 154.

not only the work of Thomas Mann but practically every major effort
and achievement of the arts and of literature in the past hundred years
or more. Besides, the author of *The Magic Mountain* is well aware of the
difficulty, so much so that the book is in parts an essay in the relation of
the typical to the unique in a world of, as it were, circular meaninglessness, a world seen in the image of Nietzsche's "Eternal Recurrence."
Listen to Hans Castorp when, lost in the snow storm, he discovers to his
dismay that after wandering about for a long time, with "the idea of
progress in his heart," he has merely returned to his hopeless point of
departure: "That was the very devil. Hans Castorp uttered heartfelt
curses although his lips were too stiff to pronounce the labials. He
stumped on his skis around the hut in order to get his bearings, and
came to the conclusion that he had returned to it from the back, having
indulged for the last hour—as he reckoned it—in the sheerest and silliest
waste of time. But there it was, precisely as the books reported it. You
went in a circle, gave yourself endless trouble under the delusion that
you were getting somewhere, and all the time you were simply describing
some big nonsensical arc that would turn back to its beginning, like the
vexatious course of the seasons. This was certainly not the way of getting
home. Hans Castorp recognized the traditional phenomenon with a
certain grim satisfaction; he even slapped his thigh in anger and astonish-
ment at the general law fulfilling itself so punctiliously in his individual,
present, and particular case." [27] And again we read, as he all but succumbs
to the temptation to lie down in the snow and to rest: "This temptation
was as great as the books reported, designating it the 'typical danger,'
which yet did nothing to diminish for him the living present and the
power of it. It asserted its individual rights, refused to be simply classified
under some general heading, and protested, as it were, that it was unique
and incomparable in its singular urgency." [28] How to equip the typical
with individuality, how to win freedom for that which is fated, and how
to give meaning and direction to a life running its course in cyclic
repetitiveness—this was the persistent problem of Thomas Mann, the
writer and thinker, ever since he realized that the leitmotif, which he
had used from the beginning, was more than a literary technique; that
it was in fact the literary symptom of a metaphysical belief towards
which he inclined.

*Q:* Towards which he inclined, or which he held?

*A:* Beliefs are not held in the ironical sphere; and in the sphere of religion it is the beliefs which do the holding.

*Q:* If it resembles Nietzsche's belief in the Eternal Recurrence, the love
of the leitmotif sounds like gloom everlasting.

*A:* Or a serene faith. Extremely gloomy, perhaps, when it expresses itself
in the parodistic return of Adrian Leverkühn's utterly sophisticated

[27] Ibid., p. 487.
[28] Ibid., p. 486.

music to archaic primitivity, or in his own defeated return to childhood. But it can also be the happiest faith. Think of those mystical re-embodiments of, say, the servant Eliezer in *Joseph and his Brothers;* every Eliezer who happens to be "in the flesh" at any given time gains life everlasting through the indestructible type his own mortal self repre-sents and he confidently says "I" even if he narrates what happened to a servant Eliezer of hundreds of years ago.

*Q:* I am not Eliezer, and I am going to do something desperate now. I shall ask you, why? Yes, why? Ah, you already look as most critics and philosophers do when asked why—like the Emperor just about not to have his clothes on. Yet I insist. Why all these changes from the cheerful Eternal Recurrence to the depressing Eternal Recurrence? Why all this romantic fuss about the aspects, and about mixing them, and about the ironical experiments, and about the duplicity of angles? Why?

*A:* Because of the great calamity.

*Q:* The great calamity?

*A:* You yourself used the word apropos Thomas Mann's "indecision," and implied it in your attack on the arbitrary "cross-references of the universe." The indecision is, of course, about what is true, and in this respect it is an old calamity. But the *great* calamity—and some would say that it is also the *new* calamity—is not to be sure even where and how to look for truth, and not to be sure whether it exists.

*Q:* Why? I mean, why should an artist be concerned with truth?

*A:* Did you not just complain about those who weren't—the "aesthetic cross-referees"? But let us assume, wrongly perhaps, that neither of us knows why they *should* be concerned with truth. Then it will be easy for us to agree that some artists *are* concerned: Leonardo, for instance, or Rembrandt, or Dante, or Goethe. Some even call themselves realists, which, if anything, means that they wish to be true to what really is. And when the great calamity is upon them, such artists are compelled more than ever to experiment—yes, to experiment with aspects and angles and mixing and mingling and "all this romantic fuss." For one can never be sure—not even about the face to make in the face of this or that. For there seem to be no faces, only masks. Death, surely, is a solemn occasion, and Hans Castorp's capacity for not remaining as mediocre as he seemed at the outset, all his latent ability seriously to learn and to grow, stems, his story suggests, from the serious and solemn lesson he has, as a child, learned from death: "One takes one's hat off to him, and goes on tiptoe in his presence. He wears the stately ruff of the past, and we do him honor in austere black." [29] But Settembrini, on the other hand, calls the power of death "strong but vicious and lascivious," so that to sympathize with it is "without the slightest doubt the most ghastly aberration of the human spirit." [30] And to be sure, death is first mentioned, on an early

[29] Ibid., p. 496.
[30] Ibid., p. 200.

page of the novel, in a grotesque context. On the way from the station Joachim tells Hans Castorp, who has just arrived, of the bob-sleigh on which, during the winter months, a sanatorium still further up in the mountains transports its corpses into the valley. And when Joachim mentions yet another oddity of the place, namely Dr. Krokowski, the assistant doctor in their own establishment, who practises soul-analysis (the dissolving attack on "form" is the link between the themes of death and analysis), Hans, already laughing at the macabre winter sport, is seized by an uncontrollable fit of merriment.[31] This is how, as soon as he arrives on the Magic Mountain, he begins to learn of the uncertain meaning of all things. And a little later he is already able to grasp what his soldierly cousin, the old inhabitant of the mountain, means when he says: "Sometimes I think being ill and dying aren't serious at all, just a sort of loafing about and wasting time up here; life is only serious down below."[32] *Placet experiri*, says Settembrini, in the humanistic hope that his disciple will discover, by way of experiment with uncertain meanings, the road to liberal certainty. Yet he himself suggests the dubiousness of all accustomed concepts when he first meets Hans Castorp, the new arrival and "mere guest." "What," the Italian exclaims, "you are but a guest here, like Ulysses in the kingdom of shades? You are bold indeed thus to descend into these depths . . ." "Descend?" asks Castorp, "I have climbed up some five thousand feet." "Upon my honor," replies Settembrini, "it was an illusion. We are deeply fallen creatures."[33] It is a parody of Mephistopheles's *"Versinke denn! Ich könnt' auch sagen: steige: / s'ist einerlei"* . . . from Goethe's *Faust II*, "Well, then, descend! Which is the same as: Rise!"—a motif which, in the form of "the revolving sphere," will dominate the *Joseph*-tetralogy, and is by no means absent from *The Magic Mountain*. In Hans Castorp's musings and dreams there is a constant merging of the ice-covered heights and the sea down below—the sea of his childhood. And soon Hans Castorp, in his deceptively mild and gentle way, begins to experiment with the uncertain levels of being— much to the embarrassment of Settembrini and his humanely experimental philosophy. And why should he? Because he feels he must find out all for himself what life is about. Did I hear you complain about the absence of "one clear and sensible truth"? Well, you remember the passage in which Thomas Mann ironically "smiles down" upon his novel and "claims the right to his own thoughts about the story he is telling." The story, at that point, is about Hans Castorp's deepening infatuation with Clavdia, his desire which in all its sensuality is yet something "exceedingly elusive and tenuous," a mere thought or even dream, "the terrifying and yet infinitely alluring dream of a young man" whose world had hitherto offered him "nothing but a hollow silence as its answer to

[31] Ibid., p. 9.
[32] Ibid., pp. 51-52.
[33] Ibid., pp. 57-58.

certain questions he unconsciously asked." It is here that the narrator breaks in with his own observations. Why has Hans Castorp been taken ill, why has he prolonged his stay on the mountain? It might not have happened, says Thomas Mann, "hazarding a surmise," if Hans Castorp's "simple soul had received from the age in which he lived some even faintly satisfactory suggestion concerning the point and purpose of the business of living." [34] This is one of the many examples of novel and novelist quoting each other, with the quotation deriving additional meaning from its new context. For the "hollow silence" was sounded before, near the beginning, when the reader was given the history of the simple young man, the "rather mediocre" hero. But his laziness was bound up with an insight, vague yet profound, which again brought his mediocrity into question. For a really mediocre young man might well be lazy, but he would hardly notice what Hans Castorp noticed: the absence of any truly compelling reason to exert himself, or, if I may quote you, the absence of "one clear and sensible truth."

*Q:* I remember. The passage in question has become weary with much use. It has been quoted so often as "marking a turning-point" in Thomas Mann's hitherto individualistic "ethos," and as a first sign of his "social awareness." But I think it merely states explicitly what was implied in *Buddenbrooks, Tonio Kröger,* and *Death in Venice.* Thomas Mann always knew that "the age" did not offer to anyone "a compelling reason to exert himself"; on the contrary, the "heroism of the age" he always represented, as you have reminded me, through "the fanatics of accomplishment" prevailing over the sense of senselessness, and making themselves heard above the din of the "hollow silence." I remember that at the presumed turning-point this is put not very differently. Here: "In an age that affords no satisfying answer to the question of 'Why?' and 'To what end?' a man, if he is to achieve something beyond and above the measure of the strictly necessary, must either be possessed of so rare a sense of moral independence and spontaneity that it borders on the heroic, or else of an exceptionally robust vitality. Neither the one nor the other was Hans Castorp's case, and thus he must be considered mediocre after all, although in an entirely respectable sense." [35] Now, is it the "hollow silence" which is the great calamity?

*A:* An age which, bustling with activity, is yet immediately beneath its energetic surface "palpably hopeless, clueless and helpless" [36] is calamitous enough. But this is not what I meant.

*Q:* Is it not? I am surprised. You always mean the age; so much so that I have come to think of you as sighing under the burden of a wicked epoch—Atlas with a global chip on his shoulder.

*A:* Do you believe in the immortality of the soul?

[34] Ibid., pp. 229-230.
[35] Ibid., p. 32.
[36] Ibid.

*Q:* No catechism, please!

*A:* If you don't, you have nothing to lose except your epoch; and if you do believe in it, it is still within your epoch that you win bliss or damnation.

*Q:* You. And I. And he. Persons. The age is an abstraction.

*A:* Far from it. It is what you and I and he and she have to say to one another. And how we say it. And what we have to be silent about. And what we do and cannot do. And what we teach and do not teach our children. *The Magic Mountain*—

*Q:* You meant to say something which you have not yet said.

*A:* Perhaps because you yourself said it a little while ago in your own inspired manner. I think you made the mistake then of blaming *The Magic Mountain,* or its author, for the age that is the theme of the book.

*Q:* So it is the age after all.

*A:* Undeniably so. For what I meant to say was that *The Magic Mountain* is about an age dispossessed of the very sense of definable meaning. Therefore all things are free to acquire whatever meaning they choose. Nothing is what it seems.

*Q:* Put like that, it sounds like a very old predicament: Plato throughout the Ages. Appearance and Reality.

*A:* Your own denunciation of European literature from the Symbolists to Thomas Mann suggests that it is more like Plato at the end of his tether: Appearances and no Reality. Hence any appearance may at any moment behave as if it had the sole claim to reality, saying, as it were: "If anything were real, I should be the *only* real thing." It is a mescalin world: the red of this tulip would be the essence of reality if reality had any essence, and essence any reality. As it is, we are merely the occasional victims of intoxication, whether it is spirit, mescalin, or art.

*Q:* What on earth has this to do with Thomas Mann? It fits perhaps Rimbaud's deranging his senses in order to sense Reality, or van Gogh's taking all the meaning which might conceivably be in the universe, and putting it into the face of a sunflower. But Thomas Mann?

*A:* The magic of *The Magic Mountain* springs from the same procedure, carried out with the latecomer's irony and the moralist's caution. The author says so himself—to the delight, no doubt, of Friedrich Schlegel, who expects a romantic masterpiece not only to do certain things but also to explain what it does: "We describe the commonplace; but the commonplace becomes very strange if it grows from strange soil." [37] The thermometer, for instance, or Hans Castorp's cigar, or the deck chair, or the glass door—they are all utensils of disquieting significance, potential messengers of important communications, and trivial usurpers of Reality.

*Q:* What next?!

*A:* Do you know that you have just named the ultimate principle of our art and learning? Where the sense of truth is as restlessly keen and as

[37] Ibid., p. 231.

profoundly unbelieving as it is with us, "What next?" becomes the master question. Every day our eyes are opened to the possible significance of something new, until they are sightless with being kept open too long. You see that we agree.

*Q:* You see too much in *The Magic Mountain.*

*A:* For instance this: "And the step to the atom proved to be without exaggeration absolutely fatal." [38] Hans Castorp's scientific musings are full of such flashes of anticipation. This, I admit, does not take us away from the epoch and its apocalyptic banalities. Let us avoid them by doing a little literary criticism. I should like you to notice how the motif of the "hollow silence" brings together three seemingly disparate things: Hans Castorp's laziness, his disease, and his love. These are the three causes which keep him on his mountain and, because they are "intertwined," keep you in a bad temper.

*Q:* Talking of intertwining, you forget his learning. For the lazy fellow, feverishly in love, reads with the zeal of a Ph.D. candidate. And still more is intertwined: music and death. Have you noticed that whenever Hans Castorp thinks of death or comes into contact with it, he looks "as if listening to music": "slightly dull, sleepy and pious, his mouth half open, his head inclined towards his shoulder?" [39] You see, I am ready for a little literary criticism. Yes, many things are intertwined. I make it seven, the magic number of *The Magic Mountain.*

*A:* Laziness, learning, disease, love, music, death. Six.

*Q:* Hollow silence. Seven. "Only connect," as E. M. Forster says. But what, I ask again, happens when everything has been connected and intertwined? You still owe me an answer to this question.

*A:* Then we are—let us agree for the time being—on the Magic Mountain, in the midst of that "lucidly handled chaos" where hardly anything remains quite itself, and in that "artistically ordered confusion" of which you are so classically suspicious, whereas Friedrich Schlegel saw in it the great merit of romantic literature. This literature, with its "enchanting symmetry of contradictions, its wonderful and ceaseless oscillations between enthusiasm and iron" seemed to him "in itself an indirect mythology." [40]

*Q:* What does "indirect mythology" mean?

*A:* I suppose it means the kind of mythology that might emerge if Oedipus, endowed with Freudian knowledge about himself, still saw fit to enact his myth; or if Moses, having read Thomas Mann's *The Tables of the Law,* were still to climb Mount Sinai and wait for the voice of God to speak. They would do it "indirectly," by way of knowledge, and perhaps in spite of it—would do it ironically or ambiguously.

*Q:* Would the voice speak?

[38] Ibid., p. 283.
[39] Cf. ibid., pp. 219 and 292.
[40] Schlegel, *op. cit.,* p. 311.

*A:* Friedrich Schlegel seems to think that it would speak more clearly even than before. I doubt it. But we are not on Sinai of the Ten Commandments. We are on the Magic Mountain of the Seven Ambiguities, which, as you can easily see, have their own improper dealings with the Seven Deadly Sins. Let us listen to Hans Castorp and what he has to say to Clavdia Chauchat. By this time he has learned a great deal—not only French but also Novalis. This is what he says: *"Le corps, l'amour, la mort, ces trois ne font qu'un. Car le corps, c'est la maladie et la volupté, et c'est lui qui fait la mort, oui, ils sont charnels, tous deux, l'amour et la mort, et voilà leur terreur et leur grande magie."* [41] Werther, Novalis, Platen, Wagner, *Death in Venice*—obviously, *l'amour et la mort* is the most German of all romantic refrains. Thomas Mann, the perfect Romantic of Schlegel's expectation, has made *The Magic Mountain* both the consummation *and the critique* of the old theme. It is the critique which you mistakenly ignore. And what is true of *l'amour et la mort,* also applies to that other romantic fascination, *la maladie et l'esprit.*

*Q:* This, surely, is a less respectable theme—the phthisical myth of *La Bohème,* tuberculosis and art dwelling together in the untidy attic?

*A:* In German it is of immaculate intellectual respectability. Thomas Mann could hardly have chosen a more suitable scene and background for his "critique of the European mind" than a sanatorium; not only because the European mind is the patient, but because mind and sickness go together within the romantic tradition of German thought. Disease is a mark of spiritual distinction, and Hans Castorp merely voices a Germanic platitude when, innocently provoking Settembrini to his first great aria in praise of the classical *mens sana in corpore sano,* he speaks, romantically, of the emotional dilemma that some patients in the sanatorium cause him by their being so ill and at the same time so stupid. Stupidity and sickness is a combination but little dreamt of in the romantic philosophy. "What I mean is, it's not right, it doesn't fit; I can't get used to the idea. One always thinks of a stupid person as perfectly healthy and ordinary, and of illness making him refined and clever and unusual." [42] This is what Hans Castorp says, and, as he is German, might indeed feel even without having read *Buddenbrooks* or *Death in Venice.* Do you know that Novalis becomes positively a Darwin of natural pathology when he meditates on disease and evolution? Listen to this: "Vegetable diseases are animalizations, animal diseases are rationalizations. Vegetation is an illness of the rocks."

*Q:* From which it would indeed follow that human sickness is an approach to divinity. The transfiguration of German measles.

*A:* A joke worthy of Settembrini at his humanistic worst. Europe had, in actual fact, no need of German romanticism in order to think that

---

[41] *The Magic Mountain,* p. 342.
[42] Ibid., p. 97.

through some denial of his animal health man might draw nearer to the divine. Novalis's romantically Darwinist fragment also says: "All diseases have this in common with sin that they are symptoms of transcendence: heightened sensibilities which strive to become higher powers. Man sinned when he desired to become God." [43] In other words: he fell ill.

*Q:* Goethe seems to have had better reasons than he knew when he identified romanticism with sickness.

*A:* On the other hand, he admired Schopenhauer—at least before the philosopher expressed himself pessimistically about *The Theory of Colors.* And as we can see from *Buddenbrooks* nothing is easier than to give to disease a very definite and very positive function in the philosophy of the Will: it weakens the Will and therefore strengthens Mind. And Nietzsche believed—at least sometimes—that an artist thrives on conditions which "are akin to, and organically connected with, the pathological, so that it seems impossible to be an artist without being sick." [44] Above all, we must not forget that Hans Castorp's education is unthinkable without his becoming ill—in a sense it is even true to say that his education and his illness are identical. Little does Joachim Ziemssen know how much he brings into question when he says to his cousin: "Oh, you with your learning! Getting wiser all the time, with your biology, and your botany . . . ! But we didn't come up here to get wiser. We came to get healthier. . . ." [45] Professor Weigand is, of course, right in saying of Hans Castorp's surrender to disease that "it has the same symbolic significance as Faust's pact with the Devil" [46]—and is almost prophetically right, or even suggestively right: Thomas Mann, much later, literally made his own Faustus sell his soul to the Devil by contracting syphilis and with it a spell of immense artistic creativity. Yet *The Magic Mountain* is also the *critique* of the romantic equation the luxuriant growth of which arouses your classical anger.

*Q:* Because critique is often merely the morally insured way of indulging the criticized fascination.

*A:* In *The Magic Mountain* disease is no longer the sure ally of mind and unfailing promoter of "spirit" which it was in *Buddenbrooks.* Frau Stöhr, the apogee of vulgarity and stupidity, is very ill, and with this *coincidentia oppositorum* confuses Hans Castorp's native philosophy of life. And true enough, before *The Magic Mountain* Thomas Mann could not possibly have allowed a sufferer from tuberculosis to say "cosmic" when she means "cosmetic." "Stupid, healthy life" is what Frau Stöhr would have been. The aesthetic proof that Thomas Mann is ironically in earnest with his critique of the old obsession is the vehement success

[43] Novalis, *op. cit.,* p. 345.
[44] Friedrich Wilhelm Nietzsche, *Gesammelte Werke* (Munich, 1926), XIX, p. 220.
[45] *The Magic Mountain,* p. 385.
[46] Weigand, *op. cit.,* p. 47.

with which the tubercular Frau Stöhr, abandoned to imbecile giggles behind her handkerchief, comes to life in the novel—indeed, crashes into life—while the man who appears to be born for the highly diseased and highly intellectual career of the hitherto typical Thomas Mann hero, Naphta, is a rather pale literary creation, and a little too obvious as the poor sacrificial tiger, that unmistakable co-author of *Meditations of a Nonpolitical Man,* who has to be killed on the altar of a spiritual conversion.

*Q:* True, what a romantic novel! *L'amour et la mort, la maladie et l'esprit* (or let's say "learning"; we are among Germans)—these are four of our seven themes ambiguously intertwined in the novel. It is easy enough to fit the remaining three into the romantic household: the "hollow silence"—or shall we say "the desperate search for meaning"? Then there is laziness—called "dreaminess" in the politer romantic idiom——

*A:* —or the Philosophy of the Good-for-Nothing in Eichendorff's *Aus dem Leben eines Taugenichts,* a book hailed as "purest romanticism" in Thomas Mann's *Meditations.*[47]

*Q:* And, lastly, music. There is the celebrated chapter about Hans Castorp's favorite gramophone records. Are they not all, although only one piece is German, about our great romantic fascinations, above all about death?

*A:* Yes, romantically played, as if by arrangement with Friedrich Schlegel, on a most advanced electrotechnical contraption. The chapter is yet another instance of the extraordinary organization of the novel. Again, it seems to retell the whole story, this time in the guise of meditations on pieces by Verdi, Bizet, Debussy, Gounod, and Schubert.

*Q:* A strange assortment. The selection not of a musician—

*A:* —but of a novelist who calls Hans Castorp's great love by the abiding name of Hippe.

*Q:* Abiding? The love story Thomas Mann tells is about Hans and Clavdia. Hippe is merely a memory. But what's in the name?

*A:* Death. Pribislav Hippe. Pribislav is a Polish name—like Tadzio in *Death in Venice;* and Hippe is the German for scythe, an instrument which belongs to the medieval image of Death. Clavdia Chauchat, to whom Hans Castorp finally "returns the pencil," which in a first boyish feat of passionate daring he borrowed from the admired schoolmate, is Pribislav Hippe's feminine incarnation. She has his "Kirghiz" eyes and husky voice, and her profound identity with him is sealed by Hans Castorp's blood.

*Q:* Blood? I can remember no such drama.

*A:* Can't you? Hans Castorp has been a visitor in the sanatorium for only a few days. One morning he ventures on a first lonely walk into the mountains. As he is lying on a bench by a stream, trying to stop an

---

[47] *Betrachtungen eines Unpolitischen* (Berlin, 1918), pp. 367 ff.

ominous bleeding at the nose (soon he will be a patient himself), his mind is suddenly invaded by the schoolyard scene with Hippe. The memory of it has the articulate presence of a vision. And only after this experience does Hans Castorp know that he is in love with Clavdia Chauchat.[48] But what is more: it *remains* the same love. The sex does not matter. Think of Hans Castorp's sleepy thoughts when, in extreme danger of falling asleep in the snow, he meditates, without any apparent motivation, upon pencils and genders in French: "*Son crayon!* That means her pencil, not his pencil, in this case; you only say *son* because *crayon* is masculine. The rest is just a silly play on words." [49]

*Q:* Do you mean to suggest that Hippe is to Clavdia as Proust's Albert is to Marcel's Albertine?

*A:* There is no need for suggestion. I merely mean what Thomas Mann not only meant but made abundantly clear: that Clavdia is to the young man Hans Castorp what Hippe was to the boy Hans Castorp. In neither case is it a passion from which marriages are made. On the contrary, it is the "unreasonable love" which Hans himself, in a conversation with Clavdia, equates with death and calls by the names of *res bina* and *lapis philosophorum,* names he has learned from Naphta, who, however, added to them "the double-sexed *prima materia.*" [50] And of Hans's passion for Clavdia Thomas Mann says that it was "a risky and homeless variety of the lovesick folly, mingled frost and fire, like a dangerous fever, or the October air in these altitudes. What it lacked was those emotions which could have bridged the two extremes." [51]

*Q:* Which two extremes?

*A:* The two extremes between which romantic love enacts its comedies and tragedies: a definable desire and an indefinably tenuous hope.

*Q:* That she will yield?

*A:* That life will yield.

*Q:* Oh, I remember: yield a meaning rather than a hollow silence. The kind of thing the Flying Dutchman expects of Senta when he sings of the "sinister glow" of which he is not sure whether it is love. No, no, he sings, "it is the longing for salvation." If only he could have it "through such an angel." I daresay you are right, and the sex of the angel makes little difference if it is salvation one wants by it, not children.

*A:* That is why I said the name of Hans Castorp's abiding love was Hippe. Death. Life is always in danger of obliteration when those two extremes touch each other and the yearning for salvation becomes fused with the desire of the senses. Listen: "The term he had set for his holiday had long since passed. He no longer cared. The thought of re-

[48] *The Magic Mountain,* pp. 119 ff.
[49] Ibid., p. 489.
[50] Ibid., pp. 596 and 511.
[51] Ibid., pp. 229-230.

turning home did not even occur to him." Why can't he ask her to return with him? Because of external obstacles? These are merely the feeble external symptoms of the inward state of affairs: Hans Castorp does not want a wife; he wants the adventure in permanence, he wants ecstasy as the daily level of living, he wants the bliss which transcends life and lasts for ever. It is the romantic variation on death and salvation. Hence he does not even wish to know Clavdia—except biblically. He seeks to preserve that yearning of which Thomas Mann says that it is "the product of defective knowledge," the exciting tension which exists "between two beings who know each other only with their eyes," and "the hysteria of suppressed communications and undeliverable messages." You remember these passages?

*Q:* I do.

*A:* You are quite wrong. Forgive the didactic trick. They do not come from *The Magic Mountain*. Of course, they might; but they come from *Death in Venice*.[52] Tadzio or Clavdia—the nature of the passion is the same. You remember how it ends: after Hans Castorp's long and patient waiting—for on the morning following the night of the Mardi gras Clavdia departed—she comes back to the mountain in the company of Mynheer Peeperkorn.

*Q:* Senta with the Flying Dutchman.

*A:* I doubt it. He needs no angel of salvation. She is his mistress, woman to a man. And Hans Castorp's passion all but dissolves. Only now has he outgrown the Hippe love the other name of which is Death. To the slight annoyance of Clavdia he makes friends with Peeperkorn, the big, inarticulate, tottering mystery.

*Q:* Yet another representative. He represents Life.

*A:* Without the slightest detriment to his own. Representative or not, admit that as a literary creation he is a surpassing success. Admit—grudgingly, if you like, but admit—that your outburst of a while ago did grave injustice to Thomas Mann on at least one point: you implied that he divests his creatures of their individual existence for the sake of their typicality. It is untrue. Thomas Mann time and again succeeds in achieving the apparently impossible—namely, in squaring Schlegel's literary circle and giving life to seemingly preconceived ideas as if they were naturally conceived children of the imagination; which is only another way of saying that you are wrong in thinking of his ideas as literally "preconceived." They belong to an imaginative order, not an excogitated scheme. Think of Thomas Buddenbrook, or Tony, or Christian! Think of Mynheer Peeperkorn!

*Q:* Who is a representative of Life.

*A:* If so, then not without irony. True, he is Dionysus, almost as painted by Rubens, and a colonial Dutch coffee planter, as unforgettably de-

---

[52] *Stories of Three Decades* (London, 1936), pp. 415-416.

scribed by Thomas Mann. But his model is not Life but Art: a poet—
Gerhart Hauptmann. Also, he kills himself.

*Q:* Yes, he kills himself. I remember an extraordinary weapon.

*A:* Specially constructed for suicide. It is a mechanical imitation of the
fangs of a poisonous tropical snake, the engineered semblance of a
demon from such a jungle as Gustav Aschenbach saw in his Dionysian
nightmare.

*Q:* An engineered demon—your Friedrich Schlegel would have loved it.
But before you draw your representative conclusions from the fact that
Life kills itself with a most intelligently and scientifically constructed
monster, don't forget that Naphta, unmistakably representative of Mind,
also commits suicide—in an act of sheer supererogation. He had never
been alive.

*A:* And is, like Settembrini, dwarfed by the advent of Peeperkorn. They
cease to exist in his presence.

*Q:* Mind dwarfed by Life.

*A:* Whereas Peeperkorn, in his Dionysian inarticulateness, cuts an excellent figure in the company of his true peers, the mighty mountain
cataract and the eagle in the sky. He acknowledges, almost applauds,
their great performances like someone who intimately knows what an
achievement it is to be a good mountain cataract or a good eagle—a
force of nature. Not to be one is to him the deepest humiliation. This is
why he must kill himself at the approach of impotence. He fears that
the tropical fever from which he suffers will destroy, or has already
destroyed, his power of answering, as he calls it, the demands of feeling.

*Q:* Life without Mind.

*A:* Your prompting is better than your intention. Life without Mind.
Then you also know why Naphta never comes to life: Mind without
Life. Peeperkorn's and Naphta's suicides may be Thomas Mann's way
of killing his oldest pair of irreconcilable opposites. Neither Life nor
Mind can exist the one without the other. "It is impossible to separate
Nature from Mind without destroying both Life and Art." [53] Goethe
knew that. Thomas Mann comes to know it again after much *"Weltent-
zweiung,"* much "sowing of categorical discord," as Hans Castorp calls
the intellectual activities of Naphta and Settembrini—or perhaps of the
author of *Meditations of a Nonpolitical Man.*

*Q:* So it is for the sake of overcoming a "categorical discord" that Dionysus has to be made sick and Priapus impotent? Irony with a vengeance.
*Placet experiri.* Yes, it pleases Thomas Mann to experiment. With what?
With all the aspects of—did you say, truth? Or did you say that all the
aspects together constitute the "hollow silence" of the age? You did speak
of "that lucidly handled chaos" of *The Magic Mountain,* where "hardly
anything remains itself," and spoke of it with a puzzling undertone of
romantic hope.

[53] Johann Wolfgang von Goethe, *Sämmtliche Werke* (Stuttgart, 1902 ff.), XXXV, 319.

*A:* Which reminds me of Novalis's saying that "true anarchy will beget religion, and religion will rise from the chaos of destruction as the glorious founder of a new world." [54] You are wrong in suspecting that I find it easy to share such cataclysmic hopes.

*Q:* But you do seem to see something positive in that chaos where everything is not itself but something else. Laziness is learning. Living is dying. Love is disease. Music is death. Clavdia is Pribislav. No amount of debate will clarify matters so hopelessly tangled.

*A:* No amount of debate. As Hans Castorp watches Settembrini's and Naphta's dialectical battles, this is how Thomas Mann describes his feelings: "The principles and points of view constantly trespassed upon one another's domains, there was no end of inner contradictions; and as it became more and more difficult for Hans Castorp's civilian sense of responsibility to make a choice between opposed positions, or even to keep them neatly apart in his mind, so the temptation grew to plunge headforemost into Naphta's 'morally untidy universe'."—Even in your most biased mood you must at least concede that Thomas Mann is far from being an uncritical supporter of this state of affairs. The passage continues: "It was the universal topsy-turvydom, the world at cross-purposes with itself, the great confusion, which, more than the 'wrong-headedness' of the partner, oppressed the soul of each disputant. And Hans Castorp sensed that this was the true cause of their exasperation." [55] These are not the words of a champion of chaos.

*Q:* The true cause of my exasperation is the virtuoso literary manner with which Thomas Mann self-consciously creates a "significant" work of art out of the apparently desperate uncertainty concerning the significance of anything. I understand that it is the vaguely sensed meaninglessness of his life which, in the novel, sends Hans Castorp to the Magic Mountain and keeps him there for seven years. This meaninglessness colors every one of his experiences, even his love. But where everything is colored by meaninglessness, of what can anything be truly significant? If I let you go on, you will say in a minute what every single interpreter of *The Magic Mountain* has said: that, among other things, it is a "symbolic novel." And as the book—how did Friedrich Schlegel put it?—"judges itself," *The Magic Mountain* probably says so itself.

*A:* It does. You may be thinking of Naphta's description of the initiation rites to which a novice is subjected if he wishes fully to enter the community of Freemasons. "Magic pedagogy," "alchemist levitation," "transsubstantiation," "hermetics," and finally the tomb, "the place of corruption" which is also "the receptacle wherein the material is prepared for its final transformation and purification"—these are the terms Naphta uses when he tells Hans Castorp of the mysteries of the mystery religion. It is clear, I think, that they stand at the same time for the

[54] Novalis, *op. cit.*, p. 738.
[55] *The Magic Mountain*, p. 468.

education young Castorp receives as the hero of the *Bildungsroman*. And
then again: "The way of the mysteries and of the purification . . . leads
through the fear of death and the sphere of corruption; and the appren-
tice, the neophyte, is the spirit of youth in person, guided by shrouded
figures who are nothing but the shadows of the mystery." [56] All this,
I am sure, is meant to reflect upon the novel itself.

*Q:* And the most shadowy of the shadows is no doubt Herr Naphta himself, the Nietzschean Jesuit and full-time mouthpiece. Yet I expect that
what is meant is the whole shrouded party of Hans Castorp's educators:
Settembrini, Behrens, Madame Chauchat, Mynheer Peeperkorn. If these
are the shadows of the mystery, pray you, what precisely is the mystery?

*A:* You don't mean "precisely," do you? Anything may be precise except a mystery. May I remind you of Thomas Mann's very Goethean
definition of "symbolic significance"? The occasion is Hans Castorp's
growing enchantment with Schubert's song of the linden tree, and his
ever clearer realization of its "meaning." The song acquires great significance for him, and Thomas Mann asks: "In what does the significance
of a significant subject lie? In the fact that it points beyond itself, that
it is the expression and representation of something general, something
universal, of a whole world of thought and feeling. . . ." [57] There is
only one "precise" way of describing a mystery, or suggesting a "whole
world of thought and feeling": to find their concrete symbols. The passages I have just read out to you are, I think, disguised declarations by
the novelist concerning the intention of his novel. Yes, he meant to
write a symbolic novel.

*Q:* You see! I am asking you how anybody can arrive at anything significant in a meaningless world, and you answer: by writing a symbolic
novel. Symbolic of what?

*A:* And what if I said: symbolic of the difficulty of writing a novel,
significant of the vital irony of an artist who produces works of art
against, and almost from, the ubiquitous suggestion that it is meaningless to produce works of art?

*Q:* It would not be an answer. It would be a joke.

*A:* You were polite enough not to laugh when a little while ago I spoke
of the *ne plus ultra* of irony in Thomas Mann's literary art from *The
Magic Mountain* onward. I really meant the same thing. However, it
would be a joke if I meant anything less than a work of art. As I mean
a work of art, it is serious. For a work of art is the vindication of meaning.

*Q:* Even if it is symbolic of meaninglessness?

*A:* If it is a work of art, it will be in some sense symbolic. If it is symbolic, it can only be symbolic of meaning—although it may say: "The
world is meaningless."

---

[56] Ibid., pp. 511-512.
[57] Ibid., p. 651.

*Q:* We are ourselves approaching the grand confusion, the *guazzabuglio* of Messrs. Naphta and Settembrini. I shall soon be as speechless as young Castorp is on those occasions.

*A:* And you will *tell* me that you are. "I am speechless," your speech will say. And it will not be unlike a work of art saying: "Everything is meaningless." If it were quite true, it could not be said—not by a work of art. The worst is not, so long as we can say, "This is the worst." There is reason for rejoicing as long as tragedies can be written. The preserved form of a piece of literature gives the marginal lie to the expressed conviction that everything is in a state of dissolution. It is an exceedingly ironical situation—a situation which has found in *The Magic Mountain* its appropriately ironical literary shape. Never before has the falling apart of all things been treated with so intensely conscious an artistic determination to hold them together.

*Q:* By the arrangement of words on a page?

*A:* Yes. And therefore as facts of the mind. And therefore as a human reality. If this were not the case, literature would not be worth the paper it is written on. The story of *The Magic Mountain* is, as it were, told twice: once as a series of incidents and experiences, and then again as a series of intimations conveyed through the very shape of the work. The arrangement between the two is not smoothly harmonious, but ironical and contrapuntal, like the two parts, the one Apolline, the other Dionysian, of the dream Hans Castorp has in the snow, the "dream poem of humanity" he composes on the verge of death, which teaches him the true state and status of *Homo Dei,* the lord of all contradictions, "between mystic community and windy individualism." [58] It would be a bad and unconvincing dream had it to rely for its authenticity only on the story told. Its proof is in the telling.

*Q:* You mean in the form, not in the content? I understand. The form, you mean, tells a story of its own, a story which stands in a contrapuntal relationship to the series of incidents?

*A:* Yes; and as a *Bildungsroman* it stands in the same ironical relationship to the rules of the genre. Wilhelm Meister, the model hero of such a novel, begins as an *Originalgenie* and ends as a useful member of society. Hans Castorp begins as a useful member of society and ends approaching the state of being an *Originalgenie.*

*Q:* Yet he eventually leaves the Magic Mountain to do his duty by his country.

*A:* Which happens to be about to destroy itself in war; and most probably will destroy its citizen Castorp. We catch a last glimpse of him amid the shrapnel of a battlefield in Flanders.

*Q:* And if he survives?

*A:* If you insist on playing this literary parlor game, my guess is that he would write a novel.

[58] Ibid., pp. 490 ff.

*Q:* I agree. With all that hermetic education in him, he cannot possibly go back to being a shipbuilding engineer in Hamburg. So he will be a writer and write a novel—most probably *The Magic Mountain*. The Eternal Recurrence—

*A:* —will not take place. For here we end our conversation.

*Q:* It is an unsatisfactory ending—a little *too* ironical. You appear to be saying two things. Firstly, that it is the aim of an education for life to produce writers of fiction; and secondly, that to acquire true identity means to lose one's identity. For you have previously told us that, according to Thomas Mann, the loss of identity is the professional hazard of literary men.

*A:* "Literature" and "nonidentity" are, in this case, the aesthetic incognito which a man, incapable of accepting a meaningless existence, chooses in a world which insists upon living as if life were meaningless. Kierkegaard meant something similar when he defined irony as the incognito of the moralist.

*Q:* Why has Kierkegaard's moralist got to use an incognito?

*A:* "Because he knows that his manner of existing inwardly cannot be expressed in terms of the world." [59] Such is our world that sense and meaning have to be disguised—as irony, or as literature, or as both come together: for instance in *The Magic Mountain*.

[59] Sören Kierkegaard, *Gesammelte Werke* (Jena, 1922), VII, p. 176.

# Joseph and His Brothers:
# A Comedy in Four Parts

*by Mark Van Doren*

To say that Mann's *Joseph and His Brothers* is primarily a comic work is to say no more than the author himself said in his foreword to the new edition of 1948. He called it then "a humorous song of mankind," an "epic undertaking" in the spirit of Goethe rather than of Wagner, a narrative written "playfully," with many "pleasantries" in it which he hoped would "cheer those who come after us," though with "pathos" in it, too, which at some later time might still be touching. He spoke of it, that is to say, as a comic poem of vast proportions. And so it is. Its "seventy thousand calmly flowing lines"—someone else might say its twelve hundred continuously intelligent pages—make up a modern masterpiece with which there are few things to be compared, though Marcel Proust's *Remembrance of Things Past* is surely one of those. That equally vast work depends equally with *Joseph and His Brothers* upon our sense of time; or, if you prefer, upon our sense of eternity; or, if you insist, upon our sense of the present moment. For when we have succeeded in giving ourselves to the present moment we are as near to eternity as we shall ever get. Eternity is not a lot of time; it is no time at all, and so is this moment that passes before we know it has come—except that we do know some moments when they come, and it is these and only these from which we learn.

The comic genius loves to speculate about such matters. It has not always done so as explicitly as in the two outstanding cases of Proust and Mann; but then ours is an explicit age which struggles to be conscious of everything, so that we are not surprised when Mann discusses at length a number of things that Chaucer, say, could take for granted. The comic genius has never been more alive than it was in Chaucer, but it does not appear that he thought he needed a theory of time, or at any rate a statable one which in effect would constitute his subject matter. Neither of course does Mann think simply that; his subject mat-

*"Joseph and His Brothers:* A Comedy in Four Parts." From *The Happy Critic* by Mark Van Doren. Copyright © 1961 by Mark Van Doren. Reprinted by permission of the author, Hill and Wang, Inc., and Nannine Joseph.

ter after all is never anything but Joseph and his father and his brothers, and the wonderful world of Egypt where he spent his most brilliant years, just as in *The Magic Mountain,* Mann's other masterpiece which deals with time, the subject matter is whatever the persons of the story talk about when their excellent brains catch fire in the cold solitude of an Alpine sanatarium. Yet it is true that Mann must think out loud as he writes, and what he thinks about is the bottomless well of time which threatens, if looked into deeply enough, to obscure every individual character and countenance—even those of Joseph himself—and to silence every event so that we who come long after may have doubts that it occurred, or in any case that it made much noise in the universe it could not manage at the end to alter. The famous prelude to the work, called Descent into Hell, might have been called instead Descent into Time. The genius of story can never dispense with time, but the genius of comic story stands in a peculiar relation to that commodity. It both believes in it and it does not. Tragedy believes furiously, even obsessively, in time; time always presses there, leaving the hero unfree to act in the wise way he might if he had the leisure. Comedy, on the other hand, relaxes and disperses time; spreads it out or draws it thin so that it looks a little like eternity. It is not eternity, and cannot ever be; but enough of it will establish the perspective that comedy likes and indeed must have. Only, given the maximum perspective, movement comes to a stop and men are reduced to resembling one another so closely, even so absurdly, that merely man is left; or, to put it abstractly, human nature.

Perhaps it was human nature that Mann lived with during the sixteen dreadful years, between 1926 and 1942, when he was composing *Joseph and His Brothers.* One could also say that he lived with Joseph, the individual upon whose image he had settled. But the image enlarged while he studied it, as did the image of every other person in the tale, so that at last he had before him something like the whole spectacle which human life provides when nothing operates to distort it. In the Germany of these years it was outrageously distorted, and there were those who said it would never regain its ancient shape. Here, though, was that very shape; and Mann has testified to the satisfaction he derived from contemplating its breadth and depth. "It was my refuge, my comfort, my home," he says, "my symbol of steadfastness, the guarantee of my perseverance in the tempestuous change of things."

Yet he would have done substantially as he did in any case. Mann's genius was entirely comic; which is to say that it was contemplative, discursive, skeptical, tender, mocking, and loving all at once. It was contemplative because it desired the oldest and the widest view of things, somewhat as they are, supposing man can know this, in their eternal aspect. It was discursive because man's mind is most at home in conversation, in endless talk that considers, measures, analogizes, and compares. No reader of Mann needs to be told how irresistibly he was drawn to language, and how much pleasure he took in imitating the various dialects of thought. The comic genius is among other things a mimic; so in America, where Mann wrote the fourth section of his epic, it was natural for him not merely to see a parallel between Joseph the Provider and Roosevelt the prophet of abundance, but also to adopt so many idioms of the time and place as to incur the charge that he no longer wrote in German, though of course he did, to the enrichment of that none too lively language. *The Magic Mountain,* like any pure comedy, tends to be all conversation; and if this is not quite true of the Joseph books, it is nevertheless true that what its people say to one another, and what Mann says about them as he converses with his reader, can be understood as carrying most of the burden. Nor can one miss the fact that Joseph's own gift, his distinguishing art, is the wonderful way he has with words, so that he entrances all who come within the sound of his voice or—the same thing—the reach of his mind. When he read aloud to Potiphar it was as if he were creating a new beauty in the text. The intellect of any person is perhaps most swiftly revealed by the way he reads a page he has never seen before. Potiphar knew the pages by heart, but never had they sounded like this. "Joseph read . . . capitally," we hear; "was fluent, exact, unaffected, moderately dramatic, with such natural command of words that the most involved literary style had a happy conversational ease. Literally he read himself into the heart of the listener; and when we seek to understand his swift rise in the Egyptian's favor we must by no means leave out of account these reading hours." He knew his way among intricate phrases as Hamlet, speaking to the players, knew his; no mind, no tongue, has ever been more nimble than that. But this was Hamlet in his comic aspect: his original aspect, which tragedy, as Ophelia divines, has already overwhelmed and lamentably deformed.

The genius of Mann is skeptical in the finest sense of an often misapprehended term. It was not that he believed nothing; he believed everything; he liked ideas, and could live with all of them at once. No sooner did one start up in his brain than another came to reinforce, illuminate, or check it. This was why he could turn so soon from tenderness to pathos, and why he could mock the very man he loved the most. These transformations of his mood will bewilder anyone who does not comprehend how serious at last the comic spirit is. Nothing in man is more serious than his sense of humor; it is the sign that he wants all the truth, and sees more sides of it than can be soberly and systematically stated; it is the sign, furthermore, that he can remember one idea even while he entertains another, and that he can live with contradiction. It is the reason at any rate that we cannot take seriously one whose mind and heart have never been known to smile. The gods do not weep; they smile. Eternity is something like the sun.

The comic spirit has a perfect sense of time, as of a good comedian we say that he has perfect timing. The comic spirit knows that time both does and does not exist; it can look like sheer illusion, though the illusion is one in which comedy will luxuriously live. Comedy takes its time, as truth and history do. The good storyteller is never in a hurry, nor do we want him to be; his digressions, his elaborations, his hesitations, his gestures are in the end more interesting than the action he unfolds; we do not, in fact, want him to reach the end, for then we shall no longer hear his voice or relish with him the way he looks at life, of which the story at hand is but one illustration. While it was being told it amply sufficed our hunger for understanding; it replaced all other stories; was, in effect, story itself, was poetry in the flesh. It treated of only a few people and things, and it treated them in some present moment which absorbed us so that we forgot the rest of time. Yet it had also something to do with the rest of time, which hung about it like a haze, beautifying and validating its apparently random, its artfully accidental details. "The form of timelessness," says Mann, "is the here and now." He can say this because he knows how to see Joseph and Jacob as men who lived both long ago and now. They lived so long ago that if time were altogether and simply real they would have no identity today; their figures, their faces, would be woefully indistinct, and the thoughts they had would be mere puffs of desert dust. But time is not that real; Joseph and Jacob can exist not only again but yet; because they existed so intensely in their moment they live always, in all moments. These things are forever happening. History, with a monotony which comedy loves rather than deplores, repeats itself ad infinitum. All thoughts, all things, all men are simultaneously true, as somehow in God's mind they are. The mind of comedy is not that great, but it is the greatest possession of the one creature made in God's image —unless, as Mann playfully suggests, man was the maker of God: in the person of Abram was none other than His father. But in that case it would still be true that the greatest thing in man is his power to know and remember many things at once; to master time; to be in a word the receptacle of the comic spirit.

Any story that is worth telling can be told either briefly or at length. Ideally these alternatives are absolute: the teller takes no time at all, or else he takes an infinite amount of it. Since neither of those miracles is possible, the narrative artist must be content with a choice between abridgement and amplitude. Mann certainly did not abridge the story of Joseph. His work is forty-five times as long as the section of *Genesis* which deals with the hero alone, and fifteen times as long as the section which covers in addition, as Mann himself does, the careers of Abraham, Isaac, and Jacob. This is amplitude indeed, and there have been those who wondered whether Mann did not achieve too much of it for any earthly purpose. The answer ought to be clear. His purpose was comic, and comedy takes its time. It insists upon leisure, of which it is confident that there cannot be too much. Also it is addicted to talk, its own and others', and entertains itself with as much of that as the subject suggests, or as we shall listen to. The subject of Joseph suggested everything to Mann; nothing he knew or thought was alien to it, and no idea was irrelevant. So for sixteen years, with major and minor interruptions, he happily spun his web until it draped like a silken veil the whole figure of the world.

Even *Genesis* had lingered over the story as it did not in the cases of Abraham, Isaac, and Jacob. There was something special about Joseph even then and there; he had nothing of the patriarch about him, and in after times his name dropped out of the *Bible*. God appeared to Moses as the God of three great men, not four. Joseph had saved the race in Egypt, but he was never to be honored as one of its founders. He was not simple enough for that. Neither in a sense was Jacob, yet Jacob's name lived on as one of the never to be forgotten three. Jacob for one thing did not become an Egyptian; he never became anything but what he was, so that when Joseph met him in the Land of Goshen there was a fantastic difference between the two figures: the younger one brilliant with linen and gold, the older one as plain as the wagon seat on which he had ridden all the way from Israel, through dust and among the remnant of his herds. It was not easy for the father to recognize his son in the splendid prince he saw step out of a chariot; nor, when the time came to talk, did he hesitate to say some things that may have sounded bitter to the young man whose mind was full of the glittering deeds he knew he had done.

> "God has . . . given you back, but yet not quite, for He has kept you too . . . He has elevated and rejected you both in one, I say it in your ear, beloved child, and you are wise enough to be able to hear it. He has raised you above your brothers just as in your dream—but He has raised you in a worldly way, not in the sense of salvation and the inheritance of the blessing . . . You are blessed, my dear one, . . . blessed with blitheness and with destiny, with wit and with dreams. Still, it is a worldly blessing, not a spiritual one. . . . Through you salvation is not to reach the peoples and the leadership is denied you. . . . You are not like the fathers, my child, for you are no spiritual prince, but a worldly one."

This is Mann writing, not the author of *Genesis,* but it is what the whole *Bible* means in spite of its silence on the subject. The *Bible* is silent like the patriarchs; Mann, like Joseph, is eloquent as civilization and comedy are eloquent. He is even loquacious, for there is nothing he would rather do than put into words what simple men suppose cannot be said, or for that matter has no need to be said.

There can be no comedy about patriarchs. They come before civilization is in flower, and comedy is the finest of the flowers. They are the foundation, for the most part hidden from sight; it is the cornice, the gables, and the roof. Or, to change the figure once again, they are the blood and it is the complexion. Mann's Joseph is all grace, all light, all intellect at its highest. He can do anything except be the silent, tremendous man each one of his ancestors was. In Egypt he remembers the faith of his fathers, and characteristically gives a lucid account of it whenever asked. But it is not a part of him; it is not in his bones as it is in the bones of Jacob. If anything he understands it too perfectly; it is one of the works of art he knows like a connoisseur; it is outside of him, and he can leave it there when he likes. He leaves it there during his sundry flirtations with other faiths and other deities: Tammuz, Ashtaroth, and Osiris. What Mann calls "the soul's love affair with matter" fascinates him if anything too much. There was a youthful moment when he almost worshipped the Moon and subscribed to its cult. "As a cult," says Mann, "it was vague, confused, and prone to degenerate—calculated to alarm the careful father—but just on that ground intoxicating, because mental and physical emotions were therein so enchantingly mixed." Egypt, the Kingdom of the Dead and therefore the embodiment of all that Jacob had taught him to abhor, was not visited by Joseph voluntarily; Jacob's other sons, the red-eyed sons of Leah, sent him there; but once there he again became the connoisseur of customs, in this case exquisite ones which the artist in him could not but admire. He did no more than admire and master this new way of life; he remained faithful to his fathers, and said so often enough; yet none of his fathers could have done what he did—could have become more Egyptian than any son of Egypt, and worn its manners like so many jewels. It is impossible to imagine Isaac, for example, flattering as Joseph did the guide who was about to take him in to his first audience with Pharaoh. Isaac would never have been there in the first place; but supposing that he was, and supposing that the guide asked him whether he knew how to salute the god, it could never have occurred to him to smile and say: "I wish I did not, for it would be pleasant to learn it of you." This was flattery, and it was mockery too; it came from the top of Joseph's mind, that touched the stars.

Joseph is material for comedy precisely because he is civilized. Both comedy and tragedy depend on civilization for their power. The stories of the patriarchs belong perhaps in neither category; they are too primitive, possibly they are too important, to be classified at all. They simply exist and tell themselves, as seeds germinate in the ground. The first fathers were to be sure the heroes of great stories; they were this side of God in whose life there are no events; but they were nowhere near as far away from absolute simplicity as Joseph was. Joseph was secular; he could believe anything and everything; he was advanced; he was free; and his only illusion was that he had none. He had several concerning himself, the chief of these being that there was no real difference between him and Jacob. Even at the end he was not too certain as to what the

difference was that Jacob had tried his best to put into words. This
supremely intelligent man did not, that is to say, know everything. And
just there is the point at which he becomes available for comic treatment. The stupid person who knows nothing is of no interest to the
comic spirit. The brilliant person who nevertheless is blind to something
as visible as the ground before his feet—he is the one upon whom wit
delights to sharpen its knives. And so with Joseph in Mann's case. Loving his hero as he loved himself, Mann still could mock him because he
was not God. And in the same breath he could adore him. He lavished
upon him all the understanding that he had, all the elaboration of
which his wit was so abundantly capable. His marvelous reconstructions
of the Egyptian court, intricate perhaps beyond any imagination but his,
and ornate as only he could delicately achieve ornateness—witness for
example the entrance of Nefertiti, "with swaying tread, faintly smiling,
her eyes cast down, the long, lovely neck thrust anxiously out: the bearer
of the seed of the sun"—still do not match the work he did inside of
Joseph's mind, where recess upon recess opens as it were into the very
caverns of genius. And this work is endless; it fills a fearsome multitude
of pages; nor was any of it done in *Genesis*. It is all Mann, all modern,
and all comedy.

Sometimes, to be sure, Mann wonders to himself about his method, and
lets us know that he does so. "There is too much abridgement and con-
densation about this," he suddenly remarks of the Biblical narrative
where it puts in two sentences the decision of Pharaoh to set Joseph over
all Egypt; "it is too dry, it is a drawn and salted and embalmed remnant
of the truth, not truth's living lineaments." Within a few lines, however, he has remembered the contrary principle. "Of course," he continues,

> "there is really nothing against condensation in itself. In the long run
> it is quite impossible to narrate life just as it flows. What would it lead
> to? Into the infinite. It would be beyond human powers. Whoever got such
> an idea fixed in his head would not only never finish, he would be suffo-
> cated at the outset. Entangled in a web of desultory exactitude, a madness
> of detail. No, excision must play its part at the beautiful feast of narra-
> tion and recreation; it has an important and indispensable role. Here,
> then, the art will be judiciously practiced, to the end of getting finally
> quit of a preoccupation which, though after all it has a distant kinship
> with the attempt to drink the sea dry, must not be driven to the extreme
> and utter folly of actually and literally doing so."

Yet three hundred pages before this he had burst out in the same way,
and in the same way had taken his words back. The question then was
how Potiphar's wife had offered herself to Joseph. "To tell the truth,"
exclaimed Mann on that occasion,

"I am horrified at the briefness and curtness of the original account, which does so little justice to life's bitter circumstantiality. Seldom have I felt more acutely the harm done to truth by abbreviation and compression. Yet let no one think that I am deaf to the reproach—whether expressed or, out of politeness, not expressed—which hangs over my account, my entire exposition: to the effect that the laconic terseness of the original text cannot be surpassed, and that my whole enterprise, which is already of such long continuance, is so much labor lost. But since when, may I ask, does a commentator set himself up in competition with his text? And besides, is there not as much dignity and importance attached to the discussion of the 'how' as to the transmission of the 'what'? Let us remind ourselves once again that before the story was first told, it had to tell itself —with an exactitude of which life alone is master, and to attain which a narrator has no hope or prospect at all. He can only approach it by serving the 'how' of life more faithfully than the lapidary spirit of the 'what' condescended to do. But if ever the fidelity of a commentator can justify itself, then surely it does in the story of Potiphar's wife and of just what, according to the tradition, she is supposed to have said."

Doubtless in such passages Mann protests too much, and in doing so loses his good humor. The comic spirit cannot afford to worry about its right to exist. And most of the time in Mann it does not commit that fault. Most of the time it is vigorous and blithe, and goes about its business with its head high in the air. Nor does it call that business commentary. It calls it story, and lets us add that it is comedy, too.

Mann's method of amplification is simple in one sense: it is the method of filling in, of stuffing interstices with matter he thinks belongs there. The Biblical narrative is famously bald; it leaves almost everything to the imagination, after of course giving the imagination great work to do. Mann cannot be said to desire that nothing be left for his own reader to imagine; he, too, gives him work, and it can be a life's work if one chooses to do it; but the reader in this case has ideas to contemplate rather than actions to complete. And the ideas are Mann's. Claiming to know in full detail what the people of the ancient tale said to one another in this crisis or that, he supplies conversations which themselves are food for the soul, so delicate and deep they are. The colloquies between Jacob and his favorite son explore the entire field of filial and paternal feeling. What Pharaoh said to Joseph tells us more about Egypt than the archaeologists can. And what Potiphar's wife confessed to him in her third-year agony of love is the climax of a whole fine novel of which she has been the distinguished heroine—though in Mann's opinion Joseph has not been its distinguished hero. He gives us that opinion—it has to do with Joseph's vanity—just as he always lays bare for us the process of his own thought. We are continuously in his confidence; the book could in fact be described as a conversation between the author and the reader, or rather as a monologue which the reader is expected to overhear. To that extent it *is* a commentary.

But the method is not as simple as all that. Sometimes it involves the addition of circumstances and deeds, the outright invention of narrative details, none of which we could have worked out for ourselves unless our talent and our scholarship had been identical with Mann's. And the richest number of these is to be found in the Potiphar section, which Mann himself called "the artistic zenith of the work." Potiphar's household becomes a fascinating world all by itself. The dwarves, the parents of the master, the eunuch master and his tragic wife—these are the central figures, and each one of them is a triumph of creation, yet they are surrounded by others still, in a busy and beautiful house which for the time being absorbs our entire attention. And none of this is in the *Bible*. Perhaps it did not need to be, but we do not think of that; and even if we did we would find nothing that contradicted or violated the primitive fable. It is simply that Mann has moved us up close enough for us to be able to see what happened in this household day by day— it may be minute by minute—during the three years it was a part of human history. There is the day, for instance, of the ladies' party, when Potiphar's wife, incapable any longer of bearing alone the crushing burden of her love for Joseph, invites her friends to come and eat oranges with her. Each of them is given a little, sharp knife with which to open the precious fruit; each starts to do so at the moment when Joseph appears to pour the wine; and down each snow-white wrist runs a stream of crimson blood. For so much beauty, so suddenly entering the hall, has captured each lady's eyes, so that her knife knows not where it should cut. And this was exactly as Mut had planned it when she told Joseph he must come in among them at such and such a moment. It is an unforgettable moment; nor did Mann need to invent it. His scholarship, which surely was enormous, found it for him in the *Koran*, in seventeen Persian poems, and in "countless renderings by pencil and brush." Those are the sources he reveals to us; but if we have access to none of them we can go to Louis Ginzberg's *Legends of the Jews* for a version graphic enough.

Not that Mann inserts the episode of the ladies' party with a flourish of narrative trumpets or with any brave show of art. Here also he is true to the comic tradition of storytelling, which plays down the narrative art. It says that history is more interesting than fiction; so history is what it pretends to write. Chaucer has his "author" whom he merely follows; Cervantes has his Arabian biographer whom he merely translates. The comic artist will not admit that he has invented anything; the truth is enough for him—Mann says "the facts"—and all truth is as old as the hills anyway; there can be no new stories, just as there can be nothing new under the sun; see the *Bible* as to that. Every man knows everything; except of course that some men forget what they know, or do not wholly realize it, and so commit the only sin that comedy is designed to deal with, namely, folly. Folly is not a fatal sin, though there are those who unaccountably grow fond of it in themselves; therefore it either can be cured or can be rendered harmless as a spectacle at which we wiser ones may smile. It is rendered harmless by understanding: the fool's understanding at last, or if this is not to be expected, then ours; and probably, too, that of several other persons in the story. The essence of comedy is its love of understanding. That is why it goes in so heavily for talk—or rather, we hope, lightly: deliciously and lightly. The dialectic of comedy may seem queer, but it is dialectic nevertheless; and they are right who credit Plato with having perfected both philosophy and comedy in his matchless dialogues. Now it would be saying too much, if not too little, to say that the essence of tragedy is misunderstanding. The errors of tragic heroes are too vast to be so trivially dismissed. Yet they do misunderstand their situations and themselves; and in the rush of events which their own blindness accelerates they do dreadful things which with more time and light they would never have done. Tragedies are dark and short; more light, more time, more talk would make literally all the difference in the world; but those blessings are not available. Whereas they are the very stuff of comedy, which like John Tanner keeps on talking though the heavens fall. But in fact they do not fall. In comedy there is neither the midnight of utter confusion nor the sudden blaze of a belated dawn. In comedy the hour is always noon.

And nothing much happens then. The action of any comedy is less interesting—certainly less memorable—than the discussions it contains. A tragedy whose plot cannot be remembered in the strict order of its events is no tragedy at all; the events create their own order, from which there is no escape, or else they have no meaning for the mind. This must have been what Aristotle meant when he said the soul of a tragedy was its plot; the action was everything. In comedy there is action too, or we should have no story; but it is most interesting for what can be said about it before and after it is done. Which throws still further light upon the fact that comic poets underplay their plots and take no responsibility for them in the first place. By the same token they are indifferent to dramatic or narrative effects; they ignore the conventional devices for securing such effects; they lean over backwards to avoid melodrama, which to be sure they may approach as a possibility, but which they would rather parody than embrace.

So Mann in his great comedy refuses to make what tragedy would make, and what the *Bible* did make, out of certain recognition scenes. The recognition scene is essential to tragedy, which lives on such bursts of feeling as it perfectly provides. There was an opportunity for Mann to contrive a meeting between Joseph and Mut-em-enet after Joseph came home from prison. But he discusses the possibility only to reject it. Romancers, he says, have tried their hands at such a scene, and the result is "Persian musk," is "attar of roses," which is to say, sweet nonsense.

For one thing "it has nothing to do with the facts." For another, their story was done. And even the recognition scenes which he is bound to accept because they come down to him and are a part of his duty—those between Joseph and his brothers at the climax and between Jacob and Joseph at the very end—he deliberately muffs, and here and there even mocks. Of course they are moving; but Mann does not want them to break our hearts, and he knows how to keep them from doing so. He wraps them in talk; the principals murmur to each other even while they weep; dialectic still holds the center of the stage. And as for the weeping, what would a tragic poet have to say of one who in the immortal scene between Joseph and his brothers transmogrifies the Biblical "he wept aloud" into: "His nose began to prickle inside, he sniffed a little, and his eyes all at once ran over"? Granted, on a later page—much later, for the scene is long—we are told that "glittering tears ran down his cheeks." This to be sure is more like drama; yet even there we are forced to suspect that the tears of Joseph *would* glitter, since everything about him shines. Nor at the moment when the great scene was preparing had the author kept us in suspense as to whether it would happen. The comic artist cares nothing for suspense, which indeed is never as indispensable to narrative as commonly it is thought to be. It is at best a second-rate device for generating interest where no interest naturally exists. At least this is true if it consists of no more than the artificial withholding from us of some information we need for understanding and would normally have. When it consists of telling us that a given thing will happen but letting us wait to see how it happens, and precisely when, it is a powerful because a natural narrative tool. And it is thus that Mann uses it, and confides to us that he does. "Joseph's suspense was great," he writes on one occasion; "on this point depended his future relations with the brothers. We, of course, are in no suspense: we know all the phases of the story by heart. . . . So in our wisdom we may smile at him." Such, remarks Mann on an earlier occasion, is the advantage of having an old story to retell. "If I were here a mere inventor of tales, what I have to tell would certainly expose me to the reproach of drawing too long a bow, and presuming far too much upon a credulity which after all has its limits. Luckily, such is not my role. I rest upon the traditional facts, which are not less sound because some of them ring as though they were newly minted. Thus I am in a position to state what I have to tell in an assured and tranquil tone that in the face of all doubts and reproaches carries conviction." A tragic poet who stopped his story to address his audience thus would instantly break his spell and lose all power to convince. For the comic poet there is no spell; or if there is one and its name is truth, it is just in this offhand way that he invokes it.

The truth about Joseph is of course a complicated thing which it is the main business of the book to convey. Mann's hero is perhaps not different from the one we meet in *Genesis,* nor is his father altered from the ancient Jacob; nor for that matter is their relation to each other built here upon ground which the original text did not at least lay out. But Mann's refinements are as many as they are marvelous. The brilliance and beauty of Joseph have few parallels in the fiction of the world. And the vanity. The problem was to make the vanity palatable, and it was solved by suggesting, not indeed in so many words, that it was like the vanity of a golden mirror which can no more help being what it is than a bright person can help being bright. Joseph might have bitten off his tongue, as Potiphar's poor wife all but did; yet he did not; he kept on saying with it the most fascinating and impudent things; and we are as glad of this as Jacob was, or Benjamin, or even the ten sullen half-brothers who in spite of themselves adored the speaker of them, too, at the same time that they wanted to kill him, or at least to remove him from their sight forever. It was Jacob, however, who resisted Joseph least; which is a mild way of saying that he committed the sin of idolatry by elevating him to the rank of favorite son, somewhat as he had committed that same sin by loving Rachel for herself and not in God. Mann is willing to say that the doting father was the chief source of his son's misery, if misery it was. Perhaps it was never that; for the pits into which this youth was cast, first in the desert and then in Egypt, yielded in every case an experience he could dramatize; and there was no exercise he loved more. In no crisis of his life did he die so that he might be reborn. He does not look to us at the end like one of those truly great men of whom it can be said, not that they have lived a lot but that they have died a lot—have been, we sometimes say, in hell. No, in some amazing way he has not been touched by the bonfires he walked through. For one thing, though he would deny this, he has never ceased to assume that others must love him more than they love themselves. The assumption had been wrong both in the case of his brothers and in that of Mut-em-enet, and now he knows that it was wrong. Yet he has not changed in the secret depths of his heart where he still knows that he is like nobody else. "Have you ever heard the voice of self-denying love?" Jacob asks him this in the Land of Goshen, and the question answers itself. When on the last page of the book Joseph insists to his brothers that they are to forgive him, not he to forgive them, he speaks in the character he has enjoyed from the beginning. "If it is a question of pardon between us human beings, then it is I myself must beg for it, for you had perforce to be cast in the villain's part so that things might turn out as they did." The hero's part had been so naturally his that he still needs no rehearsing in it.

Not that we love him less because all this is true. The triumph of Mann is that we love on every page the hero he himself loves this side of idolatry. Idolatry in Mann would have destroyed his comedy, since comedy admits no gods that are made of earth. That he resisted the sin, tempted though he surely was, is a triumph more stupendous still. The sign of his resistance is the impression of Joseph he leaves with us at last: the impression of one whose understanding is so fine that the light in his mind almost puts out the stars—yet not those stars at which his great-grandfather Abraham, that wonderful old man, stared without speaking a single word. "One can easily be in a story," Mann has Joseph say, "and not understand it." Joseph understood everything in his story except himself. His light never shone altogether inward, producing perfect silence.

# The Devil Secularized:
# Thomas Mann's Faust

## by Erich Kahler

The great novels of the 20th century, its essential books, are without exception *terminal* books, apotheoses of the narrative form. Proust's *À la recherche du temps perdu,* Gide's *Faux-Monnayeurs,* Joyce's *Ulysses,* Kafka's great parables, Musil's *Mann ohne Eigenschaften,* Broch's *Das Tod Vergils,* Sartre's *Nausée,* Camus' *Étranger*—each, in theme, is an inventory of our spiritual holdings, a moral, aesthetic, and metaphysical reckoning-up of our human estate; some of them, in form, carry abstraction to a point beyond which further evolution seems impossible. A deep, ultimate seriousness runs through them all, a seriousness which their ever-present irony increases rather than diminishes. Indeed, what is irony but the transcendence of self, a chain reaction of transcendence? Today, the spiritual, the artistic, the human itself balances on the highest peak of danger, "exposed on the mountains of the heart." So much has called it into question—how could it help questioning itself?

And indeed art has come to question its own existence—cannot escape doing so. The last veils of fiction, the last pretense of a divine plaything, are gone; the real thing invades the work of art; bare reality, of more dimensions than the individual artist can cope with, decomposes and shatters the novel. How can the artist hope to reach the central, inner-most condition of our world—which is his ultimate function—without going into its formidable factual and technical processes? How can he hope to master its growing complexity without a corresponding increase in density and abstractness of presentation, without speculative analysis and exegesis?

Thus the story loses its value as a special event and becomes a parable of the human condition; the individual character becomes a type, the symbol a model. The artist today must load the tangible with so many levels of meaning that the complete work really becomes an orchestral

"The Devil Secularized: Thomas Mann's Faust," by Erich Kahler. (Original title: "Thomas Mann's *Doctor Faustus:* 'Terminal Work' of an Art Form and an Era.") *Commentary* (April, 1949), 348-357. Copyright 1949 by the American Jewish Committee. Reprinted by permission of the author and *Commentary.* Translated by Francis C. Golffing.

score requiring a conductor—and indeed have single works of art ever before enlisted so many program notes and interpretations?

"When I hear about hearing . . ." says Adrian Leverkühn in *Doctor Faustus*. "When I read about reading . . ." would be a legitimate paraphrase: the reader cannot "follow" the theme without going one level of abstraction beyond it to embrace the entire structure, for the structure has in fact become the theme—the "what" ends up as the "how."

The traditional art forms have grown problematic through external, social, and cultural evolution, as well as through internal evolution, evolution of technique; art has become its own subject matter. And since the function of the artist and the intellectual has been called into question by the moral and social events of our epoch, the artist himself is drawn into a kind of polyphonic soliloquy on his role in our world.

It is just here that we have the content of Thomas Mann's entire work, which as a whole, bears the distinguishing traits of the great terminal books of our epoch. But in his work the terminal quality does not appear all at once; it may be watched as a process, evolving through decades.

Thomas Mann's development as a novelist comprises the whole development of modern narrative prose. He began his career with a book that, though marked by the destiny of modern art, still resembled the traditional realistic novel. Indeed, he has gone on using the comfortably circumstantial, digressive manner of the 19th-century novel right up into the latest, "structuralist" stages of his work—even in this last summing-up, his *Faust*. Yet what a long way from *Buddenbrooks* to *Doctor Faustus*. All that has happened to us, to the world, to art, during the last half-century, can be read in the course of this journey.

Mann's whole *oeuvre*, we have said, must be regarded as a single, consistent creation because, throughout, there may be felt in it an unconscious or semiconscious tendency toward a structural unity of the whole. It is a dynamic macrocosm, a more and more dense and comprehensive complex of developing motifs, exhibiting as a whole a fugal character such as is otherwise found only in single novels or works of art. Just as each work gains increasing symbolic richness by the use and intensification of a leitmotif and the fusing of several leitmotifs, so on a larger scale the work as a whole exhibits the progressive exfoliation and metamorphosis of one single, all-pervasive theme. Mann himself, in his autobiographical sketch, has pointed, not without surprise, to the relationships within the magic square: *Buddenbrooks, Tonio Kröger, The Magic Mountain,* and *Death in Venice*. Yet exact correspondences of this sort are to be found throughout his entire work.

The lifelong central theme of Mann's books has been an inquiry into the function of art and the artist, of culture and the intellectual in modern society. This cluster of problems had its origin in the 19th century, rising out of the Industrial Revolution and the political changes attendant on it, out of the mechanization, collectivization, standardization of our world, and the increasing alienation of the artist from his society.

At first the artist took a stand for threatened culture: defensively in romanticism and aestheticism; aggressively in dandyism and insolent eccentricity. But gradually, almost insensibly, his attitude began to change: his own position, the nature of art and culture themselves, became problematic to him.

It was not that his attitude toward bourgeois society changed, but that he no longer supported culture unequivocally. Instead he began to lean more and more toward a new barbarism.

Even before Nietzsche we see signs of such a development. Leconte de Lisle wrote *Poèmes Barbares*. Théophile Gautier proclaimed: *"La barbarie vaut mieux que la platitude."* With Nietzsche the problem becomes broadly apparent, and later developments branch out in many directions. One way leads directly through the brash extremism of the Futurists, of Spengler, Klages, and Jünger, to the *trahison des clercs*; another leads to the savagely defiant vagrancy of Knut Hamsun and D. H. Lawrence's glorification of the vital urges; a third leads to the ambivalent scepticism in matters cultural of tired aristocrats such as Hermann Bang and Eduard Keyserling; the last and most far-reaching way leads to the bold investigations of the contemporary novel.

Thomas Mann had an initial advantage as compared with other great novelists of his generation, an advantage without which he could not have covered the vast distance between realism and structuralism. The problem fundamental to the modern novel—the role of the intellectual within his society, a problem that, in the last analysis, is the problem of man generally, of the individual surviving precariously in a technological, collective, incommensurate world—was not a problem Mann had to realize and experience intellectually; it was given to him in his cradle as his primary experience of himself. He himself *was* the problem, by virtue of the contrasts of his origin, the conjunction of the bourgeois and the artistic. From childhood he bore within himself that tension which impels the basic theme of our era.

His earliest stories introduce this theme. They are all studies of outcasts: the misshapen or unfortunate, like little Herr Friedemann, the lawyer Jacoby (*Little Lizzie*), Tobias Mindernickel, Lobgott Piepsam (*The Way to the Churchyard*); the invalid, like Albrecht van der Qualen (*The Wardrobe*); the man set apart by religious exaltation, like the monk Hieronymus (*Gladius Dei*), the archetype of Savonarola (*Fiorenza*); and already, as early as *The Dilettante* and Spinell (*Tristan*), the outcast as literary man, the would-be-artist in his illegitimate, tragi-comic opposition to life and to the social norm. Incidentally, in both *The Wardrobe* and *Tristan* we find the germ of the motif of *The Magic Mountain*: the peculiar removal from life, the isolation and insulation that goes with illness and the atmosphere of healing. The sanitarium in *Tristan* almost strikes us as a sketch for the one in *The Magic Mountain*. Even so early as this Thomas Mann was in possession of the outlines of a work that was to be precipitated by an entirely different, unforeseeable experience, his sojourn at Davos.

These stories, as well as *Buddenbrooks,* are all what is commonly called realistic fiction. They are realistic in a cruel, often painful way that points to the influence of the great Russian novelists; they seem to result from a deliberate discipline in sustaining with exact imagination the minutest circumstances of human suffering, perverted emotion, painful embarrassment. But—and this is a wholly modern aspect of Mann's style, distinguishing it from that of the Russian novelists—all these eccentric facts have been pushed to an extreme of precision, a point of caricature, where they turn into transcendent ironies. The experience of reality has become superintensive, ironically intensive. At the same time this irony has the property of creating symbols. A perfect example is the situation in *The Way to the Churchyard*: the contentious drunkard, Piepsam, tries to push the blond, young cyclist (life) from his bicycle. Later examples are Tonio Kröger in the *Moulinet des Dames;* the carious teeth of the Buddenbrooks and the consul's collapse head-first into the gutter; Mario and the magician; and so forth. These are all extreme, vicious, ironic contrasts, and their extreme irony is what makes them symbolic. They have their root in an archetypal conflict, the ironic constitution of the artist himself.

The style of every genuine artist is originally a style of personal experience; this is true of Thomas Mann in a very special sense. There is hardly another literary *oeuvre* that bears so clear an autobiographical stamp. Mann himself has told us, for instance, in his autobiographical sketch, that every single detail in *Death in Venice* is authentic, none of it fictitious. All that happens to any individual endowed with a truly personal style of experience seems to converge into an organic system of symbols and to assume an apparently inevitable relationship to his nature. This phenomenon is particularly marked in Thomas Mann, whose fundamental problem was shaped by the circumstances of his birth. Since he experiences everything under the sign of the primary tension of his being, the raw material of life almost immediately assumes for him a symbolic character. The reciprocal irony of his psychological situation, and that further irony which transcends it, sharpen the symbolism still more. This peculiar disposition, this instinctive tendency to organize all experience symbolically, seems to account for the unique organic interrelatedness, the fugal character of Mann's entire work.

Even the works of his early, realistic period evidence a very personal system of symbolic coordinates, an irony that creates distance and transcendence. Both in *Buddenbrooks* and in *Tonio Kröger,* the fundamental personal problem is developed almost autobiographically, in the first, genealogically, from the bourgeois standpoint, in the second, individually, from the standpoint of the artist. Bourgeois and artist, each turns his gaze and inclination toward his counterpart: there is an exact correspondence between the consul Thomas Buddenbrook, who finds solace in Schopenhauer, and Tonio Kröger, with his nostalgia for the normal, blond, and respectable.

Already culture and intellect are represented as decadence, love is associated with decline; the artist is seen as a pariah from the start, iridescent with suspect hues, shading into the demon, the invalid, the social outcast, the adventurer, the criminal; already he is stranded in the ironic situation of expressing a life he himself is unable to live. And already the multiple variations the basic theme is to undergo in the later books become discernible. Tonio Kröger's identification, somehow felt by him to be legitimate, with the swindler, foreshadows Felix Krull, swindler-by-extravagance-of-fantasy, and the blasphemous hoax of the paraphrase of *Dichtung und Wahrheit* in Krull's diary. A single metaphor of Tonio's ("mufti's no use . . .") furnishes the germ of *Royal Highness,* the outcast "upward," the sublime clown who keeps directing a performance that is being enacted without him.

From here on the motifs split and ramify and rejoin, form new variations, change keys. In *Death in Venice* the conflict that had earlier appeared as an external friction between art and life is internalized; it is within the artist, indeed, within art itself: a conflict between demon and discipline. Discipline is what preserves the artist, what justifies art and keeps it in the framework of social responsibility. Once discipline slackens, the demon, the *eros,* breaks loose, and in the maelstrom of debauchery both art and artist are swept into sickness and death. The active counterpart of the passive Aschenbach is the magician Cipolla (*Mario and the Magician*), another outcast, deformed, but one who compensates and overcompensates his deformity—a deeper image of the artist seen as the irresponsible puppeteer of souls who uses his magic to cast people into the most unholy ecstasies. At this point the artist passes over into the demagogue, the dictator. He too is swept into perdition by his demon, but not because of mere passivity but because of *hubris:* unlike Aschenbach, Cipolla does not let himself go or drift, but on the contrary exercises all his powers. He is a virtuoso of the will, a fiend for the sheer joy of conquest. He does not yield to his demon but allies himself with it, indeed identifies himself with it, challenges it, incites it.

*The Magic Mountain* projects Aschenbach's psychic split into the world at large. The powers of the psyche widen out into whole landscapes. Magic expands into the magic mountain, into the sphere of an intellectual, morbid, irresponsible dissociation from life, where culture and nursing merge, and where the dissolution of dying overintensifies the stimuli of life. Discipline becomes the valley of duties, of normal, responsible action. But these too—the duties, the responsibilities, the active, normal life—lead into war and final collapse.

Here we come upon an alteration in the fundamental motif. The normality of the normal is no longer secure. Before this, Mann's work had been dedicated to the problem of life's boundaries: by means of his various outcasts he had delimited an area of healthy, normal, insouciant life. Now he discovers signs of decay on both sides of the boundary—in the world of action as well as up there on the magic mountain. Dying is part of living as living is part of dying.

The ambivalence, the paradox of all living things is at last revealed. *The Magic Mountain* opens out into an unanswered question: What *is* life anyway? What is normal? What is man and where does he stand? What is the norm of man and his measure? Goethe's question is raised once more (in a world terribly changed)—the question of *Tasso,* of *Iphigenie,* of the *Elective Affinities,* of *Faust.* . . .

In all of Thomas Mann's books after *The Magic Mountain,* there runs through the persistent motif of conflict between the abnormal and the supposedly normal, an anxious question as to the being and becoming of man. The *Joseph* novels open up the remotest layers of our mythical, totemistic past, which are at the same time the darkest layers of our psyche, the underworld of savage urges, lying ever in wait within us. Joseph rises out of these regions in a long, precarious process of sublimation, and there rises with him, within him, the sublimated, spiritualized God-image—he being the prefiguration of Jesus. He too bears a stigma from the beginning, the stigma of Grace. Grace again is full of abysses and wiles, and great discipline is required of its possessor. But, for one supreme moment, the norm seems to have shifted to spiritual man. For one moment, Joseph's counterpart was to appear, the Antichrist, the man stigmatized by the curse of spirit: Faustus.

The presentation of the Apollonian genius in *Lotte in Weimar* forms the transition. The image of Goethe emerges intact, "great, serene, and wise," as "a sacrifice—and bringer of sacrifice"; genius is preserved as an object of our reverence, sublimated as "simply the face of man." All this is still in the vein of Joseph. But behind it we see the cost, the full measure of Goethe's, of the artist's sacrifice: not only the mastering of a world increasingly packed with factual material, of days crowded with labor, and of a refractory audience, but also the ruining of many people, among them those closest to him, and the abandoning of his own everyday humanity. Discipline once more, distance, alienation, and the chill of an uncanny, transcendent irony. This brings us to Faustus, who is entirely governed by this coldness.

I have called *Faustus* the final chapter of a terminal *oeuvre.*

To start with, it gathers together all the variations and filiations of the fundamental motif, relates them in a new way, tests one against the other, and reduces them all in magnificent concentration to the old dominant theme. For what else is this Faustus but a cosmic Tonio Kröger, a Tonio Kröger expanded to his ultimate epochal and human significance? Faustus represents the extreme, the most mature fruit of the archproblem, the archexperience. The psychological split is portrayed through two characters: Adrian Leverkühn and Serenus Zeitblom—the intellectual adventurer and the "healthy" bourgeois.

The character who lives a normal life writes the biography of the one who, in the simple, human sense, is not allowed to have a life. In Adrian, Tonio Kröger's primary alienation from life, his ironic detachment from it, is pushed to its metaphysical limits. Aschenbach's demon, which operates through love and sickness, and Cipolla's demon, which operates more subjectively as *hubris* and defiant self-aggrandizement, are united in Adrian's devil. Demon and discipline are no longer seen as opposites, but discipline comes to serve the demon. Between demon and discipline, impulse and reason, death and life, there goes on the same mystical dialectic, the same reciprocal intensification that we found in *The Magic Mountain*. Besides, Adrian is really Joseph's counterpart, his spiritual kin. Adrian's elevation leads to perdition, whereas the "Pit" leads Joseph to glory; the sublimation which in Joseph's case is an act of God, in Adrian's case is an act of the Devil. From a different point of view Adrian, the Dionysian musical genius, is a counterpart of Goethe, the Apollonian, visual genius. Here too the opposites betray affinity, for both are in each: in Goethe the dark, romantic, Faustian impulse; in Adrian the lucid, visual, rational grasp of the whole. But in the last analysis the blessing and the curse seem to be contained in the contrast between word and sound, poetry and music.

Faustus is also a terminal book in point of style, the ultimate precipitation of Thomas Mann's artistic discipline. I have already intimated how this discipline, which is of North German, Hanseatic, Prussian provenance, developed through artistic filiations and the irony of an inner tension into a symbol-creating property. Discipline in art must necessarily express itself in a sharpened sense of form, an intensive striving for organic wholeness, and that means to see things symbolically.

From without, from Richard Wagner and Tolstoy, came the suggestion of the leitmotif, which in *Tonio Kröger* already is transferred from characters to ideas. Mann tells us that in *Tonio Kröger* he for the first time conceived of narrative composition as a texture of ideas woven of various themes, as a musical nexus—his affinity to music was very strong from the outset. Out of such a musical conception grows the fugal character of the later works and of his *oeuvre* as a whole.

But *Faustus* can hardly be compared any longer to a fugue; it is almost —if we may apply musical terms to a literary composition—what Adrian calls a "strict movement." It is a structure in which each detail has an exact symbolic reference, a structure of utter complexity, in which not only the various dimensions and layers, but within these each submotif and minor variation, is related to the rest and back to the fundamental motif. In spite of the semblance of ease in both invention and narrative, nothing here is accidental, nothing stands for itself alone; everything refers to everything else, each detail is determined by the whole. Correspondences run backwards and forwards, between beginning and end, upper and lower levels, in a kind of labyrinthine mathematics. From Buchel to Pfeiffering; from the father's "speculating on the elements" to the son's *Symphonia Cosmologica* and his fantastic excursions into the galactic and submarine spheres; from his actual mother Elsbeth to Mother Manardi and the ultimate mother Schweigestill; from Stallhanne to the maid Walpurgis; and from the laughing dog Suso, through the black swine at the entrance of the devil-house in Palestrina, to the dog Kaschperl (one of the devil's nicknames); from the dog's laugh to Adrian's bent for laughter and the tendency of his music to parody and "sardonic deviltry"; from the clear-wing moth to the whore; from the "greedy drop" and the osmotic, heliotropic pseudocreatures to the pathological lumbar migrations of the spirochetes and to the mannikins of the *Gesta Romanorum;* from Dürer's "Apocalypse" to Kleist's *Puppet Show;* from the destiny of Adrian's doctors to that of the Rogge sisters; and from the divines of Halle to the intellectuals of Munich who smirk at the bankruptcy of the intellect—among all these a net of converging relationships is woven, and one rational and demonic system contains them all. Even the most casual incident has its place: an emerald ring is engraved with a plumed serpent whose tongue is feathered like an arrow; an outing into the Bavarian mountains leads to Linderhof, the castle of a mad, possessed king.

The great drama of Tonio Kröger as Faustus, the drama of modern art and Germany, mirrored by the humble scribe Serenus—the impotent subject and onlooker—truly images the deeply involved Thomas Mann, ever present in the background. It is enacted simultaneously on all levels, no less in the theoretical discussions and spiritual ventures of musical technique than in syphilis, murder, and madness. The same disquieting suspense informs the descriptions of musical scores and the biographical sections; indeed the climactic boldness of the musical compositions comes to stand for the biographical climax.

We need not be surprised if readers shake their heads over the minute descriptions of a kind of music that has never been written and perhaps never could be written. People will ask: Is this necessary? Is this possible? It was necessary, and it has been done. It is both legitimate and necessary. A reader who wishes to be spared the reading of the theoretical discussions and technical details may as well spare himself the reading of the book altogether; there is no other way of penetrating to its innermost meaning. The time is past when writers could give credibility to artist-characters by letting them work for years at some monumental literary idea in color or sound and then having them perorate about the work, as Hauptmann and even Ibsen did with their artist-characters. While this procedure has always been false and threadbare, today it has become quite impossible. The progression of man today, the progression of mind, is through technical processes, and it is through them that we must seek it and understand it.

Thus the channelling of events through technical processes is not a sign of weakness or arbitrariness, not mere caprice, but an imperative requirement of the total structure giving the literary work its power of persuasion. For at the center of this book lies the problem of the destiny of artistic genius and of art itself.

But what happens in and to Adrian comprises not only the fate of modern art and the intellectual; it comprises also the tragedy of Germany that is enacted in the background, the transgression of the German character, of which Adrian partakes; it comprises the general crisis of our world. The narrative takes place within three overlapping time-spans: the time-span of Adrian, 1885 to 1941, which is extended backwards into the historical depths of medieval Germany and the German Reformation by means of the spiritual climate of Kaisersaschern where Adrian spent his childhood and by means of the humanistic-pietistic university town of Halle where he studied; the time-span of the Third Reich, whose period of incubation coincides with Adrian's prime, and whose triumph and fall Zeitblom witnesses with horror even as he writes the story of Adrian's life; finally, our own epoch, which has given birth to the crisis of modern art and of the intellectual, and which is continuing even as we read.

All these time-strata are not only homologous but also variously inter-connected. Thus the chronicle of German political events, inserted at intervals by Zeitblom into his biography of Adrian, is sometimes cross-connected with that biography, as in the discussions of the students at Halle and of the Munich intellectuals, or in the appearance of the impresario Fitelberg, who confronts Germanism with Judaism.

At the same time the book is interwoven with strands of Thomas Mann's personal history; there are long passages that are more nakedly autobiographical than any other writing by this author, who throughout his career has drawn so largely on his own life. Kaisersaschern, its form and atmosphere, the "witches" in its streets, point toward Mann's native city, Lübeck; Palestrina is the place where, under virtually identical circumstances, Thomas Mann wrote his *Buddenbrooks*. Pfeiffering and Munich both evoke familiar scenes. Mann's family, his friends, and acquaintances have been introduced into the story barely disguised, in some cases without change of name, in the fashion of montage.

This bold and rather disturbing procedure—apart from the lure and significance of parody—has the character of a radical confession of self. It is as though Thomas Mann wished to emphasize that he belongs in the story, is a part of it, that the destinies of Leverkühn and Zeitblom as well as of Germany, the intellectual, and modern art, deeply involve him. This *pro domo* applies not only to the author but also to the work. The compulsive tendency toward irony and parody in Adrian's creation; his rejection of make-believe and the "divine game" which leads to the self-abolition of art; the "never-relaxed, perilous playing of art on the edge of impossibility"; its "pilgrimage on peas"; its "strict counterpoint"; "the highest and strictest organization, a planetary, cosmic norm"; the "universal unity of dimensions"; the "calculation raised to mystery"; and finally the "thrust from intellectual coldness into the adventure of new feeling," the desire for "an art without suffering, psychologically sound, far from solemn, serenely intimate," "an art on terms of closest familiarity with mankind," and the conviction that the spirit "even in its most daring sallies, researches, and ventures, which seem to remove it from the common taste, can nevertheless count on serving humanity, and, in the end, in a very roundabout way, even actual people. . . ."—all this is the self-projection not only of the author, it is the self-projection and self-reflection of the book. If we listen closely we may even catch in the cruel narrative that *vibrato* of the voice attributed to Adrian when he speaks with a half-modest, half-haughty casualness of the artist's ultimate familiarity with mankind.

It is Serenus Zeitblom who serves to strengthen confessional to the point of self-interpretation. True, he is the author's other half, the Overbeck of the Nietzschean Adrian, a second-remove ironic reflection of the normal on the abnormal, but his true function goes far beyond all this. He is the mediator between the various spheres, not only between Adrian and life, but also between the book and the world. He is a loose personification of the author's symbolic conscience, the commentator whose fears and forebodings, queries and meditations furnish the necessary crossreferences—perhaps too many and too explicit for the acute reader, yet still hardly enough for those obtuse to symbolism. It is he who provides the additional experience of the German tragedy and integrates it with the rest; who, with his numerous reservations and confidences, makes the highly wrought craftsmanship seem easy and unobtrusive, and effects the transition to human emotion.

The creation of this character enabled Thomas Mann to maintain his highly synthetic Adrian, this cosmic figure, within the context of humanity, to make of him a real and moving character, though this is accomplished a little at the expense of Zeitblom, who often feels and expresses things that are actually outside his pale. However, the author has tried in advance to give psychological credibility to these deviations—and, indeed, man is an unstable, vibrant substance whose hidden depths may be stirred to unforeseeable effects by certain crises and stimuli. Furthermore, in this book psychology no longer counts. Zeitblom is a voice, ultimately the author's voice: "I am too close to my subject . . . but when things become serious art is left behind. . . ." Of course this itself is artifice, but it passes over into truth.

This monumental undertaking is terminal also in that it truly represents the contemporary version of the Faust problem. Valéry's *Faust,* which plays with very similar ideas, is but a fascinating existentialist idyll compared with this. Thomas Mann brings this representative symbol, not only of German but of Western culture, up to date. He treats it with finality, secularizing it and its demon, and integrating it in a purely mundane cosmos. Redemption here has become synonymous with integration. This means that the Faustian drama is revealed as the dialectical predicament of every creature, the inborn paradox of life.

This process permeates all levels of the book. Adrian's Faustian character is constitutional. The demon resides *within him* from the start, in his migraine, in his enormous intelligence which rapidly assimilates all that can be known. Thence ennui, the challenge to the ever more sublime, ironic transcendence, risibility, and a coldness both somber and blasé. The demon also surrounds him, in the father who "speculates on the elements," in the medieval German climate of Kaiseraschern, in the latent polyphony of the vast collection of musical instruments in his uncle's warehouse and the growing lure of the mathematical magic of music. The genius of the stammering organist Kretzschmar and the example of Beethoven carry him further—further still the theological studies at Halle, which Adrian chooses partly out of ascetic conceit, partly as a supreme feat of self-mastery, a braving of the highest powers.

For theology is a highly charged, demoniac field of force. It survives in our modern world as a last island of medieval spirituality, a twilight area of magical dialectics and dialectical magic. This accounts for its deep affinity with mathematico-magical music. The demon takes on greater reality in two professors of divinity, Kumpf and Schleppfuss. The baroque and blustering Kumpf, after the manner of Luther, throws bread rolls at the devil lurking in the corner of his room. But Schleppfuss, who proves by slippery, keen logic the interdependence of good and evil and the verity of witchcraft, represents, as his appearance and name indicate, the Evil One himself.

In Leipzig, whither Adrian goes later to pursue his musical studies— the attraction of music proving more concrete and immediate—the demon finally assumes an active and decisive role and starts intervening, from within as well as from without. Adrian's proud superiority, his sensitive intellectuality and primal alienation are associated with an extreme chastity, a chastity more innocent because more naïve than the pious and shrewd chastity of Joseph. It contains both a touching child-likeness and an element of cold pride.

It is just this kind of rarefied innocence that invites the deepest humiliation by sex and a consequent involvement in guilt. Indeed this presumptuous intellectuality, this ironic transcendence, constitutes in itself the Fall. The porter in Leipzig who guides Adrian to a brothel instead of a restaurant is merely an instrument of the inner demon. Love flares up at the most casual physical contact, the purest love—with a whore, love returned even from the swamp, and this love, love from the first closed to the genius, contains the poison, the demoniac involvement, the Mephistophelian pact—that in reality was concluded from birth.

Original Sin has its way; the love-poison is consumed, consciously, despite all warnings. The pact is sealed, partly out of a genuine commitment to love, partly out of proud defiance, the innate urge to self-enhancement, to the supreme act of challenge. This monstrous union of the highest with the lowest, the most solitary with the most promiscuous, of genius with *vulgus,* this union—fulfilment and treason in one— constitutes one of the most moving love stories in world literature. It also contains in germ the manifold meaning of this powerful book.

From here on tragedy takes its predestined course. The wanton, ghastly dialogue with the Devil in Palestrina, while ostensibly the center of the book, only expresses what has been clear from the beginning: "Thou shalt not love."

And another thing it makes utterly clear is the primary determinance, the biological conditioning of the spiritual drama. "You see me," says the Devil, "therefore I exist for you. Is it worth while asking whether I really exist? Is not that which acts actual? Is truth not that which is felt and experienced?" Thus hallucination and reality have equal validity, and the fellow lolling on the sofa speaks both from within and from without. The coldness that emanates from him is nothing else than the reflection of the spiritual coldness of Adrian, of that white heat that feels like ice to the touch; and the Mephistophelian wit is nothing else than Adrian's own irony. It is the same with all subsequent events: the ruin of the amorous friend whom Adrian, at once bashful and diabolic, sends as his suitor to the girl they both love; the girl's recoil; and, in his house, the death of his little nephew, the dearest of all to him, the last, tenderest Eros; set over against these, the spiritual closeness of the woman who instinctively keeps herself at a distance, whom he never sees—concord only between strangers: it is all emanated by force of that inner magic in a person which has the property of creating destiny all around itself.

Adrian's Faustian drama is set entirely within the being of spiritual man. The old cosmic drama between Heaven and Hell has been transferred into the human heart. Even the voyages into the stellar system and the submarine world are phantasmagoria nourished by science. The theological conflict is secularized; God and the Devil are secularized and made to dwell in a single body.

How naïvely chaste, how allegorically pure was Goethe's tragedy by comparison! There the theological element pervaded the whole cosmic scene, good and evil were neatly separated, and man was endowed with free choice. This contemporary *Faustus* is likewise full of theology, but theology has become a small, atavistic residue, a medieval remnant, revealed as a deeply suspect region where God and Devil fluidly merge, are mutually dependent, where the good is a *fleur du mal* and vice versa.

The Faustian man has stepped over into the secular realm of art, and his fate becomes the very fate of modern art, the fate of the alien intellectual in our mechanized world. His fate is inherent in his intellectuality and insofar as he is what he is, and does not deny himself, he has no longer any choice. In his very attempt to realize what is creatively true he finds himself today, together with art, together with all that is essentially human, in a diabolical plight, in the state of alienation, of the Fall —the Fall by rising, by ironic transcendence. What is good, what is bad? Sound or sick? What is innocence, if the purest—the spirit—is sin? Where lies the norm? All this has become difficult to resolve. Concepts and values are no longer immune, but have become tainted by each other.

Thus the drama is reduced to a point; event becomes stasis, becomes existence. Life's ambiguity, life's paradox, is revealed. The Devil resides in God and God in the Devil. Sublimest chastity becomes the easiest prey of the whore.

The German character, "threatened with being wrapt up in itself like a cocoon," with "the poison of solitude," beset with longings, with the urge to break into the world, is beguiled into a grab for world power that brings it nothing but the world's hatred, and suffering. The nation whose power of abstraction is the highest, whose spirituality is the most perfectly and perilously detached, the nation of Kant, Schiller, Hölderlin, plunges ahead of the rest into a subanimal condition. This is the nation that has created the model of a modern secularized hell, where the incredible actually happens, "without any accounting," in soundproof cellars, where torment and lust are commingled.

And what of modern art? What of this terminal book, this extreme document? Do we not find the same symptoms here? Magic has developed into the strictest structural norm, and the strictest norm—in science, too —leads back into magic. Ultimate irony, the chain reaction of transcendence, mixes with the elements and becomes deadly serious. From the furthest, cosmic, objectivity we are thrust into utter subjectivity, the confessional.

In paradoxes such as these, indeed throughout the crisis of our age, we sense the motif of Kleist's *Puppet Show:* "Thus once again we must eat of the Tree of Knowledge in order to fall back into the state of innocence." The entire effort, the supreme effort, of the contemporary spirit is directed toward this: to eat once again of the Tree of Knowledge, to make possible the impossible, finding the saving ability really to communicate with others.* And the spirit's last hope, "hope beyond hopelessness," "transcendence of despair," is that paradox of Grace: that salvation is born only of utter desperation.

* Literally "to say 'Thou' to humanity." See Martin Buber's philosophy of the "I" and the "Thou."

# The World Without Transcendence

## by Hans Egon Holthusen

> One of the finest and most splendid gifts of God is music. Satan
> is very hostile to it. With it many a temptation can be repelled.
> —Martin Luther

Thomas Mann's new novel, entitled "Doctor Faustus. The Life of
the German Composer Adrian Leverkühn, Related by a Friend," is based
on motifs that connect the following groups of themes: theology, demonology, and music; the problem of music with the problem of the figure of
Faust and the latter again with the psychology of "the German"; the
problem of genius with the motif of selling one's soul to the devil and
this in turn with the essence of music on the one hand and the problematic nature of the German soul and German history on the other. "If
Faust is to be the representative of the German soul, he ought to be
musical," the author said in a speech delivered at the Library of Congress
in Washington in 1945. At once he went on to say, with reference to the
latest catastrophe of German history: "such musicality of the soul is
dearly bought in another sphere—the political, the sphere of human
living together." In the baleful light of the Third Reich's descent into
hell, Faust's pact with the devil becomes, for the speaker, a metaphor of
the real meaning of German history; and nothing can inhibit him from
declaring to his American listeners with the most complete candor that
"today"—that is, in the spring of 1945—"the devil is literally bearing
away the soul of Germany."

What meaning, what character, what positional value (*Stellenwert*)
does the statement have, that contains the intellectual germ, the basic
notion of this book—the statement that Faust really ought to be musical?
To what region of cognition, what order of the knowable shall we assign
it? When genius dips its hand into the water of truth, it forms a sphere,
as it did in the pure hand of the Hindu woman in Goethe's "Pariah"
trilogy[1]: a creative idea is born. Goethe's "graven form that develops as
it lives," his *"Ur-plant,"* his "primal phenomenon" [1]—those are "ideas."

"The World Without Transcendence," by Hans Egon Holthusen. From his *Die Welt
ohne Transzendenz* (Hamburg: Ellerman, 1949), pp. 5-20. Reprinted by permission of
the author. Translated by Henry Hatfield.

[1] The "Pariah" trilogy is a lyric of Goethe's; a "primal phenomenon" is an archetype.

Schiller's "freedom," Leibniz's "monad," Pascal's "argument of the wager"
—those are ideas. But the statement that Faust really ought to be musical
is an *aperçu*, a bon mot, a feat of witty association. Like everything else
which the thinker Thomas Mann has produced, it comes under the
category of cultural criticism. Even the assumption, agreed upon as a
matter of course, that Faust is the symbol of the German soul, is a thesis
of cultural criticism of a very relative, perspectivist sort. It may well have
obtained for only a few decades; it has become almost a vulgar preconcep-
tion today; and moreover, it loses every shred of meaning when it is
applied to National Socialism and its brainless deviltries. Neither for
Marlowe nor for Valéry can the Faust material have had a specifically
"German" character; nor for Goethe either. He would have been the last
to interrupt the process of transforming personal experiences into universal symbols of humanity, by reflections about nationality. Only the literary historian and critic of culture can derive a national psychology from
the German tradition of the Faust motif.

The Faust figure of the old chapbooks, that was seized upon, consumed,
and transformed by Goethe's immense imaginative power and reborn as
the vessel of Goethean ideas, is an abstract mythic pattern for Thomas
Mann; he draws his analytical, psychological, essayistic circles around it,
just as he did around the figure of Goethe in *The Beloved Returns* and
the Biblical narrative in the Joseph novels. Of the "genuine" Faust
nothing remains but a late-medieval-Lutheran, demonological-neurotic
atmosphere. The true crystallization point is the aforesaid notion of the
cultural critic, with which he ingeniously connects the notion of the
Germans' characteristic musicality. Faustian atmosphere is mingled with
musical atmosphere. Thus a typical Mannian work results: for it has
always been the forte of his insinuating talent to dissolve traditional ideas
or such concepts as are "in the air" into atmosphere, or as he once called
it himself, "atmospherialia"; to reduce everything to one level by psy-
chologizing; and then, ironically or emphatically, to link everything up
with everything else. This is the secret of his stylistic brilliance in general
and his famous ironies—set in the subjunctive—in particular: for example, the secret of Naphta, the Jesuitical-Jewish terrorist, who proclaims
the proletarian *civitas dei*, or Gregorian Marxism. It is a style of thinking
and writing whose conspicuous features may be characterized as *interesting:* the style of an omnipresent intellect, restlessly experimenting, combining, and pondering, most subtle, most responsive to stimuli—indeed
dependent on stimuli and at times so much at their mercy as to lose all
autonomy.

From the beginning the theme of music occurs in Thomas Mann's
work like a leitmotif. In *Buddenbrooks* it plays a decisive role, as in the
*novella* "Tristan" and the *Reflections of a Nonpolitical Man*. It is inherent in the "Schopenhauerian" triad—"music, pessimism, humor"—

that young Thomas Mann likes to strike in defining the mood of his own life, and in the sense of "the Cross, death, and the grave" that he shares with young Nietzsche and occasionally conjures up, in the name of suffering and morality, against Renaissance aestheticism and the brutal or hectic glorification of life. As Wagnerian music it simultaneously represents the principles of modernity and of conservatism, it stands for a chromatic, analytic way of thinking, a thinking in enharmonic changes and atmospheric mixtures, and for a gloomy nonpolitical and anti-democratic stance. In *Buddenbrooks* little Hanno's musicality moves into a sphere of decadence, alienation from the burgher's world, illness, dis-solution, and death. In the *Reflections,* at the occasion of the famous analysis of *Palestrina,*[2] music appears as a Pfitznerian "sympathy with death," a motif that is united simultaneously with a German-romantic sort of nationalism, affording the author the opportunity to cite, with emphasis, a "defiant" dedication of Pfitzner's to Grand Admiral von Tirpitz.[3] In the same book certain Faust-motifs related to music are already to be found: above all the linking of music to theology, religion, and the spirit of Luther and the Reformation. "The musical education of the German," we read there, "began with Martin Luther, a pedagogue challengingly national in his basic character, theosophist, religious teacher, and musician in one; and so very much so, that in his case musicality and religiosity can hardly be kept separate, that one is equated with the other in his soul—as has been characteristic of the Germans from that time on." Typical sentiments of the reformer are cited, this one for instance: "Music I have always been fond of. It is a fine, hearty gift of God and closely related to theology." And the remark that this art is "a semidiscipline and taskmaster, making people milder and more gentle, better behaved and more reasonable."

Theology and religion, closely linked to music as they are, are viewed at the time (1917) in the light of a well-disposed conservatism, even though their contents, however opposed to nationalism Mann's intention was, appear diluted or volatilized by an extreme rationalism. "Religion," we read, "the place of worship, this sphere of the extraordinary, sets free the human element and makes it beautiful"; and elsewhere occurs the fantastic sentence: "Belief in God is the belief in love, life, and art." As to the Reformation, the forty-year-old Thomas Mann discovers that he is induced "to rever an event of genuinely German majesty" in it, which taught the German "to bear metaphysical freedom more universally." What French history lacks is nothing but a Reformation at the right time, and the revolution of 1789—here the author follows Carlyle's view —is "only the vengeful return of Protestantism, which had been rejected two hundred years before." For "freedom" here is not on the side of the Jacobins and the political West, but on that of Luther, Goethe, and

[2] [An opera by Hans Pfitzner, first performed in 1917.]
[3] [Chief of the German navy in the first World War, and an outspoken imperialist.]

Bismarck, whom Thomas Mann calls a "second Luther, a really great event in the history of German self-experience, a gigantic German fact, defiantly set off against European antipathy." "Freedom" means here a musical, reformational, antipolitical frame of mind, that insists on "denying the correspondence between the spirit and political life, or rather, recognizing the noncorrespondence of the two."

Music then, to return to the beginning of this labyrinthine and infinitely extensible chain of motifs, is the opposite of Enlightenment, "progress," politics, the attitude of the "eggheads of civilization" (*Zivilisationsliteratentum*),[4] and democracy. It is the German antidote to the rhetorical bourgeois of 1789, to revolutionary "virtue," to the "renascence of the Jacobin," and the "moralizing racket (*Moralbonzentum*) of the sentimental, terroristic, republican type." It is the "image and artistic-spiritual reflection of German life itself. "Music" is the quintessence of all German superiority, the battle cry of an enthusiastic nationalism. In its name Thomas Mann, inspired by warlike patriotic ardor, raises the Germans to the state of transfiguration—the same Germans whom, according to his testimony thirty years later, the devil will bear away. On the one hand he glorifies them in the image of Eichendorff's Ne'er-do-well,[5] who is a symbol of "pure humanity, humanely romantic humanity, to say it again: of the German"; while he encourages them on the other hand to stride forward, armed with Krupp cannons, "on the imperial path," bravely affirming their own aggressiveness. "The world-people of the spirit, having attained exuberant physical power, had drunk a long draught of the fount of ambition; it desired to be a world-people if God called upon it, *the* world-people of reality[6]—by means, if it had to be (and obviously it had to) of a breakthrough by sheer force."

"Music is a daemonic realm," the speech on Germany asserts (in 1945); "it is the most calculated order and chaotic antireason at once, rich in gestures of conjuration and incantation; it is the magic of numbers,[7] simultaneously the art farthest from reality and yet the most passionate, abstract, and mystic." Music is "calculation raised to mystery"; it is "energy per se, energy itself," as young Leverkühn once remarks, "but not as an idea, but in its reality. I would point out to you that that is almost the definition of God," he adds, without observing that he is irresponsibly overinterpreting a purely formal analogy, merely to create a "theological" mood. Kierkegaard's essay on Don Juan is mentioned, both in the speech referred to and in *Faustus* itself, but it is only the

---

[4] A term coined by Thomas Mann early in the First World War to express his bitter rejection of those German liberal or leftist intellectuals, above all his brother Heinrich, who took a pro-Western position.

[5] The charming wanderer whose sobriquet appears in the title of the romantic novella, *Aus dem Leben eines Taugenichts* (1826).

[6] I.e., the dominant world power.

[7] Mann was fascinated by numerology throughout his life. Here he refers to the mathematical relations between various notes of the scale.

theological-erotic "demonologic" *atmosphere* of this work which Thomas Mann makes use of, while its subtle and severe dialectic, its system of exactly distinguished categories fades into vagueness. "A highly theological affair, music," the devil says in his long discussion with Leverkühn, which is the nucleus of the book, "just as sin is, as I am." To put it briefly and bluntly, music is possessed by the devil. Leverkühn is driven to the peak of his musical genius by the devil, who has stolen into his entelechy via a syphilitic infection. Music, which Mann expressly praised in the *Reflections,* using Luther's words, as a "gift of God," has been stealthily transformed to a gift of the devil. It is he who gives the hero "a whole hourglass full of the devil's creative time, yes, who even presents him with particular melodies to fulfil his obligations under the pact. At one point, while reflecting on his beloved friend, the chronicler of Adrian's life asks himself: Was it one of those melodic illuminations, to which he was—I'd almost say—exposed in those days, and through which powers of whom I wish to know nothing kept their word . . . ?" Music therefore, which the author still loves passionately, now as in other days, is in league with the Evil One. Music, of which Luther said that "Satan was very hostile" to it; music, to which men have always ascribed the power to calm, make blissful, bear them upward; music, which the most ancient wisdom and mythology of mankind has quite decidedly associated with the spirit of joy, with piety and love, with the "harmony of the spheres," with the cosmogonic Eros. Was not music always the smile of the soul? Were not even the wild beasts calmed by Orpheus? Did he not move the *underworld,* "humanize" it, make it responsive to his amorous complaint?

Something "daemonic," something reminiscent of Goethe's Earth-Spirit, amoral in its natural might, does no doubt inhere in every created power, in all energies and drives of man, in all feeling, loving, and knowing, and especially in all artistic productivity. But if one wishes to understand the concept in that fashion, then the demonic is innocent, sheer existent force and vital power, and one cannot simply equate it arbitrarily with evil by blurring the boundaries between the various categories. On the other hand, if one wants to subsume under it certain enervating, intoxicating effects, hostile to discipline and filling timid moralists with dismay, the concept may perhaps be applicable to Wagner, Strauss, or certain effects of Bruckner's brasses which stir up nervous ecstasies; but it cannot be extended to Beethoven's joyous allegros and certainly not to the "Goldberg Variations," to "St. Matthew's Passion," to Mozart.

If finally the term demonic is intended to have reference to the general "irrationality" of music, its free-floating (*gegenstandslos*) passionateness and emotional power, its sweet, supermoral tenderness, its "bovine warmth," as Thomas Mann puts it, then suspicion is cast on its relation to love, its character as love; love is made demonic or even diabolical.

On this point too, as will appear, Thomas Mann has not been inconsistent. Here a problem arises which can perhaps best be characterized by the question: "Has reason alone been baptized? Are the passions heathen?" Kierkegaard, who used this quotation from Young as a motto for his *Either-Or,* in his hypersensitivity about the tension between the ethical and aesthetic pole of his thinking, characterized the "sensual brilliance," the "uninsulated eroticism" of music as demonic: a most brilliant contribution to the thorough understanding of the problem of Don Giovanni. One should however counter Kierkegaard's notion with a certain amount of the medieval realist's fidelity to the Creation and joy in sheer existence, unless one is willing to let love itself and music in general appear in a bad light.

Regarding Thomas Mann's concepts, it is easy to sink into a bottomless pit if one wants to fix, circumscribe, and place one of them. His concepts have no definite boundaries, no locus, no region where they obtain without ambiguity. As concepts they are not to be taken at all seriously, they are to be understood only as continuously varying atmospheric values and psychological stimulants. Mann, with his enormous stylistic energy, devotes great care to combining them, reworking them, and employing them effectively. A sort of superessayism is at work with an unbounded, unscrupulous lust for making new associations or combinations, an ambiguous and subtle art of distorting and confusing concepts, of arranging them in a montage. Thus it is possible that, according to the mood of the author, music appears at one time as "a gift of God," at another as black magic; the nature of the Germans at one time appears transfigured, in the light of a humane romanticism, at another as miserably abandoned to the pact with the devil.

Music, theology, the Reformation, and the problem of the German are again combined in a chain of motifs, and only in this context does the "demonism" of music reveal its entire meaning. Luther, the "musical theologian," "a gigantic incarnation of the German character (*Wesen*)," still has quite the same importance as before, but now the accent lies in the other aspects of his character: the "choleric and churlish," and his passionate, immediate relation to Satan. As evidence of his spirit we get to hear, this time, only violent phrases that leave the content of his theology completely obscure: "The devil's sow, the Pope," and similar things. His modern parody and caricature is Ehrenfried Kumpf, professor of theology at Halle, a foul-minded "man of the people" and a devil of a fellow, who hurls a roll at a nonexistent Old Nick, roaring out *"Apage!"* He is an "all-out nationalist of the Lutheran type," who raves to his students about "Hell and its pit" in a strangely mannered, very crude Old German with sixteenth-century reminiscences, and replaces theology with demonology. The meaning of Lutheran exorcism is perverted and reversed by deleting the God-concept of Luther's impassioned prayers and leaving Satan as the only "theological" figure.

Side by side with Kumpf teaches Eberhard Schleppfuss, the *Privat-dozent* [8] in the psychology of religion, an even more cunning champion of the idea of the devil. He has settled upon the psychological aspect of religious life—more precisely, the sexual, neurotic aspect—as his field; he senses in the objects of his discipline "only the almost irresistible provocation to defilement," only "the stimulus to blasphemy which emanates from the sacrosanct," and ostentatiously relates unpleasant and sadistically erotic tales about the witch-burning period. In this case the science of divine matters has become spiritual lewdness. All interest in theology seems to be born of bitter resentment against what is holy. The devil is more interesting than God, and the Satanic Nay is more stimulating intellectually than the triumphant Yea of Creation and Revelation. The lower element is mobilized against the higher; psychological knowledge supplants ontological and metaphysical knowledge. Sigmund Freud is proven correct, over against the mighty tradition of occidental theology from Augustine and Thomas Aquinas to Luther, Pascal, and Kierkegaard. Transferred to a critique of moods, this attitude means: melancholy is truer than joy; when melancholy one perceives things as they are.

All this, devised most slyly and with great technical competence and insinuatingly presented, amounts to theology's being compromised as a diabolic science, which then in turn involves music's being made suspect as an art very close to theology and the demasking of the Germans as a people especially vulnerable to theology and music. The element of the German character evoked in the cosmos of *Doctor Faustus* is not the "classic" which rejoices in reason and form, the bright, the humane: not Mozart[9] and Goethe, not Kant, Schiller, Lessing, or Hölderlin. Nor was it the lovably romantic, the element which appeals to the inwardness of one's nature: Eichendorff, Schubert,[9] Caspar David Friedrich,[10] and Mörike have no part in it. The strength and grandeur, devotion and ardor of the German Middle Ages play no part. Not a word is said of all this. But the element of violent immensity, of fatal *hubris* and perilous temptation is conjured up: everything which could be by hook or crook connected with Satan—thus the "Faustian," thus Luther, certain of Beethoven's traits, above all Nietzsche, whose career has to serve, even in many details, as a pattern for the biography of Adrian Leverkühn. Here "German" connotes above all the atmosphere of late Gothic architecture and of the age of the Reformation—to be sure without the concept of God of those periods—a world full of apocalyptic unrest, hysterical eccentricity, and syphilitic infection. These things are "German": "the urgent pilgrimage to the Holy Blood at Niklashausen in the Tauber valley, children's crusades and bleeding Hosts, famine, the Peasants'

---

[8] Roughly the equivalent of an American assistant professor.

[9] Austrian, not German.

[10] A romantic painter, 1774-1840.

Revolt, war and the pestilence in Cologne, meteors, comets, and significant omens, stigmatized nuns, crucifixes . . . A fine time, devilishly German time!"

On this occasion it is not Weimar that is "German," but Kaisersaschern, Leverkühn's home town, Lübeck[11] transfigured, a Lübeck shifted to the region of Naumburg, the landscape of Nietzsche, Bach, Händel, and Thomas Münzer;[12] it is a town psychoanalytically understood, of which it is said: "In the air there was still something of the attitude of the human spirit in the last decades of the fifteenth century, the hysteria of the dying Middle Ages, something of a latent psychological epidemic." And further: "Symptomatic of such archaic, neurotic depths and the secret psychological disposition of a town are the many 'originals,' eccentrics, and harmless half-crazy types who live within its walls and make up the image of the place, as it were, like the old buildings."

Against this atmosphere, where Luther, music, and the devil are at home, where Nietzsche-Leverkühn grew up, the classical philologist Serenus Zeitblom protests in the name of Thomas Mann, just as the author himself, in his speech about Germany, protests against Luther in the name of Giovanni de Medici. Zeitblom represents a humanism without brilliance, aged, and a bit Philistine; he is the philological element in Nietzsche, which connected him with Erwin Rohde and Jacob Burckhardt;[13] he is the spirit of Weimar if one thinks of this translated into the realm of pedantry and gloom. Therefore, in the puzzling game of concepts, the values "Goethe" and "Luther," "Humanism (*Humanität*)" and "music" have dissociated themselves and become mutual enemies. If moreover in former times the spirit of Mazzini, of political devotion to ideology and to the French Revolution appeared as the quintessence of horror and a prodigy of inhumanity, things have become thoroughly different now. "Democracy" and "humanism" have been united, and the classical philologist and humanist Zeitblom is also a little Settembrini—without his Italian fieriness, to be sure.

Seen in this perspective, the Reformation inevitably loses much of its "genuinely German majesty." "The renewal through reform of a religion which was already withering away, already regarded with general indifference" necessarily causes profound displeasure. "And a man of my type," Zeitblom writes, "may well ask himself whether these ever-recurring rescues of an element already on the point of perishing are actually to be welcomed from the cultural point of view; whether the Reformers are not rather to be viewed as reactionary types, harbingers of misfortune." Yes, yes, the Thirty Years War! If one re-

[11] Thomas Mann's birthplace.

[12] A German Anabaptist, much to the left of Luther during the Reformation; beheaded after the defeat of the Peasants' Revolt.

[13] Actually neither of these scholars was a mere philologist, or lacked brilliance.

gards world history as a bowling alley on which everything automatically follows a predetermined course, and where specific political catastrophes necessarily ensue, every time, from specific intellectual causes, then the Thirty Years War "necessarily" grew from Luther's actions, as National Socialism did from Hegel and Nietzsche and the Bolshevik Revolution from Hegel and Marx. Such a way of viewing matters mostly results in the distortion of history and in ideological montage. It disregards the element of freedom in all history, the mystery of spontaneity in every moment of history. It ignores the element of "translation," which mediates between the idea and actuality. It underrates the irrationality of matter-of-fact reality, the obscure, incalculable way things operate in the geologic movement of historical masses and forces.

Thomas Mann himself, in his speech about Germany, carries Zeitblom's resentful rejection of the Reformation to its extreme when he remarks: "Its results for Germany were the Thirty Years War, which depopulated it, caused a disastrous cultural retrogression, and probably, through its immorality and pestilences, made something different and worse of German blood than it was perhaps in the Middle Ages." Then the German classic and romantic movements, our music, our philosophy, are products of inferior blood? A truly despicable sentence, a fantastic indiscretion! But with these characteristics, I admit, the "devilishly German period" of the Reformation retains hardly a trace of any good quality. The author has taken over everything from Dürer's picture "Knight, Death, and Devil" *except* the figure of the knight. Luther himself, once praised in a challenging tone as a godly musician and the man who educated his people to attain metaphysical freedom, now appears, with his mouth full of crude invectives, as the deathly foe of real, that is political, freedom and the prime example of all our political doltishness. "He was a hero of freedom," says Thomas Mann, "but in the German manner, for he understood nothing about freedom. I'm not referring now to the 'Freedom of a Christian Man,' [14] but to the political freedom of the citizen—that not only left him cold; its stirrings and demands were profoundly repugnant to him."

It is remarkable that Mann's way of setting up political and "culture-critical" problems has not changed since 1917; it has remained on the same plane and is orchestrated in the same taste and style of thinking and with the same stock of concepts and motifs. What has changed is the position of the writer, his political "opinion." What has changed is the distribution of plus and minus signs, the recipes for arranging, polarizing, and accenting values, master images, and concepts. The disparity between the intellectual and political life of the Germans: here it appears again, but regarded critically and from without. In those days evidence of German maturity and superpolitical humaneness (*Hu-*

---

[14] Title of Luther's famous tract, 1520.

*manität*), it is the opposite today: namely stubborn provincialism, "romantic counterrevolution," peevish imperviousness to the ideas of the "European religion of humanity." The "quintessentially German divergence between *national* impulse and the ideal of political *freedom*" (Thomas Mann, 1945) corresponds exactly with the assertion that the German authoritarian state of the Bismarckian type was the citadel of true freedom and social progress, and with the polemical protest (of 1917) against the "baldly abstract" concept of freedom held by the political West, against the "system of parliaments and parties, that affects all of a nation's life like a pestilence." In 1945 we read: "The Reformation, like the rising against Napoleon later, was a *nationalistic* movement towards freedom"; for the Reformation (that had as much connection with nationalism as Robespierre's "virtue" with the Gospel) has slid in the meantime over to the side of German liabilities. The French Revolution, formerly seen as an unsuccessful attempt to make up for the lack of a reformation, an attempt that very quickly degenerated into ideological terrorism, has now become the epitome of political freedom, although, we are told, it actually brought forth the concept of the nation. "The 'nation,'" Mann now states, "was born in the French Revolution; it is a revolutionary and libertarian concept that includes the human; its domestic policy is freedom, its foreign policy is—Europe. All the attractiveness of the French political spirit is due to this fortunate unity." The whirligig of concepts is functioning splendidly. For now it is Napoleon whose "policy is Europe," while the Germans, otherwise of so cosmopolitan and European a disposition, were so morally stupified by music that they actually committed a "nationalistic" revolt against Europe when, allied with England, Russia, and Austria, they freed Europe from Napoleon's domination. For "the German idea of freedom is 'folkish' and anti-European, always very close to barbarism." With this, the bastard ideas of Hitler and Rosenberg are blithely projected upon the totality of our political and intellectual history; and phenomena like the Storm and Stress, Schiller, Kant, Beethoven's *Fidelio,* Stein, Marx, Uhland and the Forty-Eighters[15] are ignored in the most cavalier way. Thus, for better or for worse, he reaches the following conclusion: "A people which is not inwardly free and responsible to itself does not deserve external freedom; it has no say about freedom and when it does use that sonorous word, it uses it falsely. The German concept of freedom was always directed outward. . . ." Outward —to be understood as the "breakthrough by main force" to becoming the "world people of reality." In 1917 it was Thomas Mann who so brilliantly instrumented the ideological musical accompaniment to that attempted breakthrough.

---

[15] Here the author is listing movements, men, and so forth, all of which were products of the decades between 1760 and 1850. Nearly all of them were liberal, indeed libertarian.

# Variations on Picaresque (*Felix Krull*)

## by *Robert B. Heilman*

### I

There is a sense in which it is not surprising that Thomas Mann, having begun a picaresque story at the age of 36 and left it unfinished when the special demands of its style became burdensome, should never be able to dismiss it wholly from his mind, should at the age of 68 debate with himself whether to take up again the tale of a rogue or to begin work on the great Faustus theme, should in the eighth decade of his life return to the "artistic jest," as he once called it, and at 79 publish a continuation which was still not a conclusion, and should plan to go on from there. This persistent attachment to the story of Felix Krull is understandable if we remember Mann's tendency not to forget themes that had once got into his imagination, his delight in facing new technical problems, his zest in the unexpected or the daring, and, of course, that sense of the playful and the comic which we may lose sight of when, as may happen to the philosophic novelist, adulation focuses only on the portentously vatic.

Yet that Mann, after *Magic Mountain,* the Joseph series, and *Dr. Faustus* should at 80 be going on with an apparently trivial tale—think of Shakespeare after the tragedies returning, say, to *Taming of the Shrew* —will, somehow, evoke a question. And surely the basis of the question is the fact that the picaresque tradition is a relatively thin and discontinuous one, with few great works and fewer great practitioners. On the whole it seems meant for the writer, like the Byron of *Don Juan,* who will not or cannot encompass experience in its densities. If it be argued that *The Transposed Heads* and *The Holy Sinner* raise the same problem, or else eliminate the problem entirely by showing that Mann periodically tried a jocular hand at slight and slender forms, the answer must be that *The Transposed Heads* and *The Holy Sinner,* however far they go or do not go in themselves, nevertheless belong to the realm of fable, fairy tale, and fantasy where all depths are possible; while *Felix*

*Krull* is in a mode that is not only "realistic" but deliberately limited in its realistic scope.

## II

In picaresque a "rogue" is "hero," and we may define rogue as one who lives by his wits. The word *rogue* suggests such other words as *scamp* and *rascal,* the family of terms by which we designate the person who lives partly, though not threateningly, outside communal standards of responsibility. It is, of course, part of his way of life to simulate insideness; when he achieves a partial insideness, not by a specially designed facade, but by aspects of personality that elicit a spontaneous warmth of response, he is likely to be called "lovable rogue"—a term that, though it suggests some actual paradoxes of human make-up, is likely to denote a sentimental stereotype. "Lives by his wits," popular phrase though it is, has substantial defining value. For one thing, it suggests the wit that characteristically belongs to the picaro—the instant readiness of mind, made evident in repartee, manipulation of ideas, or extemporization of apt words or actions. More important, it states affirmatively his central modus vivendi, and thus it simultaneously implies the lopping off of those elements of personality characteristically lacking in the picaro. Living by wits implies knowledge of "the world," a sharp insight into responses that may be played upon advantageously, a mastery of the techniques of playing upon them, the ready appraisal of life by what Charlotte Bronte might have called "the organ of computation"— in a word, the apparatus of a "lightning calculator." Since in the life of "wits" certain functions of the mind dominate, this life also means a diminution, if not total elimination, of emotional depths and moral concern. The rogue is without conscience or superego or the inhibitions created by the community's sense of right and wrong; not so much that he is the enemy of these or falls short of an expectable standard by which we judge him, as that he lives in another world from them. He lives outside the "ordinary" feelings of the community: his hypertrophy of practical intelligence replaces a full emotional development. Not that the picaro is entirely "heartless" or without feelings; it is aesthetically necessary that he be not a monster. His self-love gives him some link to the rest of mankind; he can fear; he may have transient fidelities. But if he is afraid, his fear does not deepen into terror. He may experience disgust, but not horror. He is likely to be well endowed with sex, but he hardly experiences passion or serious jealousy, and least of all love. He may find people difficult, objectionable, or annoyingly skeptical, but he does not hate.

The key is shallowness, which in this case is to be seen not as a defect but as a fact, like the size of feet, and understood to have both advantages and disadvantages; in shallowness lies the clue not only to the degree but also to the direction of his feelings. Ordinarily, rather than earning an emotional identity by experiencing a complex of rejections, acceptances, and modifications, he simply takes over available patterns of feeling, and these are most likely to be conventional or orthodox. (In the presence of the articulate, energetic off-center sexuality of Diane Philibert, Felix Krull sounds almost like a proper young man.) In their different ways, Jack Wilton and Moll Flanders are unprincipled conservatives, who automatically identify with lords or dominant classes; a Communist picaro, though a private entrepreneur in his roguery, would be Marxist in feeling. As a wearer of old school ties the rogue is still the shallow man, responsible for nothing and free to act as unconservatively as he pleases; for instance, to pick the pockets of his tie-brothers. If the picaro tries unpicaresquely to discover an individual order of feeling, his shallowness leads him into a foamily sentimental outsiderism (if this is not a redundancy) in which we can see resemblances, at a great distance, to bohemians, Robin Hoods, etc.

In looking at the man who lives by his wits, we do not use words such as *villain, revenge, cunning, malice, bitterness,* or *trouble-maker,* for these imply a profundity of feeling or an intensity of commitment foreign to this kind of schemer. Words like *crook* or scoundrel vary with context and intonation; they may denote either a picaro or a serious attacker of the moral order. *Criminal* seems to me not to belong to the vocabulary of picaresque, though I say this with some diffidence, since the word is used by good critics of Mann, and even by Mann himself, to apply to the Krull-world. True, criminal and picaro both break laws, and there are other subtler affiliations which we must observe later. But *criminal* implies earnestness, the will to disturb, seize, and violate; deliberateness or "engagedness" in an attack on the will of others or on the public order; ruthlessness; illness. *Picaro,* on the other hand, implies flippancy; harassments rather than serious attacks; the trick-or-treat prankster; seduction rather than rape; the securing of and playing upon the victim's consent; a relish of the game as such; in Dantean terms, less the perversion of right feeling than a nonfunction of right feeling. Let us say that both are "psychopathic personalities," one with a distorted soul, the other with a rudimentary one. The picaro is the literary equivalent of that familiar abnormal type that must use talents, which are often extraordinary, not for murder but for masquerade; who must take by trick what he could earn by effort; who must dazzle rather than seek respect; to whom the world is a theatre rather than a school; who by spectacular fakery can get by as a physician or even surgeon, but who would never take a medical degree. Though many variations, degrees of development, and overlappings are possible, the criminal has kinship with Iago, the picaro with Falstaff.

So much for the rogue as such; now for the rogue as "hero." The picaresque writer has the interesting technical problem of securing, for an extralegal operator, "sympathy" and even "identification." He can do this by giving the picaro certain generally admired qualities—good nature, charm, an ironical view of himself. Or he can do it, as in *Lazarillo de Tormes* and *Guzman de Alfarache* and initially in *Moll Flanders,* by making the rogue somewhat a creature of necessity, maltreated by others and by circumstances; though here the scent of the "problem" story, the bouquet of pathos, and the perfume of the sentimental threaten the true picaresque mode. A sounder method is negative: giving no place, or at least no prominence, to other characters who, by being larger or nobler people and thus having a stronger claim on our "right feelings," might usurp the sympathy due the picaro. One way of "protecting" the picaro is to endow representatives of right feeling and "right thinking," if these get into the story, with disagreeable personal traits—pretentiousness, complacency, and so on. But in this method the danger is that the work may slide into satire, which, though it may have a role in picaresque, is, as a mode, a different thing, generically related to melodrama and therefore calling upon another area of aesthetic responsiveness. Though neither picaresque nor satire is essentially unstable, either one may, if the tone is not skillfully controlled, lapse into the other. Sinclair Lewis's Elmer Gantry, intended as an object of satire, is treated with so little depth and thrust into such a frenzy of misdeeds that the moral critique is somehow transformed into a tale of adventures inviting a relish of successful rascality. Becky Sharp, conversely, is transmuted from picaresque heroine to object of satire: this happens when sympathy for her piquant gamesmanship is allowed to shift to her victims, who are shown fully enough to draw us in on their side (Rawdon as father, for instance). For the most important method in picaresque is to keep the victims out of sight, lest they threaten our alliance with the rogue (thus we never see the candy-store owner that Felix robs). Or the victims can deserve what they get, through graspingness, or foolish pride, or a gullibility which is an affront to all good sense—the area in which satire may transiently enter picaresque. Or most subtly the writer can, as I believe Mann does, convey a sense of the positive satisfaction accruing to the "victim" in his experiences with the rogue. Here analysis of picaresque would take us close to the general realm of that singular victim —dupe, seducee, or even murderee—who must unknowingly convey his unknown readiness to the trickster or evildoer who will fulfil him.

The rogue-hero determines not only the treatment of other characters but also the scene and structure. Such a hero precludes extensive analysis of a situation: while retention of sympathy for him means a cursory treatment of other characters, his own shallowness forestalls prolonged study of his own nature. Instead of depth and rigor we have speed and multiplicity: since without "character" a story cannot indefinitely be spun out of one set of circumstances, one situation must soon be replaced by another; and since living by wits alone is not conducive to long residence, one scene normally gives way to another without much delay. Picaresque is naturally cinematic and episodic. However, the familiar use of *picaresque* as if its basic meaning were *episodic* is quite inaccurate, for, while it is virtually impossible to be picaresque without being episodic, it is entirely possible to be episodic without being picaresque, as in *Joseph Andrews*. Though in criticism *episodic* has usually a pejorative sense, nonetheless the continual change of scene inherent in picaresque has compensations: the form is made for the travelogue-novel. Mann may well have had this sense of the picaresque, for Felix Krull loved "the world" and was evidently intended to explore a good deal of it. In the end the potential of the episodic travelogue-fiction depends on the endowments of the world-tourist. The man who lives by his wits can have any amount of wits the author chooses, any amount of descriptive and analytical intelligence; he can be a brilliant mirror of life in the world. Often Mann confers upon Krull the gifts of his own recording and exploring, even of his searching, mind; indeed, even a measure of his creative imagination. Among his exploits in this book he must indeed have enjoyed making the charlatan something of a philosopher, the masquerader an exemplar of his own industrious, even cataloguing, encyclopedism.

## III

The form which cuts off the larger dimensions of human reality appeals by affording a relief from responsibility. For the reader it bans scruple and passion, offering aesthetic pleasure freed of the moral concern or emotional trials that are, in whatever way, a part of the aesthetic pleasure of "great" fiction. The writer of picaresque enjoys, apparently, freedom from the most severe imaginative demands; his mind can roam like a picaro, commenting where and as he will. He need reconcile the free flow of observation and opinion with only slight demands of structure and with the most easily obtainable consistencies of character. Mann can have a free hand here without our impugning his sense of form as we are inclined to do in his other novels.

But since picaresque is not the only fictional holiday from the full self, we must seek its uniqueness in another function. This, I suggest, is the catharsis of rascality—catharsis, certainly not as purification; perhaps as elimination; but primarily in the sense that it gives free "play" to certain human impulses. Or we might shift to the opposite metaphor and say that it permits these impulses to "work," and even, if one should want to argue for that end result, to "work off." (The end result, the psychic and moral residue of aesthetic experience, is outside the scope of this paper.) Through the picaresque hero a seamy side of man, the tricksy side, has a fling—that persistently present, though conscientiously kept-under, side, where there lurks a universal impulse to escape the shadows of guilt and to put things over on others or the world, to be nimble of foot, and hand, and head. One need not be a wit to feel the charm of living by wits: in the rogue world every deed is a repartee of action. The reader put off by the gay libertinism may find a comparable satisfaction in the "success story," for Algeresque is really picaresque transposed into another key: a fragmented personality still gets the booty, but now he is an insider operating by the latest edicts of the central rules committee. Since now there are no reckonings, Algeresque is a much more misleading imaginative exercise.

In picaresque another quality has a fling, the quality which I will call the "instinct for episodes." The very episodic structure which, as we have seen, derives from the nature of the picaresque hero, shows us something about the aesthetic functioning of the form: it appeals to a longing to reduce the muddled continuum of life to episodes manageable by cleverness alone. And here we run into counterimpulses called into play by an apparently simple literary genre: for that control of life by ingenuity which is offered by picaresque is secured by a reduction of reality, and that reduction itself implies a yielding, a going-under. For the "instinct for episodes" means a secret inclination to discontinuity, to hit-and-run raids on life, the impulse to shun the long and exacting unity, to live instead by episodes. If this "instinct" for the episodic becomes dominant, that is, gets out of balance with counterforces in our psychic equipment, it produces the "episodic character": he may find, within the norms of society, a way of life marked by many breaks and shifts, each perhaps eliciting a momentary burst of energy; or, outside the lines of conventional esteem, become a rolling stone, a gypsy or a "floater," or find some other style of "life by episodes."

At this point the orbit of the picaresque comes fairly close to another attribute of Everyman that is less likely to be recognizable because it is more held out of sight and rendered inoperative—namely, a certain vague proneness to degradation (perhaps a variant of the death wish). This appears normally in an impulse to relax the guards that give form to life or even in a taste for polite humiliation that is not restricted to eccentrics; radically in the life of the *clochard* or "bum" or in pursuits of a psychopathological sort; even sentimentally in certain flattering disguises—for instance, when dirtiness appears to its possessor to be an incisive critique of the falsities that may accompany cleanliness. But in what is necessarily a very oblique tapping of this element in the psyche, picaresque could very easily slide over into scatology or satire or a simplistic cynicism.

Finally, though I have argued that rogue and criminal must be distinguished, it may be profitable to consider the rogue a kind of denatured or sterile criminal, for we could then understand picaresque as releasing even the radically rebellious impulses. Since the conscious rebel finds all the direct voices he needs, the liberating picaro would speak only for those who in ordinary consciousness would take for granted their own unreserved sympathy with legal and moral order. The criminal, as it were devitalized in the picaro, could evoke the responses of the "good man" like an expressionistic symbol that passes through consciousness to engage other nonconscious powers. An exponent of catharsis doctrines might argue, from the tolerance of the picaro, for an analogous permissiveness of criminality by the social order generally, a "consent" through need, a letting-go to be followed by the imposition of penalties which are also a self-punishment. The analogy doubles us back again to fiction: in picaresque the nonmoral holiday always comes to an end; the picaro is reformed or is jailed; and in the aesthetic experience the rascal after his play period retreats within the citizen.

The operating hypothesis of picaro as residual criminal (true outlaw passion neutralised, as in the making of a serum) has another utility. The man who lives by his wits has usually a vigorous instinctive life; he somewhat paradoxically combines natural man and the sophisticated schemer. In this he is cousin, in however attenuated form, to some of the great embodiments of evil in literature: Goneril and Iago: the union of animal passion and exorbitant craft of mind.

## IV

Though living by wits suggests immediately sleight-of-hand and verbal skill, it should also suggest the older meaning of *wit*; that is, mind or intelligence in a general sense. For the picaro is in his way a creature of "mind"; his family tree is that of Ulysses rather than that of Prometheus or Hercules or Roland or Romeo. The picaresque experience is in one sense an exercise of mind, really a reveling in the mind as conqueror, a relishing of power through purely mental rather than physical or political or social means. The picaresque hero, a solitary victor with weapons of intelligence, corresponds to a desire in Everyman, a desire essential enough to insure, even in an anti-intellectualist atmosphere, endemic dreams of mastery by brain power, e.g., "control of nature." When, in ruminating about the picaresque mode, I first thought of the picaro as an imaginative representation of the instrumental intelligence, I felt immediately that there must be another artistic version of the dream of power—a version in which the impulse was not transposed into terms of playful rascality or seen in the intermittent flash of episodes, with the habitual picaresque flight closing off the full potential of energy in the idea only partly tapped by the fractional rogue-figure. In the other version, the theme would have to be, not living by wits alone, but living by brains alone, an earnest, total commitment to the exercise of power through the operations of mind. To complete the formulation was to identify the imaginative form of it: the Faustus myth. And to spot this cousinship, these divergent developments from a common starting point, was also to see further into the contrasting aesthetic experiences of picaresque and tragedy: in the picaresque, the free tasting of private power, easily summoned and applied as occasion came; in the Faustian, living in power while discovering the consequences of acquiring and regularly wielding it; in the former, indulging some of the self but happily cut off from the parts whence self-awareness and guilt would come; in the latter, being thrust by the fable of total self-indulgence into the depths of self where total knowledge is the final burden.

At this point I came across Mann's *Die Entstehung des Doktor Faustus,* and in it his account of his hesitating, after the completion of *Joseph* in 1943, between two possible subjects for his next work. It now seemed extraordinarily significant, more than a simple uncertainty between unconnected alternatives, that his choice lay between the Faustus theme and a continuation, after many years, of the Krull story. Then comes his climax: he reread the Krull materials—"with singular result," namely, "insight into the inner relation of the Faust-material with it (depending upon the solitariness-motif, here tragic-mystical, there humorous-criminal); . . ." In this exploration of the picaresque it seems to me worthwhile to record these independent conclusions, very close despite the difference of emphasis, on the affinity, illuminating as I hope it is, between the picaresque theme and the great tragic theme, or at least between the Mann versions of the two. One cannot note the bond without wondering whether Mann, in giving Krull the name Felix, of the meaning of which much is made, happened to recall that the Latin adjectives *felix* and *faustus* are synonyms. And one remembers, inevitably, the theory that in Hamlet and Falstaff a common theme is explored in different styles.

In all the literature that deals with the wit-conducted life there is, ultimately, ambiguity. Perhaps only detective stories naïvely exploit the passion for the mind's control of existence. Tragedy and picaresque set this passion in play; yet, though tragedy endows it with all the dignity of which it is capable in the completely presented human being, and picaresque lives by exercizing the human delight in this control, both are penetrated by a sense of the failure of mind alone. Oedipus finds mysteries he cannot solve by taking thought, Faustus learns the destructive price of power by knowledge. Picaresque heroes, at their best almost infinitely clever, nonetheless fall prey to sex, covetousness, prodigality, carelessness, vanity, in a word, to the irrationalities of human nature, and to accidents, the irrationalities of circumstance.

## V

Within the limits of picaresque a novelist can do little or much. As one would expect of the writer who saw in Felix Krull a version of the Faustian solitary, Mann used his form very richly. Compare Simenon, also of international fame: his nondetective fictions have a great air of searching the soul, but in the end we have only psychological mechanisms and banalities; whereas Mann, with the air of one intent only on a literary gambol, convinces us that more is going on than meets the eye—which is precisely what does not happen in most picaresque. Not that he does not observe the basic conventions of his form: Felix's career falls into episodes, and we know that the law was to puncture his felicity. Yet the episodes are developed with unusual fullness, they have certain dramatic interconnections, and Felix periodically finds in one experience a reminder of something earlier, a linking image or concept or feeling; in these ways the book moves toward a unity that itself suggests complications beyond the picaresque. Felix's fall is long postponed; the moral guardian always hovering fretfully over traditional picaresque is less present; and in this increase in picaresque "purity" we sense an original amplification of the rogue tale. Felix's own intelligent perceptiveness drives us to seek the intentions behind the mask. We find, too, a sense of character that goes beyond picaresque habits: Susanna Kuckuck, for instance, is in several ways quite reminiscent of Aglaya Yepanchin in Dostoievski's *Idiot*.

A stylistic mode of enrichment is self-evident—a grandioseness that is a parodic reminder of serious autobiography. So it is not surprising to find Mann describing the "fantastic intellectual charm in the burlesque idea of taking a much loved tradition—self-portraiture in the Goethe manner, the introspective 'Confessions' of the born aristocrat—and transferring it to the criminal sphere." That Mann found an immediate stimulus in the memoirs of a living confidence man makes an enlightening parallel between him and Fielding. Fielding found in the life of the criminal Jonathan Wild the genesis of a fiction ironically employing traditional ideas of greatness; Mann found in the autobiography of Georges Manolescu the genesis of a fiction ironically employing the traditional manner of great autobiography. But whereas Fielding was at heart an angry homilist who fell into laborious irony, Mann's method is akin to that of Joyce: placing the heroic and the contemporary in an ambiguous juxtaposition marked more by ironic interplay than by satirical undermining.

In amplifying picaresque Mann took another Joycean tack. Felix is not an isolated Mann character but is another figure in the study of rascality with which Mann was infatuated; Felix has some kinship with Joseph. Mann says that he wrote the Joseph story because of an interest in "the eternally-human, eternally-recurring, timeless, . . . the mythical." It is clear, I think, that the Krull story was taking on a mythical dimension, and that in some way it would have continued the Joseph theme. Joseph is many things, Mann says, "but then he perceptibly slides into a Hermes part, the part of the mundane and skillful business man and the intelligent profit producer among the gods, . . ." It is fascinating to see how Hermes persisted in Mann's imagination, for Hermes comes into the Krull story as the patron deity of Felix as thief, and his name is repeatedly mentioned. Indeed, it is not only by being a thief that Felix is a Hermes-figure: he is identified with luck, travel, theft and trickery, priapism, eloquence, and the arts—over all of which Hermes presided. Mann was clearly infusing into picaresque something of the mythic that absorbed him; indeed, we might say that he was constructing "the picaresque myth."

Goethe had noted the possibilities in the Joseph materials, Goethe was the model and rival in the use of the Faust materials, Goethe was, if not exactly the target, at least the figure that contributed some of the meaning to the amiable joke in *Felix Krull*. There is at least a little complication in Mann's attitude to Goethe; beside the *"imitatio Goethe,"* as it has been called, there is a sly impulse to twitch up the prima donna's skirts in front of the audience—not to expose but to get a laugh from dignity undone. Mann says that *Felix Krull* represents "my attitude toward tradition, which is at once kindly and destructive" (elsewhere, "sympathetic and detached"). How true, we feel. But another meaning intrudes here: since Mann "identifies" with Goethe and tradition, the words "kindly and destructive" also imply something of his attitude to himself. Indeed, in the same sentence from which I have just quoted, Mann says that *Felix Krull* "may be the most personal" thing he has done. These words written in 1930 have a peculiar applicability to the whole work, the fragments already written and the major additions of almost twenty-five years later: Mann's most daring exploitation of picaresque is to model the hero partly on himself. In *Felix Krull* are his own fantastically jocular *Dichtung und Wahrheit* and *Wilhelm Meister* (Wilhelm's son, incidentally, was named Felix).

Nor is it too hard, keeping in mind the necessary reservations, to conceive of *Felix Krull* as autobiographic. Critics often allude to the elements of self-portraiture in Mann's works, and Mann himself speaks of an artistic work as "a realization . . . of our individuality," even as "the sole and painful way we have of getting the particular experience." But if, even after Mann himself says, "A work must have long roots in my life, . . ." Mann-as-picaro seems inherently improbable, we can at least note the parallels between the Krull story and the Mann story as Mann himself traces it in *A Sketch of My Life*. Mann reports that he

was an indifferent student, given up by the school, but condescending
to his fellows, becoming a young man of "indolence, bad civic conscience,
and the sure and certain feeling of latent powers." Felix hated school,
played truant skillfully, and always felt superior to others. The elder
Mann died when Thomas was 15, the elder Krull committed suicide
when Felix was 18. Mann says that the family business had not been
going well, the Krull business had gone bankrupt. Thomas went to
Munich and worked in an insurance office directed by a friend of his
father, Felix went to Paris and took up a hotel job secured for him by
a family friend. Thomas hated the army (his "determination to free
myself was prompt, deadly, and in the event irresistible"), developed an
ankle inflammation in which there appears to have been at least a psycho-
somatic ingredient, and thus through medical connections secured a dis-
charge after three months. To Felix, military service was an "unpleasant
problem" that "weighed heavy on my heart"; his godfather "did not
have any sort of connection with army doctors" (as Mann's family did);
but he succeeded in having himself declared unfit by faking an epileptic
attack. While working in the insurance office, Thomas "secretly . . .
wrote my first tale"; from his secret life, of course, sprang his career.
While working at the hotel, Felix had also his secret life as "gentleman"
—the beginning of his basic way of life. An untried author, Mann persuaded the hesitant Fischer firm to take *Buddenbrooks* on his terms, and
this was good for both. Felix, a novice thief, persuaded a receiver-of-
stolen-goods to give him something like his own price, and both profited.
It is most difficult not to see the autobiographic in Felix's comments on
the expatriate's feelings about his native land—his tendency to senti-
mentalize it, to give it an undue authority, "especially when one's home-
land has behaved unkindly, unjustly, and obtusely toward one," and
eventually to "yield to the temptation" to return and "show himself to
its narrow view in all the glitter he has gained abroad," and, "with
mixed anxiety and derision in his heart," to "feast upon its astonish-
ment—just as, in due course, I shall report of myself."

And so on. Beyond the discovery of factual parallels, which I suspect
could be carried into greater detail, the most interesting quarry for the
biographer would be the oblique self-revelation by the author. What,
for instance, is to be made of the fact that Felix's Lisbon friends, his
tutors in diverse ways, are in one striking way reminiscent of Mann's
parents: the husband is German, and the wife Portuguese? The difficulty arises when Felix makes love to the wife (as well as her daughter),
but this difficulty is no greater than that of dismissing the German-Por-
tuguese marriage as a coincidence, since Mann was not the writer to
stumble into such patent resemblances of fable to life. Though biographical interpretation is not my object, it might be helpful to work
from Henry Hatfield's proposal that *Buddenbrooks* is "a sort of reckoning with the father image by the young man who has broken with family

tradition" and treat Senhora Kuckuck's passionate embrace of Felix as
an establishment of Thomas in the maternal approval, whether the
mother symbolizes the family tradition or the artistic impulse sometimes said to have been transmitted to Thomas through his mother. But
this would be only part of it. What of Kuckuck, whose name fittingly
suggests both "cuckold" and "rote," and who embodies something of
Mann's own encyclopedism? Again, Felix is an alter ego for the Marquis
of Venosta, who is also something of a Mann-figure: just as Mann's long
visit to Italy was the symbolic break with family tradition, so Venosta
breaks with, or at least resists, his family by *not* taking the grand tour
planned for him. Mann here reverses the family history in much the
same way as he does in transmuting the splendid funeral of his father
into the paltry rites for Felix's father. The Marquis (the insider who
wants to get out) and Felix (the outsider who wants to get in) are in
part opposing sides of Mann, complementing each other somewhat as
do Serenus Zeitblom and Adrian Leverkühn, the contrasting masks of
the author of *Dr. Faustus,* that sober twin of *Felix Krull.*

If we look for "oblique self-revelation," we must face the tantalizing
question of Mann's motive in rendering some phases of private history
in picaresque, of the "secret connections," as Mann himself puts it, that
"must lead from it [a work of his] to earliest childhood dreams, if I am
to consider myself entitled to it, if I am to believe in the legitimacy of
what I am doing." For one thing, picaresque would be the least expectable mode of autobiographic fiction; it would permit surprise, it
would be new and daring, it would be ironic and vastly playful—all
ends that Mann valued. It would disarm the audience, and, as an antidote to self-love, it would be an extraordinary means of securing detachment, of providing a wonderful distance and even freedom. The
most convincing guess about Mann's leaving *Felix Krull* long unfinished
would rely on his remark that *The Magic Mountain* could not have
been written ten years earlier, since for the work he needed certain experiences which had "to ripen within him." Surely this would be true
for *Felix Krull,* in which the severely limited view of man would be
possible to an artist of profound perceptions only when long experience
would make possible a curbing of his total vision, and of which the
comically disillusioned perspective, held serenely rather than with queru
lous cynicism, is possible only to an artist of the mature assurance con
ferred by long personal and professional growth. Through such control
he might give voice to self-criticism or guilt, perhaps effect a catharsis.
If, as Hatfield says, "Werther and Aschenbach die in order that their
creators may live," it may be that Felix had to live on in order that his
creator might live with himself. Might not the disillusioned artist large
enough to include himself in his own disillusionment say, "How like a
rogue's life mine looks!" Within the capacious irony of the rogue's tale
there lies, we may conjecture, humility: partly an oblique confession

partly an assumption of Everyman's rascality, a discovery of the heart masterfully transfigured into an urbane jest.

## VI

In his remarkable expansion of picaresque, Mann, ever *"novarum rerum cupidus,"* as he put it, altered tradition most strikingly by making *Felix Krull* "the story of an artist." This interpretation by Mann is not inconsistent with the other readings that I think the book requires—with the Hermes-myth suggested by the textual evidence, with the Goethe-parody that delighted Mann, and with the variation on autobiography that it is difficult not to infer. And if the picaro is, as I define him, one who lives by his wits, this definition also reflects much of the artist's professional modus vivendi—his skill, ingenuity, working with head rather than body, with individual artifice rather than group planning.

Mann's public wrestling with the problem of artist vs. *Bürger* has shaped a large body of criticism. In the *Krull* chapters long available for study, Mann's view of the artist strikes critics as denigratory. Though this view is open to argument, I wish less to debate than to distinguish two critical problems, both legitimate: one concerns the relation of a given work to the history of the writer's opinions on a given subject; the other concerns the kind of illumination of the theme by the unique work. The former problem belongs to biography; the latter, on which I want to work, to literary analysis. The assumption here is that the author is less recording an attitude, which may change tomorrow, than he is exploring a theme in the terms provided by the chosen form. This does not deny that he is recording an attitude, but it proposes that what is said is more than an attitude, and less impermanent. We might argue that *Felix Krull* says, "The artist is only a picaro," or, conversely, "The picaro is really an artist." The problem, however, is less one of contending for the deflation of one character, or the exaltation of the other, than of seeing what steady light is shed by the insistent pursuit of the analogy.

Mann's statement that Felix is an artist-figure is documented by many aspects of the story that need only be quickly mentioned: Felix's love of and skill in make-believe, costuming, and acting; his precocity and sensitivity; his flight from school to dreams; his sense of audience, whether he is staging scenes or doing daily jobs; his identification of himself with the "artists" at the circus; his taking on diverse roles with such ease that priest and soldier would claim him, and a whore thinks him "predestined for the service of love." Mann's technique is no less striking but goes deeper when he raises a serious problem of the artist. Early in the book Schimmelpreester complains that though they admire talent people never want to accept the "oddities that are always associated with it, and perhaps are essential to it," and shortly afterwards Felix himself is shocked when, after being charmed by a talented actor, he meets him without benefit of make-up and finds his face repulsive and his back covered by "horrible pustules." For the theme of the discrepancy between artist as artist and artist as person, the picaresque is an ingenious choice, for the hero's rascalities are a vivid comic symbol for all the "oddities" that accompany talent. Mann never forgets the duality of the artist, but, with characteristic novelty, he fuses two perspectives of the duality: the maculate man behind the charm of art, or, conversely—and more emphatically—the specialized conscience behind the consciencelessness in ordinary life.

This novelty is a key to the book, which Mann surely wrote with the love of novelty to which he refers more than once. For him the subject was old, but the method a total innovation. Early in the book Felix uses the words, "as one should see everything—that is, with a fresh eye undimmed by habit," and near the end he elaborates: "One should always try to see everything, even the most commonplace, the most completely matter-of-fact, with new, astonished eyes as though for the first time. In this way it wins back its power to amaze, which has faded into matter-of-factness, and the world remains fresh."

Take the traditional view of the artist as lonely, isolated, outside the community. This can become a romantic or sentimental truism. But exhibit this solitariness in the man who lives by his wits, outside the ordinary responsibilities and reciprocities, who never settles down but always travels, and it begins to take fresh outlines in a hard, untouched-up light. Show this solitariness as at once instinctive and finicky, calculated and prudential, vain and protective, the aloofness of a rascal who in his felt superiority schemes against the world. Combine an almost racketeering toughness with a constant aesthetic awareness. Paint the picaro despising the majority, fearing that if "[I] spent myself in a loose sociability—I should literally do violence to some secret part of my nature," separating himself from the circus crowd and feeling that he belongs to the "profession" of "entertainer and illusionist." To picture loneliness without sloppy clichés, let the picaro study the circus "artists," have him ask, "Are they really human at all?", have him deny that they can love, lest the lions revolt and the acrobats "pitch headlong toward the ground into disgrace and death." Have the Marquis of Venosta tell the picaro: "You always hold something back. . . . You seem to me the type who is more loved than loving." Here are the outsider and his essential unresponsiveness, but also the devotion evoked by art and the artist.

Yet this solitary astonishingly seeks not pure contemplation but power, power in the very world withdrawn from. True to the picaro type, Felix is a lover and pursuer of things found only in the world—material things, physical comforts, society and high places; he even has a "natural instinct for good form." The solitary as man of the world—an inconsistency?

Mann faces right into this, maneuvering his comic tale toward the inherent contradictoriness of all serious things. Felix says at one time that
his basic "withdrawal from the world" can go "amiably hand in hand
with an eager delight in the world"; at another time that "My basic
attitude toward the world and society can only be called inconsistent."
What we see in the dramatic action is the paradox that withdrawnness
is often an attribute of the power-holder, that art must succeed in the
world, that the artist is despite himself a strange marriage of bohemian
and bourgeois.

How freshen up the fact that as technician the artist works through
the concrete, that unlike the hermit he must cling to the immediately
perceived and felt surfaces of life? Again make him a lover of the world,
of all palpable and visible reality; make him an amorous observer and
recorder of sensory surfaces, an embodiment of visual and olfactory and
tactile passions. Let him stare into shop windows and lust after pastries
and jewels, carpets and clothing; let him exclaim, ". . . the enticing,
educational aspects of the world, . . . O scenes of the beautiful world!"

To fulfil himself as artist he must possess that world, take what he can
as he can. But of course. How give life to a copybook maxim for the
aspiring writer? Let Felix be a thief—of bonbons, jewelry, money; even
of the life and family history of another, at once ornamenting it and
himself and so delighting an audience. The "ruthlessness" of the artist
as artist appears with equal originality when Felix sharply rebuffs "honest
Stanko" by refusing to join in a projected robbery, since he "was not
born to be anybody's accomplice." Mann refines upon the artist's acquisi-
tion of materials in the two "robberies" from Diane Philibert: in the first,
with a minimum of active effort, Felix takes what chance has offered; in
the second, he takes what she offers herself; in each case what he gets is
used shrewdly, not thrown away prodigally. When Diane insists that he
"steal" from her for her own singular pleasure, in effect she is the individual begging the artist, "Use me."

In a well-known sense the artist must "love" all people, for hate leads
only to polemics. So let the artist appear as the picaro Don Juan: let Felix
love Genovefa the maid; Rosza the prostitute; Diane Philibert the blue-
stocking writer; both Senhora Kuckuck and her daughter Zouzou—old
and young, arrogant aristocrat and "prickly" Puritan. Then a double
reverse: let each bed-affair be a growth, a learning, even a symbolic statement. Let the prostitute be praised for giving her lover "refinement . . .
*through* love." Let Diane, in that wonderful erotic scene in the hotel,
embody at once the ambivalence of parental and sexual relations, a
Jocasta candidly seeking youth (richer far than Cocteau's querulous
neurotic), the "intellect [that] longs for the delights of the non-intellect,"
"spirit" yearning to glorify "beauty" and to be at one with the elemental,
a highbrow humanity romantically possessing, in an "eternal instant,"
through the ageless art of which the ingenious youth is a symbol, the

potency and completion not offered in everyday life. Let Zouzou, a remarkable character, be no less than a character, but attach to her the
chill odor of literalist common sense, scientific reductionism, and Puritan
squeamishness: art must woo even this, striving to release its underlying,
though incomplete, inclination to be at one with art. Thus Felix breaks
inevitably into the home where "order, reason, and intelligent planning
prevail"—breaks in, not to court but to seduce, for with none of them
can he live after they have served him, and he them.

Felix does not merely use others; he gratifies them. From beginning to
end he never loses the intent to give pleasure or the pleasure of giving it.
Mann's view of art is Horatian, but here again he is entirely original.
Don't show Felix as an insipid allegory of benevolent sweetness, but let
him be seen blissfully inhaling applause for successful costumings, mim-
ings, masquerades; report with satisfaction how much everyone likes him,
even when he despises them; boast of the extraordinary pleasure he gives
in sexual intercourse; have charm, not the Grandisonian kind, but the
kind that charms men out of jobs and money, and women out of their
clothes; please people not only by courtesy and attentiveness, but by
funny stories, an "agreeable voice," a beautifying pronunciation of names,
by flattery, and even pimping. But combine all this with indispensable
self-restraint: like a Machiavellian prince, Felix must use all means that
serve his end but cannot deviate into private self-indulgence. Excessive
sexuality "impoverishes our capacity to charm, since only he who desires
is amiable and not he who is satiated." But the art of pleasing is at once
narcissistic and altruistic: ". . . I loved myself—in a way that is really
socially useful, self-love turned outward as amiability." No sonorousness
here of "self-respect" or "integrity." Yet what is dramatized is a stern,
demanding, antiromantic view of the artist, disavowing the crabbed
hermit who writes or paints only to gratify himself, contemptuous of an
unresponsive public.

Mann paints the artist as nonmoral man; then he completes the storyteller's "double twist" by painting the morality of the nonmoral man.
If the artist always "shapes himself to please," nevertheless playing to the
public on its own terms will not do; again Mann might have come from
a reading of Horace to write that "a performance . . . had to be masterly
if it was not to be ridiculous." Not only must art "work"; it must have
a kind of excellence which is found in what it communicates beyond
itself; Felix has contempt for "every deception which fails to have a
higher truth at its root and is simply a barefaced lie." In this we do not
see him as either smirking or self-deceptive, any more than we do when
he keeps emphasizing the necessity of "discipline." He has a sense of
vocation, and he talks repeatedly of avoiding the cul-de-sac, the "shortcut
to happiness." He rejects the love of wealthy Eleanor Twentyman and
that of Lord Strathbogie, who by bribery would possess the artist personally, for he "rebelled against a form of reality that was simply handed to

me and was in addition sloppy" in favor of a life "dependent . . . only on imagination." "The way" is virtually a basic metaphor with him, and his "reason" calls masquerading as Venosta a "bypath" and a "dangerous road." But he is won by the "charm of the adventure, an adventure that would call upon all my talents"—a response to a challenge that Mann as artist might have used of himself; besides, he feels a connection between this great disguise and his boyhood costumings and games of imagination, so that we are to see here not a detour but the main line of vocation.

But let us suppose that to serve his sense of excellence the artist must have something else besides Horatian learning and discipline and studiousness to please, that is, the *je ne sais quoi*, the mysterious spark, the nonrational gift of Ion—how give it a new, untrite phrasing? Let a worldly priest and a lustful woman independently praise Felix for an "agreeable quality of . . . voice," and an army doctor attribute to him "astounding hyperacuity of hearing." Let him assert that what he did, in acting an epileptic fit, "happened as though without my cooperation . . . to my own momentary amazement." Let him show "natural adroitness" in hotel work, know a waiter's skills "by instinct," make an impressive report on unseen architectural beauties, and show an "amazing and mysterious" gift for languages, chattering in virtually unknown tongues with an "almost ecstatic feeling of being possessed by a foreign spirit." Let him burst into a highly articulate rhapsody on love and "swear" that "it just came to me," that he was "inspired." Let him plunge recklessly into tennis, a new game to him, and through sheer daring and bravado balance his "hopeless errors" by "occasionally performing feats of pure genius"—the doctrine of "inspiration" in joking understatement.

Besides the fine comic representation of inherited ideas about art—the morality of vocation, the union of imagination and discipline, snatching a grace beyond the reach of art—there are exciting inquiries and speculations. More than once Mann grapples piquantly with the sensations of imaginative life. When the "starry-eyed" Kuckuck talks of cosmic space and time, Felix has a "feeling of significance and vastness"; Kuckuck's tale of origins produces a "feeling of expansion that almost burst the limits of my nature." This strange excitement Felix goes on to declare "identical with" what as a child he called "The Great Joy," a "secret formula" of vague meaning but "soon endowed with an intoxicating breadth of significance." He had first mentioned an "incomparable expansion of my whole being" in describing the robbery of the candy store ("the carrying over of my dream treasure into my waking life"), and this in turn he identified with a "nameless sensation," "a yoking of emotions and fancies" which he called "The Great Joy." Though this is in some way connected with sex also, he insists that the sex act is only "the grosser part" of The Great Joy. Mann suggests links among childhood imaginings, theft, sex, and new knowledge. Whatever the center of the ultimately

undefined association—mysterious transformation, initiation, creation—
what is unmistakable is the groping for the symbolic continuity among
diverse experiences.

The finding of links, the quest of oneness, is an insistent theme, announced plainly or given imaginative, even strange and puzzling, forms.
If art is "universal," the artist is a unifier; he has something in common
with all. Felix is to travel, it appears, to many countries; he is a master
of many tongues; but our attention is more caught by the fact that, although his active maleness is not questioned, he has a delicate attractiveness that puts him aesthetically between the two sexes ("And I was," he
says, an "extraordinary being in between"), so that he excites homosexual
impulses in the hotel owner and other men and infatuates Lord Strathbogie—a bold symbolic way of attributing to the great artist the human
inclusiveness that lies behind the universality of his work. If Felix is
equally attractive to all, he himself feels a singular attraction, not to one
person or even to a succession of persons, but to pairs of persons, to what
he regularly calls the "double image"; this appears first in a brother and
sister whom he sees on the balcony of a Frankfort hotel and who strangely
excite his imagination; then in the mother and daughter Kuckuck, who
remind him of the Frankfort pair; and near the end Felix tells us of a
Lisbon toreador who was to reappear later in his life "as part of a double
image." It would be unfair to the spirit of Mann to see in Felix's fascination with doubles, given fantastic form in his simultaneous wooing of
mother and daughter, anything less than a double meaning: say, the
sexual overlapping of apparently discrete experiences, as well as the
artist's need to be at one with, to win, men and women, old and young;
or possibly a reflection of the artist's own duality. But overlying all other
meanings is the quest of oneness; in the kinship of different beings is a
clue to unity. In Felix's mind the mother-daughter pair are imaginatively
allied with the brother-sister pair, and he ultimately concludes that in
the "double" of which he dreams there is "a significant whole blessedly
embracing what is beguilingly human in both sexes." The "esemplastic"
quality of Felix's imagination, striving to put two things into one, the
"significant whole," or at least to discover unifying analogies, carries him
even outside the "beguilingly human." In Kuckuck's lectures he is aware
of the impulse to find unity in vast reaches of natural history; he hears
that "men and animals are closely related," that man and nature are
analogous, that in "playfully crossing the line from one domain into
another" (organic and inorganic) nature "was trying to teach us that she
was one," and that "All's well when Being and Well-Being are in some
measure reconciled." When he praises love to Zouzou, Felix argues climac-
tically that the kiss is "the pledge of that marvelous release from separateness" and that love always tries to "raise it [closeness] to the actual
oneness of two lives, . . ." The story moves toward more paradoxical

intimations of unity when the aristocratic Senhora Kuckuck, who a little later will accept Felix as lover, undergoes a mounting passional excitement as the bull is fought and killed at the *corrida*. Felix glances "from her surging breast to the living statue of man and animal" and concludes: ". . . more and more the stern and elemental passion of this woman seemed to me one with the game of blood below." In the "game of blood" life, death, and art have a strange nexus; and in the same game, what is more, the professor traces links between Christian beliefs and practices and those of a rival blood-worship cult in which the god lived both in the bull who was sacrificed and in the man who killed him—a teaching that joined believers "in life and in death; and its mystery consisted in the quality and identity of slayer and slain, axe and victim, arrow and target."

What *Felix Krull* dramatizes is the working of a Joycean artist, if not finally putting all things into one, at least pursuing with fascination all the subterranean connections that reduce the multiplicity of the phenomenal world. The artist as artist does many things, but universality is his need, and unity his obsession. Such is the oneness ironically concealed behind the narrative disunity of the picaresque, the acquisitive and amatory episodes of the mobile rogue; these are the wonderfully original design for that part of the old *ars poetica* traditionally assigned to the *poeta*.

## VII

The story was to end conventionally: the picaresque hero exposed and jailed. A romantic might argue that this would be society's inevitable rejection of the artist, a positivist that society eventually got its feet on the ground and rejected illusion; but both of these would be foreign to Mann, above all to the Mann of this book. It is safer to guess, I think, that imprisonment would have been a symbol of some failure of Felix's own—perhaps too great a fondness for "high life" in the "man of the world," a decline from that use and mastery of the world which are legitimately his into an unpermissible worldliness, such as tasteless pandering, being corrupted by material things, choosing local glory instead of moving on alone—or perhaps a nobler failure, an attempting of that ordinary humanity, of those personal devotions, which at the circus Felix theorized might mean the destruction of the artist. Or there is another possibility, and a more tempting one, that even within the confines of rogue comedy Mann might have explored another kind of flaw, such as vainglory and pride: for Mann did see Krull as a counterpart of Faustus, and one can imagine this audacious experimenter attempting a comic and yet not unheroic version of another artist who undertook too much.

At one time Felix believed he "had improved upon nature, realized a dream," and with "strange and dreamlike satisfaction" he rested from his "creative task."

Here we have to look at the *raison d'être* of the confidence man, who is distinguished among outlaws in that he requires the consent of his victims. Though we must not discount entirely the profit motive in the victims, it would account only in small part for confidence men, since there are better—i.e., safer or more intoxicating, as the individual's nerves require—ways of seeking gain. What we must postulate, I am convinced, is a basic need to confide, to show faith, to yield belief: in a word, a debased religious feeling (one would expect confidence men to flourish in skeptical ages). Here is a distant secular echo of *credo quia impossibile*, or, as a practicing Christian put it to an outsider hesitantly sticking a toe into Jordan, "I believe because I want to." We must also theorize that, whatever the eventual disillusionment and outraged outcries, the relation with the confidence man (the ritualistic exchanging of wallets, which is just what Venosta and Felix literally do) exists because the actions that constitute it are in some way satisfying or fulfilling in themselves. Now traditionally the writer of picaresque puts us on the side of the "con man" or "false god"; and this enjoyment of power becomes aesthetically possible because, as we have seen, the victims are not shown. But a greater writer of picaresque, who understood all the implications of "confidence," would surely mediate between the man of wits and those who believed in him, between the man of wits who not only took but in some way gave, and the faithful who not only were taken in but in some way fulfilled. Now is not this precisely what Mann does in *Felix Krull?* We see Felix energetically striving for, and eliciting, confidence; but whatever his ends, we also see his believing followers in some way rewarded or satisfied, finding, whatever the discrepancy between appearance and reality in Felix, a physical or psychic fulfillment—all the people for whom he works, Diane Philibert the novelist, the Marquis of Venosta, Luxembourg ambassador and Portuguese king, lecturing professor, and, on the evidence of an unfinished story, presumably his wife and daughter whom Felix strives to seduce. We see less victims than seekers and finders, tricked, yes, but served.

Now if the picaro is also thought of as artist, this theory of the confidence man is plainly relevant. Like the confidence man in real life and the picaro in fiction, the artist must win assent or confidence; the former must find the will to believe, the latter a comparable state of mind—namely, the willing suspension of disbelief. How boldly Mann puts it as he has Felix describe an audience's response to a skillful actor: "What unanimity in agreeing to let oneself be deceived! Here quite clearly there is in operation a general human need, implanted by God himself in human nature, . . ." Picaro and artist serve this need analogously, and for the "deceived" there is clear profit. When the actor left the stage,

Felix reports, "shoulders slumped, and virtue seemed to go out of the audience." "Confidence man" and "audience" supply a need for each other: what happens between them is, in Mann's words, "a mutual fulfilment." What is here put theoretically is expressed dramatically in all the episodes of Felix's life.

In the foreground, we see an analogy between picaro-victim and artist-audience; and in the background, if my analysis is sound, a third relationship analogical to these two—that of deity and mankind. Does Mann, in all his kindly-ironic speculations on the need for belief and the fulfilment of believers, bring these ultimate terms into play? I believe that in part he does. When, in a childhood feat of imitative artistry, Felix delights his audience, he is called "an angel child and an amazing little devil." The casual terms of praise suggest the "inspiration" in which Felix always believes, and on another occasion this is emphatically construed as noncelestial; as an artist in epilepsy Felix suggests that he must have been under "a satanic influence and impulse"—a theory to which he devotes a half-page discussion that is a joke and yet not a joke. The intimation of the more-than-human comes in most strongly in the account of Andromache, the circus artist. Was she "really human," he asks several times. He "worshipped" her, the crowd "worshipped her"; their "lust for her was transformed into awe"; she was a "solemn angel," the vision of whom was "painful and uplifting at once." Though man was closer to the animals, she "was a chaste body, untainted by humanity, and stood much closer to the angels." This thoughtful contemplation of the circus divinities, with whom Felix identifies himself, seems entirely earnest, uncolored by the deadpan ambiguities so characteristic of the book. The tongue-in-cheek treatment of the more-than-human appears with greatest verve when Diane Philibert pours forth raptures as Felix undresses and joins her in bed: ". . . catch sight of the god . . . *prêt pour la chapelle* . . . your divine limbs . . . The holy breast . . . you angel of love . . . you young devil." Her "intellect longs for . . . the divinely stupid, it kneels before it, it prays to it, . . ." For her, "the divine, the masterpiece of creation" is Hermes, *"le dieu voleur,"* and thus she confers upon Felix a new identity that he never quite forgets. To him, Kuckuck praises Hermes as "an elegant deity" whose brain-cell fabric "must have assumed especially artful forms."

Thus in a jest, and on one occasion less gamesomely, Mann gently pushes the picaro-artist a little way toward the analogous divinity-figure. And there, perhaps, he would have dropped it. But a tempting possibility comes to mind: suppose the rogue attempted the ultimate deception, the confidence man got too much confidence, the artist set out to provide fulfilments beyond the reach of art? Suppose the master-builder aspired to too great heights in his "creative task," or the herald of the gods mistook himself for Apollo or Zeus? This might have been the climax of "picaresque tragedy"; it would have been entirely consistent with the complex terms of the story as far as Mann has taken it; as a "kindly-destructive" reflection on the religion of art, it would have been of a piece with the philosophical jesting of the work; and the jail where we know Felix was to land would have been the right purgatory for a hero whom, despite some divinity in the dimensions, the author was determined to hold in a fresh picaresque perspective.

"Only the episodic," Mann has Kuckuck say to Felix, "only what possessed a beginning and end, was interesting and worthy of sympathy because transitoriness had given it a soul." Mann has taken a standard episodic form, one very likely to be tedious, and discovered in it a soul: not an allegory, but, beyond its outer liveliness, an inner continuity and vivacity that encourage speculation about its generic form and about the artfulness of its fabric.

# Aspects of Contradiction:
# On Recent Criticisms of Thomas Mann

*by Bernhard Blume*

Among the effects a great artist produces, one must include the resistance to himself that he evokes. This is not always a matter of mere
misunderstanding: even an unjust attack may on occasion yield insights
that are more fertile than simple-minded praise. What interests us the
least about Novalis' objections to *Wilhelm Meister* is the question of
their "correctness"; Kierkegaard's negative attitude towards Goethe,
Santayana's criticism of *Faust,* the objection raised by Ortega y Gasset
in his famous essay "Asking for an Inner View of Goethe": one-sided
comments of this sort are definitely able to further our understanding of
a great man. In any event, they accomplish one thing: they put our
judgment to the most severe test precisely when it is an affirmative one.
Therefore it may not seem inept to turn one's attention to the foes of
Thomas Mann's work in the hope of deepening one's understanding of
it. Such a procedure is all the more natural in view of the fact that
Thomas Mann is quite obviously the most violently debated figure of
twentieth-century German literature. Yet in applying it, one must impose
definite limits because the mass of critical comment and polemics is vast.
In this study I shall discuss only a few criticisms, published during the
last decade,[1] that can claim, because of the talent or the point of view
of their authors, as it were a representative or symptomatic significance.

First of all, it is remarkable that the most resolute foes of Thomas
Mann are to be found in Germany; in other countries he occupies almost
the position of a German classic. This disparity in his reception is all the
more remarkable in that German literature otherwise suffers rather the
opposite fate: again and again, for some reason, German writers of high
rank, Hölderlin, say, Kleist, Eichendorff, Stifter, are by no means fully

"Aspects of Contradiction: On Recent Criticisms of Thomas Mann," by Bernhard
Blume. *Germanic Review*, XXXI (1956), 175-190. Copyright © 1956 by Columbia Uni-
versity Press. Reprinted by permission of the author and Columbia University Press.
Translated by Henry Hatfield.

[1] That is, since 1946.

recognized beyond the German borders. In contrast, Thomas Mann represents German literature abroad: together with Rilke and Kafka he stands for German literature of the twentieth century. But in Germany itself it is precisely this representative role that is denied him.

One will not be mistaken in seeking political reasons first for this incongruous state of affairs. The great debates that have been carried on in Germany about Mann have by no means been focused on the peculiarity, the difficulty, the possibly questionable nature of the form of his novels. Always in these feuds the issues have been political, from the thirty-eight-and-a-half pages by which the *Reflections of a Nonpolitical Man* were shortened when they were included in the collected edition of his works, to his trip to Weimar in 1949 and the Goethe Prize that he then accepted from the Communist potentates. Apparently the time is not yet ripe for a full discussion of this series of events. Nevertheless it is surely no accident that the best contribution to the theme "Thomas Mann and Politics" was made by a Swiss critic. Near enough to comprehend the passionate excitement of such battles, and far enough away not to be implicated in them, the Swiss observer can follow the conflict calmly. In the disinterested perspective of such a distance, the *Reflections of a Nonpolitical Man* is transformed from a polemic, for or against which one takes a stand, into an "essayistic educational novel (*Bildungsroman*)." [2] This change in emphasis most felicitously makes clear what matters in critical discussions of Thomas Mann: insight into his nature as a *literary artist (Dichter)*.[3] Only this really concerns us, and for its sake one would indeed wish to be able to omit any consideration of criticisms of Mann made for political reasons. Only if political criticism were nothing but criticism of *political* statements, could this easily be done. Frequently however it occurs that a commentator discusses, or thinks he discusses, Thomas Mann's *literary* work while the real reasons for his rejection of it are to be sought in the political sphere, though at times he is completely unconscious of this self-deception.

In my opinion, a typical case of this sort is the criticism of Mann that the *Frankfurter Hefte* published in 1948. Undoubtedly the relationship between the writer and a great part of German public opinion was a most painful one at this time, nor was it a simple matter of the front line dividing the supporters and opponents of National Socialism. The invitation to return to Germany that Walter von Molo had sent to Thomas Mann in 1945 and its brusque rejection led to unpleasant debates. Harsh words were spoken by both sides. For a while, it seemed impossible to publish comments on Mann which were not at once appropriated by one

---

[2] Max Rychner, "Thomas Mann und die Politik," *Neue Schweizer Rundschau*, N.S. XV (1947), 465; also in *Welt im Wort, Literarische Aufsätze* (Zürich, 1949).

[3] [The word *Dichter*, often translated poet, denotes a writer in any genre who has real creative power; it is often opposed to a "mere" writer (*Schriftsteller*).]

of the hostile armies. When the editors of the *Frankfurter Hefte* gave space to a foe of Thomas Mann for a passionate attack on him,[4] and simultaneously tried to keep this attack insulated from the very resentful atmosphere of Germany, they must have been highly conscious of this state of affairs. A preface by the editors declared that Mann had many "low (*schlechte*) opponents," and they emphatically distance themselves from these low opponents. According to the editors, the objections raised by Ulrich Sonnemann in his essay have less than nothing to do with "hate-ridden resentment." They ask the question whether it would not have been better to make an attempt at "judicious objectivity," only to answer it immediately in the negative. It was necessary to *take sides* in Mann's case, they maintained; this could not be done *sine studio* nor by any means *sine ira;* certainly "not without exact knowledge and careful seriousness, but by no means without passion." It is easy indeed to be convinced that Sonnemann argued his case with passion. Less obvious is the absence of bitter resentment, despite the testimony of the preface. From what other source can the inclination to invective derive; what can it be but "bitter resentment," when the expression "roguish pedant" runs through the author's statements like a leitmotif? The phrase is Goethe's, and it is immediately explained: in *Wilhelm Meister's Wanderjahre* Goethe mentions pedants who are also rogues; these, he remarks, are "the worst of all." Roguish pedantry, an inorganic combination of the characteristics of Goethe's Mephisto and his Wagner, is the formula with which Sonnemann repeatedly describes Thomas Mann's nature. He definitely assures us that he loved Mann's work, at least until *The Magic Mountain,* although (as he immediately adds) Mann presents no "real people" compared to Dickens' or Balzac's characters; rather, it is "fate, process, the course of events" that carry his characters along. The author is at the point of saying that it is "life" that carries them along—in fact he does say so, but then he corrects himself: rather, it is the "leitmotif-like rhythm of the sentences . . . a music in the mood of twilights and rain which . . . transforms life into a vapor." Reading this, one is reminded of *The Beloved Returns,* that is, of the ambivalent admiration with which Riemer speaks of Goethe, again and again setting out to praise and ending by taking exception. In just this way Sonnemann emphasizes the great and potent "spell" which Tonio Kröger and Aschenbach cast on his generation; but, he then implies, this influence was an ominous one: through it Thomas Mann drove German youth into Hitler's arms. To be sure, he does not assert this quite so bluntly; what he does say is rather: "that the great bulk of this generation would not have let itself be led so disastrously astray, led towards spiritual and social ruin if the narcotic of self-abandonment, the inclination to abandon oneself

---

[4] Ulrich Sonnemann, "Thomas Mann oder Mass und Anspruch," *Frankfurter Hefte,* III (1948), 625-640.

to nothingness, the coy flirtation with death had not first deeply penetrated the consciousness of its elite groups, who regarded this tendency
as an essential source of aesthetic pleasure."

It is no wonder, he continues, that such "magic of decay," such coy
enticement finally forces death to appear; it obeys the conjurer, even
though in strange shape—"in the shape of one possessed," that is, one
"marked by a forelock and a little black moustache." And now we understand the intention of this angry demurrer. It seems to call out to Thomas
Mann, in 1948: don't distance yourself so pharisaically from those who
stayed in the fatherland; you yourself enticed the demons even if now
you claim to have been uninvolved.

But the author breaks off to return to his real task, the characterization
of Mann as an artist. No longer considering only his early works, he seeks
for a more inclusive formula. Deriving it from *Felix Krull,* he finds it in
the phrase "magical swindling (*magisches Hochstaplertum*)." Harsh words,
one feels; but, Sonnemann explains to us: " 'Swindling' as the characteristic of the artist is Thomas Mann's own term; he had the courage to
coin it himself." Sonnemann does not further concern himself with the
ironic lights that flicker about this term as it appears in Mann's work,
but the reader remains aware of them. What is *swindling,* he asks himself,
as the world uses the word? Well: misrepresentation, masquerade, deceit,
the control and skilful exploitation of external forms to which no actual
rank and value correspond. Now we understand the polemical title of
Sonnemann's essay: "Thomas Mann or Measure and Presumption."
*Measure and Value* was Mann's title for the journal which he edited
during his exile in Switzerland; "Measure and Presumption" is the title
Sonnemann chose for his essay. "Presumption," one seems forced to conclude from this confrontation, sheer presumption takes the place of
genuine "value" in Mann's work, and just that is swindling. The essence
of his Goethe novel is a swindle too, indeed most emphatically that, in-
asmuch as Thomas Mann does not play his own part here, but "puts
words into Goethe's mouth," all through the book. Thus the greatest
German poet serves in Mann's novel as the "silver background of a
mirror, in which roguish pedantry is not loath to see itself reflected";
he becomes a "foil," a "mask," that must be used to "pass off" Mannian
"loquacity" as the wisdom of Goethe's old age; above all—and here we
are in the realm of politics again—to cull the expressions of displeasure
and anger from Goethe's remarks about Germany and the Germans and
to "expatiate on them"; and thus to make clear that "while of course
everyone knows of these things today, Thomas Mann really knew of them
over a century ago." But before Sonnemann pursues this line of thought
further, he addresses himself again to Mann's creative work, to *The Magic
Mountain,* a book "magical here and there in its intellectual depth
(*Geist*) and humor, also in individual poetic touches of considerable
power." To be sure, he at once pushes aside Settembrini and Naphta,

calling them "debating impossibilities"—also "the lazy and by no means natural [or spontaneous—*naïve*] Hans Castorp, who stays so long in secondary school," and the figure of the "highly morbid" Clavdia, "who alas is only sketched in, as a leitmotif." Yet the critic approves of one figure, indeed "the best, most lasting personage whom this writer has ever achieved." It is Mynheer Peeperkorn. For the sake of this one character Peeperkorn, Sonnemann is inclined to a certain indulgence even; or, strictly speaking, not he himself but "some later generation" will "forgive Thomas Mann much, for Peeperkorn's sake"—he is convinced of that. Before that point is reached, we naturally hear again the "but" à la Riemer. For posterity will not fail to note "a significant circumstance: the only great figure in whom . . . the narrator rises above himself . . . can only stammer; he is not articulated." And thus, after all, the real "experiential substance" of this figure, with its "engagements (*Verpflichtungen*) that passionately demand to be fulfilled," is not really expressed. To be sure, it is part of the profound humor of the novel that Peeperkorn cannot speak. It also is related to its contrapuntal nature. Imagine the author granting the wish of his critic, giving Peeperkorn the talent for articulated speech—to Peeperkorn, the "symbol of majestic inadequacy"[5] (and how easily Mann could have arranged that!)—how utterly would the structure of the whole have been destroyed! For it is based on precisely the circumstance that on the one side, the "talkers," the intellectuals, lack "life"; whereas those "men of vital potency," on the other side, lack intellect. And the fact, regretted by Sonnemann, that even Peeperkorn ends as a suicide, is most precisely in accord with this structured order.

In the suicide, Sonnemann, to be sure, sees nothing but a "no exit" situation—"no exit" for the author, not his characters—a situation moreover which is already old-fashioned; for, he claims, the "onrushing reality of the century" has long since left the nihilistic author behind. The proof of this he finds in Mann's political writings, which he calls clumsy and intellectually thin. Yet even if they were of dazzling intellectual brilliance, that would be just as irrelevant to an evaluation of Thomas Mann's creative achievement. Therefore it is unnecessary to attempt a political evaluation of Mann, an end to which Sonnemann devotes almost half of his essay. That does not mean that his political opinions are tabu; like everyone's opinions they are open to criticism and contradiction. But it is a different matter when the passion of political *engagement* takes over the aesthetic sphere and political attack appears as artistic judgment. Certainly, it is one of the tiresome evils of political struggle that one cannot attack an opponent without running him down. Wherever literary criticism becomes the prey of this usage, it can lead in my opinion to no real advantages.

[5] Thomas Mann, *The Story of a Novel* (New York, 1961), p. 199.

In any case, the criticism which might be directed against Thomas Mann's political views would not, in my view, be addressed to details but to their lesser validity generally. That may sound strange; but compared to the multiplicity of levels and dimensions possessed by *The Magic Mountain, The Beloved Returns, Doctor Faustus,* Mann's more direct, unambiguous, definite manifestos and polemics are of secondary rank, I think; they lack the perspectivism and the irony that characterize his creative work. To the degree that the political questions about which Mann took a stand lose their immediate relevance, the real situation will become clear; this seems a safe prediction. Then it will appear that the observations of Zeitblom, say, which can already be found in Mann's speech "Germany and the Germans," are not thus simply established as his "real belief," but rather that this "real belief," by being put in the mouth of a fictional character, is relativized, indeed possibly parodied. Therefore let me assert, in opposition to the usual view, that "direct" statements of a creative writer, say in diaries, letters, or essays, have a lower, not a higher "truth content" than his creative work.

This "truth content" is the matter at stake in a basic, radical attack launched against Thomas Mann by a distinguished essayist, Hans Egon Holthusen.[6] He too complains again and again about Mann's political beliefs, deploring now his partisan rigidity, now his inconsistency. Here he continually plays off the *Reflections of a Nonpolitical Man* (1918) against "Germany and the Germans" (1945) and *Doktor Faustus.* Yet one is inclined to apply to Holthusen's own work what he says of the "thematic arrangement" of *Doctor Faustus* as "cultural criticism": that is, it is most rewarding when it avoids political matters. Above all, philosophical (*weltanschauliche*) defects provoke him: what he cannot find in Mann's work is truth. But what is the "truth" of a creative writer? Well, in Mann's case, as Holthusen says, it is "something transitory, non-binding, and highly suspect. It is conceived of without 'eternity' and quite without objectivity." He cites from the *Reflections* a remark of Mann's to the effect that all truths are relative to a given time. "The intellect," Mann writes, "is the courtier of the will, and the needs . . . of a time present themselves as 'insights,' as 'truths.' " Obviously this derives from Nietzsche. Holthusen also stresses it, a bit condescendingly, as a "discovery of the era of Schopenhauer and Nietzsche, now pretty dated." Here it "is being popularized in a *feuilletonistic* way," as he puts it. Now Thomas Mann was not the first *feuilletonist,* after all, to popularize Nietzsche's doctrines; the "consistent relativism" which Holthusen so categorically censures in Mann is a basic characteristic of the age.[7]

---

[6] Hans Egon Holthusen, "Die Welt ohne Transzendenz," *Merkur,* III (1949), 38-59 and 161-180. Also published as a brochure (Hamburg, 1949).

[7] Holthusen has no difficulty in defending himself when the charge he made against Mann is turned on him. Thus: "Someone asked how it came about that I awarded the laurel to the Catholic philosopher Haecker at one time, and at another to the nihilist

"There are no definitive statements any longer," Wilhelm Emrich has declared in an analysis of the contemporary novel, "neither in Kafka, nor Musil nor Thomas Mann, since the multiplicity of possible reflections and insights approaches infinity." [8] This is precisely the point, and Emrich accordingly does not waste his time by informing us whether he welcomes or deplores this situation, but rather indicates how this multiplicity of possible reflections and insights necessarily produces new artistic forms and "structural models." Thomas Mann's tendency "to connect everything with everything else," which bothers Holthusen so much, rises from his awareness of this situation; and when Holthusen states that Mann's concepts have "no definite boundaries, no locus, no sphere in which they are valid without ambiguity," he will be contradicted on one point only: that is, in his conclusion that therefore they are "not to be taken seriously." The much-cited irony, the "ambiguity" of Mann's style and attitude, is by no means only the result of changes in his mood, as Holthusen seems to assume. Rather, it is the necessary expression of an artistic view in which there is nothing unambiguous, but only perspectives which endlessly cross and intersect one another.[9] Inevitably, anyone who expected to find the "simple statement of great wisdom"—the absence of which Holthusen deplores—in art of this type will be frustrated. In general, concepts like "wisdom" or "eternal truth" are equally unusable as aesthetic criteria; for, as Hofmannsthal put it as a young man: "the value of a poem does not depend on its meaning (otherwise it would be wisdom, say, or learning) but its form." [10] Still sharper is Nietzsche's formulation: "To be an artist, man pays the price of experiencing the element which all nonartists call 'form' as *content,* as 'the thing itself.' " [11] Just this is the price Thomas Mann paid to be an artist. It is an inescapable fact that such an artistic existence is problematic. Just how problematic it is appears in Nietzsche's sentence which follows the aphorism just quoted: "Thus, to be sure, one becomes part of an *inverted world,* for content becomes something merely formal —and this includes one's own life." Undoubtedly Mann was aware of

---

Benn. For after all, a man's intellectual world must be unambiguous, a definitely bounded system. . . .

"I accepted the challenge, put the word 'truth' in the plural and asked in return why it should not be possible to owe fealty to different, even opposed truths in the same degree, if not at the same time, if one affected my consciousness no less strongly and centrally than did the other.

" . . . I distinguished between a truth 'for me' and a truth 'per se'. . . . " *Ja und Nein* (München, 1954), p. 267.

[8] "Formen und Gehalte des zeitgenössischen Romans," *Universitas,* XI (1956), 51.

[9] Compare also Max Rychner's statement: "The concept ambiguous . . . means . . . in Thomas Mann that a phenomenon partakes of two antithetical spheres of meaning." *Die Neue Rundschau,* 1955, Heft 3, p. 270.

[10] *Loris. Die Prosa des jungen Hugo von Hofmannsthal* (Berlin: Fischer, 1930) p. 265.

[11] *Der Wille zur Macht* (Leipzig, 1930), p. 552.

these profound problems; the pact which Leverkühn concludes with the devil is evidence of this. We remember the condition the devil makes: "Thou shalt not love!" Basically it is superfluous, for Leverkühn has always fulfilled it. Actually he *cannot* love, his purely formal existence in which everything becomes art makes this impossible. This is his guilt, tragic guilt if you will, for it is presupposed in his own being. As we know, Mann encountered it in his own existence. From the beginning, "ironic distance" from life has been regarded as a basic theme of his personality and his creative work. In the last analysis, even his political emigration can be regarded as the logical continuation of an attitude whose decisive trait has always been "not being involved." It is not meant in a completely positive way but still stated with respect when Hans Paeschke declares: "Indeed, it is no laughing matter when a man who was an outsider all his life . . . an emigrant from life even before his emigration, is finally sought out by his most essential archetype as Leverkühn was by the devil." [12] (Paeschke's critique of Mann, in this as in other matters, is distinguished by his objective mode of argumentation.) Thomas Mann himself called *Doctor Faustus* "a penance for having been away." [13]

By citing this "being away" some writers have tried, *tout court*, to deny Mann any right at all to treat a theme like that of *Doktor Faustus*. In a negative discussion of the book, Walter Boehlich declares that the author lacked "the soil to which he owes all"—German soil, that is—when he was writing *Doctor Faustus*, and therefore the novel inevitably had to "fail." "To the degree to which he no longer understood Germany he had to misunderstand the symbol of Germany [that is, Faust]." For far from Germany, on American soil, no such symbol can be forged, for America "a country without a great literature, without a poetic tradition, without vital criticism . . . seems not to be a country in which symbols can flourish." Also it is difficult, Boehlich holds, to describe such matters as the developments in Germany from 1933 to 1945, unless one has "experienced" them; by "experience" he means physical presence, "being there." At the close Boehlich reaches a sarcastic climax in alluding to a famous remark[14] of Goethe's: "It was an epoch of world history, and Thomas Mann can say that he was not there." [15]

It is delightfully ironic that the most valid reply to Boehlich's claims comes from Holthusen. On the question of "experience" and "being there" he declares: ". . . it is not 'experience' that makes the creative writer, but imagination." Further explaining his position, he writes: "I

[12] Christian E. Lewalter and Hans Paeschke, "Thomas Mann und Kierkegaard. Ein Briefwechsel über den *Doktor Faustus* und seine Kritiker," *Merkur*, III (1949), 933.

[13] "Die Aufgabe des Schriftstellers," *Neue Zeitung*, 26 September, 1947.

[14] [Goethe's remark was made after the army of revolutionary France checked the invading allied forces at Valmy in 1792.]

[15] Walter Boehlich, "Thomas Manns *Doktor Faustus*," *Merkur*, II (1948), 588-603.

have read bundles of poems that were written in concentration camps, and there was barely one of them which could not have been written by a third-class, sentimental lyricist of the school of Emanuel Geibel.[16] On the other hand, two or three pages by an important writer, who never saw a concentration camp from within or without, seem to me the best, as literature, that I have read on this topic."[17] These remarks of Holthusen follow almost immediately after Boehlich's article in the same journal. To be sure, they do not refer to it nor to Mann, but that does not prevent them from being relevant.

But quite apart from the question of how Thomas Mann may have conducted himself in life, distance from life, "coldness in life" is one of the great themes of his *work*. At the end it undergoes a grandiose heightening (*Steigerung*) in the figure of Leverkühn and in his pact with the devil. Yet parting from life and renouncing love make up only one side of the diabolic pact. The other is the alliance with illness. Here it is not simply that intellectual heightening is linked to the weakening of vitality, genius with degeneration, as occurs again and again in Mann's work from *Buddenbrooks* on. Now it is rather that this linking is consciously engineered. What Leverkühn is ready for, what he desires in the depth of his being, is heightening of productivity at the price of self-destruction. Basically the spirochetes are only the drastic expression of a condition which under certain circumstances could also be brought about by drugs. "Illumination" as a toxic frenzy, inspiration reached at such a price, is a crime, a pact with the devil. Holthusen makes his strongest objections to the pact with the devil as the intellectual center of the novel—and thus appears again in the ranks of Mann's opponents. If one makes the countervailing point that the appearance of the devil must be regarded as a dialogue imagined by Leverkühn (which Holthusen obviously failed to see) it is correct as long as one remains in the psychological and rational sphere.[18] This is the sphere of Zeitblom, the fictive narrator of the story, whom Holthusen continually confuses with Mann.[19] Erich Brock, with his statement that the devil of *Doctor Faustus* is "one of those ambiguous marginal concepts which cannot exist and yet must exist," comes closer to the paradoxical complexity of this figure. He is, Brock says, "the most extreme element of our self, and precisely for this reason he is wholly alien to us."[20] In this sense it could be maintained that the devil in *Doctor Faustus* simultaneously exists and does not exist, that Mann does and does not believe in him. That is not simply ironic am-

---

[16] [Nineteenth-century writer; here a symbol of derivative mediocrity.]

[17] "Exkurs über schlechte Gedichte," *Merkur*, II (1948), 605.

[18] Lewalter, *loc. cit.*, p. 925.

[19] Compare Hanns Braun, "Welt ohne Transzendenz? Zu einer Kritik an Thomas Manns *Faustus*," *Hochland*, XLI (1949), 597.

[20] "Die ideengeschichtliche Bedeutung von Thomas Manns *Doktor Faustus*," *Trivium*, VII (1949), 123.

biguity; basically the situation of Goethe's Mephisto is very similar. But precisely by comparing *Doctor Faustus* with Goethe's *Faust* Holthusen attempts to depreciate the novel. In Goethe, he declares, the devil is "finally overcome by the Yea of eternal love. In *Doctor Faustus* he has become autonomous and no longer has a divine opponent to fear." Or, as Holthusen says elsewhere, the "idea of God" is "not to be perceived" in Mann's works. Even if that were the case, it would not indicate anything about the actual value of Mann's novel. But quite aside from that, when the devil appears in a novel and God does not, that still does not mean that God is not present. It is well known that there are countless stories in which the devil appears and God is not even mentioned; this does not weaken their Christian character. In this case the term "negative theology" has rightly been used. No one would derive from this the statement that Thomas Mann "believes" literally in the figures of Christian mythology. That the Evil One exists may reasonably be doubted; not that evil exists.

The pact with the devil in *Doctor Faustus* signifies that aesthetic existence is viewed under the aspect of *guilt*. Yet it does not mean that music, regarded in the *Reflections* as a gift of God, is now, as Holthusen puts it, "briefly and crudely put, possessed by the devil." Rather, it partakes of both realms; music is an instrument which belongs to the higher and lower powers and therefore is ambiguous; everything depends on the spirit of the man it serves. These thoughts are not as wholly new and unheard-of, as wholly off the track, as Holthusen's objections might lead one to believe. There is that *Kapellmeister* Berglinger whom Wackenroder imagined in order to exorcise the doubts and anxieties in which his passionate love for music involved him. When Berglinger speaks of the "criminal" innocence of music, of its "terrible obscurity, ambiguous as an oracle," [21] when his author says of him that the "mere *health* of the soul did not satisfy" [22] him, when he himself declares: "My lustful artist's joys are poisoned deep in the very germ; I wander about, sick in my soul, and from time to time poison pours through my veins," [23] those are turns of phrase in which the themes of *Doctor Faustus* are already sounded, as it were in a prelude. The author, Wackenroder, had a soul of childlike purity and piety. No one has ever doubted it, but precisely in unlimited abandonment to the divine beauty of art he saw the temptation to stray from the path of living up to the Christian and moral demands of life.

In Thomas Mann's case there is naturally no question of his accepting the basic Christian dogmas in a similarly unquestioning way. Whether

[21] Wilhelm Heinrich Wackenroder, *Werke und Briefe*, ed. Friedrich v.d. Leyen (Jena, 1910), I, 194.

[22] Ibid., p. 127.

[23] Ibid., p. 274 (by Tieck). On the figure of the demonic musician in the romantic period, cf. also Korff's discussion of Berglinger, in his *Geist der Goethezeit*, III (Leipzig, 1949), pp. 60 ff. and of Kreisler, vol. IV (Leipzig, 1953), pp. 544 ff.

one should cover with scorn, however, the undogmatic "religiosity" that he indeed inclines to claim because it does not correspond to one's own "transcendental" position, is another matter. We cannot perceive the "truth" of a creative writer's work in its transcendence or immanence or elsewhere; but rather, in the exact place in which Holthusen, at the end of his essay, sees the "Archimedean point" of Mann's world: in the personality of the author himself. Of course, Holthusen thinks that he has made an annihilating pronouncement; in my opinion rather, his metaphysical rigorism[24] reminds one of the embarrassment which Charles Du Bos used to feel when faced with the question whether this or that thought of a writer was "true." Something within him, Du Bos declares, would then at once answer: "Undoubtedly, since it is *his* thought." According to Max Rychner's elucidation of this remark, this means that "one must read every statement of a poet physiognomically, with reference to that 'truth' which is given with the personality itself and need not be translatable into generally valid terms." [25]

Such physiognomic comprehension will not be achieved by any approach that applies its own political or metaphysical criteria to the poem from without. This is also true of the *moral* aspect, to which Felix Rahn has subordinated his critique of *Felix Krull* and Mann's late work in general.[26] Above all, his attack is centered on the "shamelessness" of *Krull,* by which he does not mean, at least not primarily, the shamelessness of the hero but that of the author. This is stated, half withdrawn, supported by a variety of evidence and yet qualified again, by a critic who is obviously concerned not to be confused with the crude, undiscriminating opponents of Thomas Mann. In a prefatory note he declares that it is not his intention "to disparage the admired *oeuvre* or the honored personality of a creative writer." Any negative criticism is directed against a "legend," the "image which, with the influence of the international press, has become current in our contemporaries' consciousness." True, Mann has relativized this image himself, but in such an "ironically sly way" that he was not believed. Thus a "claim to greatness and authority" still clung to him which provoked opposition. Of course, not everyone had the right to such opposition." "But if," Rahn declares, "knowledge, suffering, and love entitle one to take a stand, I may proceed with a good conscience."

[24] This rigorism has naturally provoked an equal rigorism against itself: see Lewalter's remarks (*loc. cit.*, p. 927) on Holthusen's concept of transcendence: "These are the *idées fixes* of theological supernaturalism; until now I had assumed that since Schleiermacher, they had existed only as a historical curiosity." Precisely "transcendence" is what Erich Kahler claims for Mann: "What is irony but rising above oneself, but a chain reaction of transcendence." "The Devil Secularized," *Die Neue Rundschau,* 1948, p. 186.

[25] "Erinnerung an Charles Du Bos," in *Welt im Wort* (Zürich, 1949), p. 328 f.

[26] "Das Spätwerk Thomas Manns und die Frage der künstlerischen Sittlichkeit," *Neue Deutsche Hefte,* I (1955), 174-194.

Here is a critic with scruples, then, a polemicist who denies aggressive intentions and who moreover—one can't express it otherwise—has been entranced by his opponent. He seems to realize it himself. So unexampled is Mann's art of depiction, he assures us, so great his "joy of playing" that it is able to tinge even the sentence structure of the critic who is reproaching the writer for his "mannerism." Not only his sentence structure, I think. In contrast to Mann's other opponents Rahn is tied to the object of his criticism by a sort of love-hatred or at least definite ambivalence—"stretched to the breaking point in the cleft between admiration and revulsion." Obviously, an instinctive malaise is primary here, which, while it is hunting for justifications, is repeatedly called to order by a trained aesthetic intelligence. Here one can observe that the critic is himself by no means free of the weaknesses which he censures in his author. Like many another he deplores the writer's lack of a fixed position, and yet cannot find the "firmly established point of view" from which the world of his opponent might be overthrown. "A kingdom for a point of view!" he exclaims, not without self-irony. Until it is found, the most varied *possible* points of view are found, and so the manifold objections appear which are also found elsewhere in criticisms of Mann: his profound "lack of seriousness," his "destruction of the Christian image of man," his "denial of all faith, of all metaphysics," the "dreadful discrepancy between talent and essence," his "flirting with his own virtuosity." Rahn does not associate himself absolutely with any one of these objections (or with many more which have been raised). Very often they appear in question form, introduced by an "if," in the guise of the subjunctive; they are uttered in the debate between admirers and rejecters of Mann's work, relativized by "We are assured" or "Some say, others reply"; in fact, Rahn goes to the length of having a (naturally imaginary) Thomas Mann say his say and judge his own work. An ambivalent judgment results. At the same time the critic always refers to the "overwhelming artistry" and "gleaming richness" of the writer and repeatedly overrules his own objections. Granted that he speaks of the "disreputable" charm of *Krull,* of the "sophisticated methods of an art which is . . . meretricious"; granted that he finds it "treacherous and despicable" to admire such—but he continues that it would be a "ruinous delusion" to think that one "could dispose of the phenomenon of Thomas Mann as thinker and artist . . . with remarks of this sort." "What an artist!" he exclaims, "whose masterful presentation makes us forget how thoroughly his work undermines our belief in man." As soon as he becomes again aware of the poet's lack of metaphysics, he does indeed feel "caught out in premature admiration," ends by summing up his objections, leaves no doubt that they are moralistically grounded, in that they all derive from "a standpoint of personal morality," and himself finds that this standpoint "is not quite satisfying." Why not? Because the same arguments would force us "to reject many other literary works whose rank has never been doubted." Still in search of a reliable criterion, the critic finally addresses his questions to aesthetics and summarizes his aesthetic theory in seven (very plausible) theses, only the fourth of which is quoted here: "It is a potentiality of literature but not its mission to improve the reader morally and edify him religiously. The effect of moral betterment, of education through aesthetic values, is no measure of the value of a literary work."

It is clear that here moral argumentation on the aesthetic level has become untenable, as Rahn fully realizes. There are art works of the highest rank, he declares, which are morally and religiously vulnerable, downright scandalous even. After citing a number of examples, he continues: "What women, members of the school boards, . . . and public prosecutors decide in this matter does not have the slightest relevance to the literary value of such works." But who then has the right to a judgment? "No one," answers Rahn, "except the history of the human spirit; during its course a work of art either shows the staying power to assert itself against the changes of time, taste, and social views, or falls prey to oblivion."

As is well known, history does not pronounce any final judgments; it knows only unending retrials and revisions. Nor does the selection of the "lasting heritage" take place of itself, but through the vigorous effort, the articulated feelings, the communicated understanding of many individuals, who do not wait for history's sentence but are among the forces influencing it. There is something mysterious in the spiritually creative energy that radiates from a poetic work, encounters receptive spirits again and again and repeatedly compels them to occupy themselves and come to terms with the work, and to give an account of it. Should not the indestructible vitality of a "decadent" work like *Buddenbrooks* suggest caution to those who, as repeatedly happens, confuse the creative writer with his subject and take the presentation of decadence as decadence of the work itself? For not only poetry must maintain itself in the stream of time; a critical judgment must also do so. "Criticism is . . . always hazardous," Ernst Robert Curtius rightly said.[27] Indeed it takes no small courage to see in Thomas Mann, some fifty years after the publication of *Buddenbrooks,* nothing but "the prima donna in the great literary dance of death," to dismiss him, as Muschg does, as the most successful representative of "bastardized creativity (*Dichtertum*).[28] Bastardized literary creativity: that signifies what is generally called, not quite so crassly but still contemptuously enough, the work of mere literati (*Literatentum*). "Is he a *literatus* or a poet (*Dichter*)?—throughout all his . . . work Thomas Mann has been unable to supply the answer," the *Annals of*

[27] *Kritische Essays zur europäischen Literatur* (Bern, 1950), p. 300.
[28] Walter Muschg, *Tragische Literaturgeschichte* (Bern, 1948), p. 254 f.

*German Literature* declare.[29] Thomas Mann is, in Joseph Nadler's judgment "no poet, a mere writer" [30]—a "writer" who "reflects only a very small section of the German being," Wilhelm Grenzmann's *German Poetry (Dichtung) of the Present* states.[31] In the willingness with which he accords the title of "poet" to authors like Kolbenheyer, Blunck, Thiess, Waggerl, and many others, Grenzmann offers a particularly revealing example of a use of terms that is not without polemical undertones. It would be worthwhile to trace some day, and not only in Mann's case, the contrast between the terms "poet" and "writer," which has been repeatedly made in critical and literary-historical writings in recent decades. The distinction intended was that of the creative against the manufactured, the intuitive against the conscious, the soul against the intellect, faith against irony; in many cases it protected and exalted simple-minded provincialism.

This concept of the poetic had remarkably little to do with language; in fact linguistic mastery was usually conceded to Mann even by his opponents, at least in the sense of virtuosity, artistry, bravura of style, as if language were a sort of varnish with which the content, unpleasant in itself, were covered at the last moment to make it acceptable. However, nothing remains of a poetic work if one subtracts its language; it exists only as language and can be judged only as language, by criteria that are intrinsic to it. Responsible critics know this. When Joseph Kunz, for instance, feels that he is forced to state that there is an "inner flawedness" in Mann's work, he does so with express reference to a criterion derived from the work itself, and without casting doubt upon the "towering greatness of Thomas Mann's achievement." [32] It would be highly rewarding to follow more exactly the stylistic line which Holthusen has drawn from Heine, via Nietzsche, to *The Magic Mountain* and *Doctor Faustus*. The parallel of two undeniably great figures, who are also characterized in part by "flawedness," could yield very valuable insights. Compared with Kafka, to whom he is considerably related in the "ambiguity of his themes" Thomas Mann does not possess an equal perfection of thoroughly structured form; while in Kafka all the raw material has been recast into crystals, as it were, in Mann amorphous masses repeatedly occur, scattered within the artistic substance of his work. To see this point and others is the legitimate task of criticism; objections to Mann's work are possible and have been raised. Yet as to its rank and significance as a whole, I share the view of a critique which recently appeared in the journal *Die*

[29] Hans Schwerte, "Der Weg ins zwanzigste Jahrhundert," in: *Annalen der deutschen Literatur*, ed. Heinz Otto Burger (Stuttgart, 1952), p. 749.

[30] *Literaturgeschichte der deutschen Stämme und Landschaften* (Regensburg, 1928), IV, 761.

[31] (Frankfurt, 1953), p. 72.

[32] "Thomas Mann," in *Deutsche Literatur im zwanzigsten Jahrhundert*, ed. Hermann Friedmann and Otto Mann (Heidelberg, 1954), p. 229.

*Gegenwart.* There Thomas Mann is described as a man "who has preserved the continuity of German literature, beyond partisan hatred and
partiality, who has indeed represented it as a part of world literature." [33]
In my opinion this sums up concisely and pertinently the exceptional
component in the lifework of Thomas Mann.

[33] "r.h." in a review of Erika Mann's *The Last Year Die Gegenwart,* XI (1956), p. 348.

# Humor and Irony

*by Thomas Mann*

[Mann's remarks in a radio discussion, September 15, 1953]

Yes, my dear Herr Jancke, I shall do my best to give you a little help in clarifying the concepts which you just mentioned in your introductory remarks. I noticed in your words the implied question as to how I see the difference between irony and humor and what role these two elements may play in my own work. Well, one could easily be tempted to consider irony the higher principle, towering far above humor in dignity and spirit. I recall a sentence of Goethe's which has always made a deep impression on me. He said on one occasion: "Irony is the grain of salt, without which the food set before us couldn't be enjoyed at all." A very remarkable statement. We could conclude from it that Goethe makes irony almost coincide with the artistic principle as such. We could say—we could conclude from it that he equates irony with that artistic objectivity for which he strove all his life, that he equates it with the distance which art keeps from its object, that irony is just this distance, in that it hovers over things and smiles down upon them, no matter how much it also entangles the listener or reader in them, draws them into its web. We could equate them with the Apollonian principle, to use the aesthetic term for it, for Apollo, whose arrows strike from afar, is the god of farness, the god of distance, of objectivity, the god of irony—objectivity is irony—and the spirit of epic art; one could address him as the spirit of irony.

Now let me say something more. You have probably already noticed in occasional private observations of mine that I always feel a bit bored when critics assign my own work so definitely and completely to the realm of irony and consider me an ironist through and through, without also taking account of the concept of humor, which in my case, I think, cannot and should not be completely ignored. Let me put matters in an extreme way. Irony, it seems to me, is that spirit in art (*Kunstgeist*) which draws a smile from the reader or listener, an intellectual smile, I

"Humor and Irony," by Thomas Mann. *Gesammelte Werke*, XI, *Reden und Aufsätze* 3, pp. 801-805. Copyright © 1960 by S. Fischer Verlag. Reprinted by permission of Joan Daves, agent for the proprietor. Translated by Henry Hatfield.

might call it; while humor induces the laughter that wells up from the heart. This I personally rate higher as the effect of art and welcome it more happily when it is the effect of my own productions than the Erasmus-like smile which irony evokes. I must say—you know that I have read aloud a great deal in my life, and every time my reading evoked a hearty laugh in the auditorium, I was the most pleased and felt happiest on the platform.

I don't think that readers will find irony predominant in *Budden-brooks,* the book of my youth which in a sense laid the foundation of everything that was to follow. Rather, it is a book of pessimistic humor —forgive the perhaps paradoxical combination—a book whose sources and ingredients are not only Schopenhauer and Wagner and the French, Russian, and English novel, but not least the Low German sense of humor as it is expressed in the work of Fritz Reuter,[1] one of my very first literary impressions, which left a definite mark on this book.

I am always pleased when people see in me less an ironist than a humorist, and I believe that it will not be difficult to point out the humorous element in what I have written. Take the figure of Jacob in the *Joseph* tetralogy. Well, he is a figure full of deep feeling, and yet no doubt every reader feels that he is surrounded by a peculiar humor. Even in a scene which ought in itself to be utterly tragic, like Jacob's lament for his favorite son who, he thinks, has been rent to bits (that is in the conversation with Eliezer where Jacob expostulates with God and reproaches him for having failed to keep up morally with the development of the human heart), even there one finds humor which cannot be confused with irony; it is something essentially different.

Or take another example which has just occurred to me. In one of the later chapters of the memoirs of the swindler Felix Krull, there is a scene in which a professor of the natural sciences teaches the young pseudomarquis that the lovely, soft, slender arms of a woman, which on occasion embrace a man—if he is lucky—are nothing but the claw-like wings of the primal bird and the pectoral fins of the fish. To this the so-called marquis answers: "Yes, *Herr Professor,* in the future I shall keep this in mind." You see, when this passage was read, there was always hearty laughter in the auditorium; it was one of the passages whose effect gave me the sense of satisfaction which a humorist feels when his public shows that it is amused.

Well then, I'll try to think of another example. Good: there is *Doctor Faustus,* certainly a melancholy, deeply serious novel. Is it credible that humorous elements have stolen into this book, even into this book? They did not steal in; I very consciously put them in, well knowing how necessary this element would be in just this book. Look: even the idea of putting the narration of the life of the hero, the composer

---

[1] 1810-74. Best known for his novels in dialect.

Leverkühn, into the mouth of the good humanist Zeitblom or letting it flow from his pen, even the notion of having the daemonic pass through a pronouncedly undaemonic medium, even this idea is a pronouncedly humorous notion with humorous intentions, which are I think realized —at least to a considerable degree, in the first part. So, on the spur of the moment—we are improvising after all—I have given you three examples which can if need be bear witness that I am a humorist.

But now I have already talked too long and will give our friends a chance to speak. Of course the whole thing is a gamble: we are conversing as if we were in our own homes and we try to forget, and really do forget, that hundreds and thousands are listening to us. It is a gamble, but after all there are four of us, and a four-leafed clover is said to bring good luck. So it will doubtless go wrong.

[Remarks by other members of the panel, Oskar Jancke, Werner Weber, and Carl Helbling.]

There you are quite right; forgive me for interrupting you so soon. In just this connection a little story occurs to me which has always amused me. It is about the composer Ditters von Dittersdorf, who had a talk about Haydn with the Emperor Joseph. The Emperor asked Ditters: "But what do you think of Haydn's pieces for chamber music?" Then Ditters: "Well, your Majesty, that they have been a sensation in the whole world, and quite rightly so." Thereupon the Emperor asks him: "Doesn't he often trifle far too much?" And Ditters replies: "He has the gift of trifling without abasing art." Well, I can only say: if I have occasionally trifled with language, I must hope that in so doing I have never seriously abased art.

# Chronology of Important Dates

| | |
|---|---|
| 1875 | Born in Lübeck, June 6. |
| 1893 | Moves to Munich; works first in a fire insurance company, then on the satiric magazine *Simplicissimus*. |
| 1896 | To Italy for about a year (spent largely with his brother Heinrich). |
| 1898 | *Little Herr Friedemann* (collection of *novellas*) |
| 1901 | *Buddenbrooks* |
| 1903 | *Tristan* (collection of *novellas*, including *Tonio Kröger*) |
| 1905 | Marriage to Katja Pringsheim |
| 1909 | *Royal Highness* |
| 1912 | *Death in Venice* |
| 1918 | *Reflections of a Nonpolitical Man* |
| 1924 | *The Magic Mountain* |
| 1929 | Awarded the Nobel Prize, mainly for *Buddenbrooks*. |
| 1930 | *Mario and the Magician* |
| 1933 | Emigrates to Switzerland. |
| 1933-43 | *Joseph and His Brothers* (tetralogy) |
| 1938 | Moves to the United States, living first in Princeton, then in Pacific Palisades, California. |
| 1939 | *The Beloved Returns: Lotte in Weimar* |
| 1947 | *Doctor Faustus* |
| 1951 | *The Holy Sinner* |
| 1952 | Returns to Europe; lives in Kilchberg near Zürich. |
| 1954 | *Confessions of Felix Krull, Confidence Man*, Part I |
| 1955 | *Essay on Schiller* |
| 1955 | Dies in Zurich, August 12. |

# Notes on the Editor and Authors

HENRY HATFIELD, the editor of this anthology, teaches German literature at Harvard and is the author of books on Goethe, Thomas Mann, and Winckelmann.

BERNHARD BLUME is Kuno Francke Professor of German Art and Culture at Harvard. Among his scholarly works are books on Thomas Mann's relation to Goethe and on Arthur Schnitzler; he has also published dramas and prose fiction.

ANDRÉ VON GRONICKA, professor of German at the University of Pennsylvania, is the author of a book on Henry von Heiseler. He is particularly interested in Russo-German literary relations.

ROBERT B. HEILMAN, professor of English at the University of Washington, is known particularly for his studies of Shakespeare.

ERICH HELLER, a professor at Northwestern University, is particularly interested in German and Austrian literature of the nineteenth and twentieth centuries, and in lyric poetry. His books *The Disinherited Mind* and *The Ironic German: A Study of Thomas Mann* are both widely known.

HANS EGON HOLTHUSEN, one of the younger German men of letters, has shown his versatility in many fields but is perhaps most prominent as an essayist.

ERICH KAHLER is recognized both in this country and on the Continent as a critic, essayist, poet, and scholar. Of his many books, *Man the Measure* is perhaps the best known in this country.

RAINER MARIA RILKE is considered by many observers the greatest lyric poet who has written in the German language during this century.

MARK VAN DOREN is renowned as poet, critic, essayist, and teacher.

HERMANN J. WEIGAND, Sterling Professor of German Literature Emeritus at University of Massachusetts is, by common consent, the first among those who know Mann's work. His book on *The Magic Mountain* is the most helpful analysis of that novel.

E. M. WILKINSON, professor of German at the University of London, is the author of a book on the eighteenth-century critic J. E. Schlegel and of exceptionally brilliant essays devoted to various works of Goethe and to Schiller's aesthetic theories.

# Selected Bibliography

Du Bos, Charles. "Homage to Thomas Mann." Translated by W. M. Frohock. *Germanic Review,* XXV (1950), 275-284.

Gronicka, André von. "Thomas Mann and Russia," *Germanic Review,* XX (1945), 105-137.

Hatfield, Henry. *Thomas Mann: An Introduction to his Fiction.* (Rev. ed.) Norfolk, Conn., 1962.

Heller, Erich. *The Ironic German, a Study of Thomas Mann.* Boston, (1958).

Kaufmann, Fritz. *Thomas Mann: the World as Will and Representation.* Boston, (1957).

Levin, Harry. "Joseph the Provider." In *The Stature of Thomas Mann,* pp. 211-217.

Lukács, Georg. "In Search of the Bourgeois." *Ibid.,* pp. 469-473.

Mann, Erika. *The Last Year of Thomas Mann.* New York, 1958.

Mann, Thomas. *A Sketch of My Life.* Paris, 1930; New York, 1960.

Neider, Charles, ed. *The Stature of Thomas Mann.* New York, (1947).

Oswald, Victor A., Jr. "Thomas Mann's *Doktor Faustus:* The Enigma of Frau von Tolna." *Germanic Review,* XXIII (1948), 245-253.

Rice, Philip Blair. "Thomas Mann and the Religious Revival." *Kenyon Review,* VII (1945), 361-377.

Stock, Irwin. "Mann's Christian Parable: A View of *The Holy Sinner.*" *Accent,* XIV (1954), 98-115.

Thomas, R. Hinton. *Thomas Mann: The Mediation of Art.* Oxford, 1956.

Weigand, Hermann J. "Thomas Mann's Gregorius." *Germanic Review,* XXVII (1952), 10-30, 83-93.

Weigand, Hermann J. *Thomas Mann's Novel "Der Zauberberg."* New York and London, (1933).

Wilkinson, E. M. "Aesthetic Excursus on Thomas Mann's *Akribie.*" *Germanic Review,* XXXI (1956), 225-235.

Yourcenar, Marguerite. "Humanism in Thomas Mann." *Partisan Review,* XXIII (1956), 153-170.

## TWENTIETH CENTURY VIEWS

# Other Titles